EMU and Political Science

Europe's Economic and Monetary Union (EMU) celebrated its tenth anniversary in 2009. Before its birth many observers were concerned about its viability. This volume examines a number of noteworthy concerns that were heard a decade ago and it assesses what has become of them. The contributors to this volume examine various topics. Has EMU been a failure or success? Does EMU require more political integration? What type of deeper integration in the financial market has occurred because of EMU? Does the public like EMU? Does EMU cause a decline of the welfare state, reduce the role of labour unions and are adjustments now made mainly through the labour market? Do countries in EMU become more similar over time? Is EMU sustainable in the long-run? Will EMU survive the global financial crisis? The contributors to this book are leading Political Scientists in the field, and draw on a wealth of research and experience.

This book was published as a special issue of the *Journal of European Public Policy*.

Henrik Enderlein is Associate Dean and teaches Political Economy and Economics at the Hertie School of Governance, Germany. He was awarded the Max Planck Society's Otto-Hahn Medal in 2003 for outstanding achievements by young scientists, and in 2007 was Fulbright Distinguished Chair at Duke University's Political Science Department. He has published numerous articles on economic policy-making in Europe and beyond.

Amy Verdun is Professor of Political Science, Chair of the Department of Political Science, Director of the Jean Monnet Centre of Excellence at the University of Victoria, in Canada. Some of her earlier books include (as author or editor) *Britain and Canada and their Large Neighboring Monetary Unions*; *The Euro: European Integration and Economic and Monetary Union*, and *European Responses to Globalization and Financial Market Integration: Perceptions of EMU in Britain, France and Germany*, and (as co-author or co-editor) *Ruling Europe: The Politics of the Stability and Growth Pact*; and *EMU Rules: The Political and Economic Consequences of European Monetary Integration*.

Journal of European Public Policy Series

Series Editor: Jeremy Richardson is a Professor at Nuffield College, Oxford University

This series seeks to bring together some of the finest edited works on European Public Policy. Reprinting from Special Issues of the 'Journal of European Public Policy,' the focus is on using a wide range of social sciences approaches, both qualitative and quantitative, to gain a comprehensive and definitive understanding of Public Policy in Europe.

EMU and Political Science

What Have We Learned?

Edited by
Henrik Enderlein and Amy Verdun

Routledge
Taylor & Francis Group
LONDON AND NEW YORK

First published 2010 by Routledge
2 Park Square, Milton Park, Abingdon, Oxon, OX14 4RN

Simultaneously published in the USA and Canada
by Routledge
270 Madison Avenue, New York, NY 10016

Routledge is an imprint of the Taylor & Francis Group, an informa business

This book is a reproduction of the Journal of European Public Policy, vol. 16, issue 4.
The Publisher requests to those authors who may be citing this book to state, also, the
bibliographical details of the special issue on which the book was based

Typeset in Times by Value Chain, India
Printed and bound in Great Britain by TJI Digital Ltd, Padstow, Cornwall

British Library Cataloguing in Publication Data
A catalogue record for this book is available from the British Library

ISBN10: 0-415-57482-X
ISBN13: 978-0-415-57482-2

Contents

Abstracts

EMU's teenage challenge: what have we learned and can we predict from political science?*

Henrik Enderlein and Amy Verdun

We review the initial predictions and claims regarding economic and monetary union (EMU) in Europe against the evidence of its first ten years of existence. We argue that pessimistic views on the creation of EMU have proved to be wrong. Yet EMU's success is rather puzzling, since it is based on a peculiar institutional structure not thought to lead to success. EMU has generated redistributive effects and may have increased business-cycle synchronization. Those effects have not translated into the expected decrease of legitimacy or a widespread democratic deficit of EMU. At the institutional level, EMU has coped well with an asymmetric framework, largely decoupling EMU from political union. There have been neither major spill-over effects pushing for further political integration nor conflict and disintegration. The main question for the future is whether this institutional structure will stay the same in the aftermath of the global financial crisis.

EMU and political union: what, if anything, have we learned from the euro's first decade?

Dermot Hodson

The road to Maastricht and the eventual launch of economic and monetary union (EMU) fuelled debate among scholars and policy-makers about the relationship between monetary and political integration in Europe. This article revisits a selection of these arguments ten years after the launch of the euro. It finds little evidence to corroborate claims that EMU will spur political union either out of functional necessity or the intentional choice of euro area members. If anything, the projects of monetary and political integration in Europe show tentative signs of decoupling.

On consensus, constraint and choice: economic and monetary integration and Europe's welfare states

H. Tolga Bolukbasi

This article reassesses the theoretical expectations and empirical findings in the political economy literature on the impact of economic and monetary union (EMU) on European welfare states. After summarizing the literature which views EMU as the symbol of the primordial conversion to neoliberalism, the article identifies the underlying hypothesis, assumptions, and predictions of the earlier, largely apprehensive literature of the 1990s which was based on ex ante convictions on EMU's social consequences. Then it reviews more recent ex post studies pointing to dynamics of welfare state resilience informed by new empirical evidence that became available and new theoretical approaches that became influential. After highlighting the conditions under which welfare reforms have taken place and the role played by EMU in these processes, this article concludes by re-evaluating the earlier expectations in the literature in light of the empirical findings and draws lessons for the discipline of political economy.

EMU's diverging micro foundations: a study of governments' preferences and the sustainability of EMU

Tal Sadeh

The political economic literature on EMU suggests that its sustainability depends on the consolidation of the member states into a political community, based on shared beliefs in neo-liberal values, as well as the development of strong EU institutions and a well-integrated and liberalized common market. Have national governments in the EU become less favourable to policies that accordingly contribute to the sustainability of EMU? A dataset including 15 pre-2004 member states during 1990–2006 shows that, while the member states of the euro zone have in recent years converged in support of macroeconomic policies that are important for a sustainable EMU, they have also become more divergent about imperative microeconomic policies, and their scepticism with regard to the authority of EU institutions has become more consensual. This may challenge the sustainability of EMU. This study is innovative in its original government orientation analysis and large dataset.

Economic interests and public support for the euro

Susan A. Banducci, Jeffrey A. Karp and Peter H. Loedel

Although economic theories have been advanced to explain public support for the common currency, we know very little about how public support for the euro has been affected by its economic impact. We hypothesize that concern about rising prices following the introduction of the euro may have dampened enthusiasm for the project. We use Eurobarometer data from 2000–2007 to examine how rising prices and other economic factors have shaped support for the euro. We find that while inflation has had a negative impact on support for the euro, this is offset by the positive effect of diffuse support for the European Union. This support, along with the impact of a strong currency, has led most (approximately two-thirds) of Europeans to be generally positive about the euro.

EMU: the last stand for the policy convergence hypothesis?

David H. Bearce

This paper explores the extent of euro area policy convergence during the third stage of EMU. The policy convergence hypothesis from international political economy posits that euro zone national economies should become more similar over time in terms of economic growth, employment and inflation outcomes as a result of using a common currency and taking the same regional monetary policy. Yet the descriptive data show little evidence of euro area policy convergence post- 1999. One possible explanation for the lack of macroeconomic convergence within the euro zone is advanced (fiscal policy divergence), and the implications of policy divergence for the long-term viability of EMU are discussed.

Wage inflation and labour unions in EMU

Alison Johnston and Bob Hancké

This paper examines different levels of wage moderation in EMU member states since the introduction of the euro. Most arguments examining wage restraint have done so relying on the assumptions that relations between EMU member states are symmetric and that wage-setting systems are similar across sectors within one country. We introduce one innovation to these approaches and develop a second existing one. The paper adopts a dual-sector approach, where exposed sector unions are still tied to a competitiveness constraint on wages, while sheltered sector unions neither face a hard monetary constraint imposed by the central bank nor are subject to a competitive one. Wage moderation is higher in countries with wage-bargaining institutions which tie wage-setters in the sheltered sector to the exposed sector through a co-ordination mechanism. The second innovation is that of asymmetries between Germany and other EMU member states.

Political science and the 'Cinderellas' of economic and monetary union: payment services and clearing and settlement

Lucia Quaglia

So far, political scientists have paid very limited attention to the 'plumbing' of economic and monetary union (EMU), that is payment services and the clearing and settlement of securities. This paper evaluates the analytical leverage of 'bureaucratic politics' approaches – in particular, the 'bureau shaping' theory – against the empirical record of a variety of policy initiatives taking place in the two fields mentioned above. It is argued that an adapted version of the theory of bureaucracy sheds novel light on to the policy process and the bureaucracies involved in it, namely the Commission and the European Central Bank. This research also highlights the politics involved in these seemingly 'technical' activities.

Notes on Contributors

Henrik Enderlein is Professor of Political Economy and Associate Dean at the Hertie School of Governance, Berlin, Germany. Amy Verdun is Professor of Political Science, Jean Monnet Chair and Director of the Jean Monnet Centre of Excellence at the University of Victoria, Canada.

Dermot Hodson is Lecturer in Political Economy at Birkbeck College, University of London, UK.

H. Tolga Bolukbasi is a Lecturer in Economics at the Middle East Technical University, Güzelyurt, and Research Associate in the Centre for European Studies at the Middle East Technical University, Ankara, Turkey.

Tal Sadeh is Senior Lecturer in the Department of Political Science at Tel Aviv University, Israel.

Susan A. Banducci is Associate Professor and Head of the Department of Politics at the University of Exeter, UK. Jeffrey A. Karp is Associate Professor of Political Science in the Department of Politics at the University of Exeter, UK. Peter H. Loedel is Professor and Chair of the Department of Political Science at West Chester University of Pennsylvania, USA.

David H. Bearce is an Associate Professor of Political Science at the University of Pittsburgh, USA. His work in international political economy focuses on international monetary politics and the politics of foreign aid effectiveness.

Alison Johnston is a Ph.D. candidate in political economy at the London School of Economics and Political Science, UK. Bob Hancké is a Reader in European Political Economy at the London School of Economics and Political Science, UK.

Lucia Quaglia is Senior Lecturer in the Department of Politics and Contemporary European Studies at the University of Sussex, UK.

Preface

1 January 2009 marked the tenth anniversary of the start of the third stage of economic and monetary union (EMU) in the European Union (EU). Research in political science was very active during the run-up to EMU and its early years in assessing its possible consequences. The end of the first decade marks an excellent opportunity to take stock of the research in political science. This book contributes to this debate.

The idea for this book was born at a Council of European Studies roundtable discussion in Chicago 2006, which also involved Kevin Featherstone and Nicolas Jabko. Since that day, the project has materialized thanks to the generous financial support of the Claus M. Halle Institute for Global Learning which allowed us to organize a conference on 'Ten years of EMU' in Berlin in April 2008. We thank especially Mark Hallerberg for helping us to establish the link to the Halle Institute and for co-organizing the conference with us. We thank all the participants of the workshop, many of whose papers could not be included in this book, but we all benefited from their contributions and comments. We are grateful to almost 30 referees who helped us in the selection and improvement of the papers. Special thanks go to Gabriele Brühl for invaluable support during the whole process and to Josyln Trowbridge for editing support. Finally, we are particularly grateful to Jeremy Richardson who continuously encouraged and supported us during the preparation of this book.

We look forward to the next decade of EMU and to a continuation of the fascinating research on this wonderful political and economic endeavour.

Henrik Enderlein and Amy Verdun
Berlin and Victoria, February 2009

EMU's teenage challenge: what have we learned and can we predict from political science?[*]

Henrik Enderlein and Amy Verdun

INTRODUCTION

Teenage years are always challenging ones. But for economic and monetary union in Europe (EMU) the start of the second decade of its existence could prove to be even more difficult than that. In the face of a major economic crisis, this historically unique economic and institutional endeavour of initially 11, now 16, nations sharing a single currency is threatened in its very existence and will have to demonstrate particular resilience (e.g. *Financial Times* 2009). Is EMU sufficiently strong to face this crisis?

Finding an answer to this question necessitates a backward-looking assessment of the successes and failures of EMU and a forward-looking analysis of the challenges likely to arise. During the run-up to EMU and its early years of existence, research in economics and political science was very active, formulating core predictions and research questions on the basis of conceptual foundations which at that time were mainly analytical, sometimes historical. Today, those predictions can be assessed against the evidence of ten years of EMU and new analytically founded claims can be made on what we expect for the future.

The purpose of this article is to embark on that stock-taking exercise with a particular focus on the findings in political science. While we believe that it is impossible to draw clear disciplinary boundaries in research on a topic that obviously transgresses the realms of politics and economics, we will nonetheless make the attempt to summarize and review critically a certain component of the political science literature which focuses on the nature of the linkage between politics and economics. Therefore, we do include some of the literature that originates outside of political science but which has been discussed at some length in political science for the purpose of our assessment of EMU. We identify three key themes in this research, which we consider to be of particular relevance in the context of the current economic crisis and which we place at the centre of our analysis: (i) questions on the redistributive features of EMU; (ii) questions on the overall legitimacy of EMU; and (iii) questions on the political power structure in EMU. We will first justify the selection of these three themes, before analysing each of them in separate sections, and end by offering a brief conclusion that looks at the implications of the current crisis for the second decade of EMU.

The core claim of this article is that almost all of the highly pessimistic views on the creation of EMU have proven to be wrong. Yet EMU's success is rather puzzling, since it is based on a peculiar mixture of outcomes that no one predicted, and which was not thought to lead to success. We find that EMU has generated redistributive effects and may well have increased rather than decreased business-cycle synchronization. Yet those effects have not translated into the expected decrease of EMU's legitimacy or a widespread democratic deficit of EMU. At the institutional level, we find that EMU has coped well with an asymmetric framework, in which EMU remains largely decoupled from political union. We have not seen spill-over effects fostering further political integration – but nor have we seen conflict and disintegration. The big question for the upcoming decade is whether this peculiar mixture of outcomes will stay the same even in the aftermath of the global financial crisis.

1. POLITICS AND ECONOMICS IN EMU – IS THERE STILL A MISSING LINK?

A key theme in both academic research and practical politics during the run-up to EMU was whether monetary union could be successful in the presence of high economic heterogeneity across the participating countries (non-fulfilment of the 'optimum currency area' criteria: Mundell 1961; Sachs and Sala-i-Martín 1992; Eichengreen 1993) and in the absence of a strong political authority capable of steering the currency union ('asymmetry' between economic and political union: Verdun 1996, 2000; see also Howarth 2007; Jones 2002a; Padoa-Schioppa 2004). Much of the initial discussions therefore rested on the chicken-and-egg issue of whether political union had to precede monetary union or vice versa (for a review of theories concerning the origins of EMU, see Sadeh and Verdun 2009). In political discussions, this issue was most prominently raised in the opposition of the primarily French approach to monetary union under a *gouvernement économique*, as opposed to the primarily German view that political union had to precede a successful monetary union (Dyson and Featherstone 1999; Verdun 2000; 2003). In the economic literature, a similar issue was discussed in a debate opposing the view that a single currency would create a lower synchronization of business cycles as a consequence of increased specialization in production and therefore an increase in so-called asymmetric, or sector-specific, shocks (Krugman 1993), as opposed to the view summarized under the heading of the 'endogeneity of optimum currency areas', arguing that increased trade integration was likely to create business-cycle convergence in a currency union (see Frankel and Rose 1998).

What came out of those debates in both political science and economics was an arguably gloomy overall picture on the future of EMU. It was based on a few key claims, such as that EMU was in the interest of the largest member states only (Moravcsik 1998); that it could not survive without a common identity of the European citizens (Risse *et al.* 1999); that it would lack legitimacy ('democratic deficit': Majone 1998; Verdun and Christiansen 2000; 2001); that it would end the continental and Scandinavian welfare state models (Leander and Guzzini 1997; Rhodes 1997; see also Scharpf 2002; Hodson and Maher 2002); that it would give rise to numerous collective action problems amongst member states, mainly free-riding in fiscal policy (Eichengreen 1995), and ultimately lead to a weak currency (Cohen 1998) administered by a weak central bank (Gormley and de Haan 1996). Taking all of those points together, the US economist Martin Feldstein famously made the following statement: '[T]he shift to EMU and the political integration that would follow it would be more likely to lead to increased conflicts within Europe and between Europe and the United States' (Feldstein 1997: 61).

With hindsight, it is striking how little understanding or even solidly grounded assumptions there were on the nature of the spill-over effects from the economic side to the political side and vice versa. Instead, many authors offered mere scenarios, sketching out possible domino-effects (such as Feldstein 1997: 61 arguing that in the beginning there would be 'important disagreements among EMU member countries about the goals and methods of monetary policy', which would then be 'exacerbated whenever the business cycle raised unemployment in a particular country'; these disagreements would then trigger 'distrusts among the European nations', and ultimately, 'new conflicts would reflect incompatible expectations about the sharing of power').

Obviously, such scenarios look simplistic – and they are. Indeed, if there is one core message in the preceding list of arguments, it is that the complexity of the various economic, political, and social transmission channels deriving from the single currency is very high. We can easily conclude that none of the many negative scenarios on the future of EMU predicted what really happened.

The goal of scholars of EMU after its first decade should be to take up this complexity, try to assess where assumptions were right or wrong, and then reduce it again to a few updated claims and research questions for the next decade(s). We seek to make a contribution to this discussion.

Our approach is to re-examine the initial discussions on EMU under three broad questions. First, there is the overall question as to whether EMU has triggered redistributive effects amongst member states. This question encompasses several of the points referred to above but can be reduced to a few simple and testable claims. It also allows us to draw clear policy conclusions: if redistribution takes place, there are good reasons to allow for rebalancing activities. Various suggestions have been made about how to achieve them (ranging from fully-fledged fiscal federalism to rebalancing activities via the European Union (EU) budget). The second key question is, what is the appropriate type of legitimacy for EMU? Pareto-improving policies, i.e. policies that improve overall aggregate welfare without making anyone worse off, can generally be legitimized on the basis of their result only ('output legitimacy'; e.g. Scharpf 1999), whereas welfare distributing policies either require a direct type of procedural legitimacy ('input legitimacy') or a very strong collective normative basis (often a common national identity). Finally, our third main question is, what is the power structure in the politics of EMU? Do member states only act on their direct interest (Moravcsik 1998) or has EMU given rise to independent actors or mechanisms working not only in the direct interest of the largest shareholders in the system but also maximizing collective utility. This question obviously touches upon the roles of the European Central Bank (ECB), the EU Commission and the Eurogroup; it also asks whether spill-over effects in typical neo-functionalist fashion have started to materialize.

2. WELFARE EFFECTS OF EMU: EFFICIENCY INCREASES VS. REDISTRIBUTION

Every monetary union that is far removed from being an 'optimum currency area' will at one point face the challenge of its own distributive implications, calling for some kind of rebalancing through redistribution (Mundell 1961; McKinnon 1963; Kenen 1969). Economic historians give several accounts of how the trade-off between preserving monetary union and preserving national cohesion ended in the break-up of a previously politically integrated area, even though one has to acknowledge that the causes of the break-up of national monetary unions are typically found in political developments rather than in purely economic forces (see Bordo and Jonung 2003 for an overview). In EMU we can differentiate between three main channels of welfare or redistribution effects. The first channel is the overall welfare generating effect from a single currency; the second is the redistribution effect emerging when there is a primacy of the real interest effect over the real exchange rate effect; the third is a redistribution effect from welfare state policies and possible retrenchment as a consequence of EMU.

Welfare enhancing effects

First, EMU has certainly triggered some welfare generating effects. Not surprisingly, the most complete summary of those positive effects can be found in the Report of the EU Commission email: 'EMU@10' (EU Commission 2008). In this report, the main emphasis is put on (i) the successes of monetary policy in anchoring inflation expectations, (ii) progress in fiscal consolidation in EMU member states, (iii) economic and market integration in the euro area, (iv) financial market integration, (v) resilience against external shocks, (vi) accelerated catching-up processes in lesser developed member states, (vii) the success of the euro as an international currency and the euro area as an integrated 'pole of stability' in the world economy, and (viii) job creation with employment in the euro area having increased by 15 per cent since the creation of the euro.

Whether all of those effects can be causally linked to the creation of EMU is of no crucial importance for our assessment. There are various welfare enhancing effects that at least partly confirm the high expectations that were voiced in the run-up to EMU, mainly in the 'Delors Report' (1989; see also Commission of the European Communities 1990, 1991), even if the EU Commission in current assessment puts much less emphasis on trade creation than in its ex ante justifications of the creation of a single currency.

Redistribution as a consequence of the real interest rate

Besides welfare enhancing effects there is also increasing evidence that EMU has generated welfare distributing effects. The EU Commission itself acknowledges such effects (2008: chs 1–4), even if the wording chosen in the report is careful, probably because of the Commission's awareness of the consequences that such effects might trigger; see below.

The key mechanism behind welfare distribution in a currency union is the primacy of the real interest rate effect over the real exchange rate effect. As the ECB does not take into account economic developments in single member states but rather targets the euro area as a whole, its 'one size fits all' monetary policy may destabilize those domestic cycles whose economic fundamentals are not in line with the euro area average. Member states with higher inflation rates than the euro area average face low real interest rates generating higher rates of investment and consumption. These effects drive up the domestic growth rate beyond its long-term potential, thereby generating even higher inflation rates, further reducing real interest rates, and ultimately generating cyclical overshooting and price bubbles. Similarly, in a context of low inflation and high real interest rates, growth rates are likely to fall below potential growth, thus triggering even higher real interest rates and potentially generating a textbook-type bust cycle.

Prior to the start of EMU, most theoretical analyses of monetary unions assumed that the real exchange rate effect would have primacy over the real interest effect and that domestic stabilization would therefore be generated automatically (Frankel and Rose 1998). This approach was built on the assumption that domestic prices (and thus also real interest rates) in a monetary union are bound to converge given the mobility of goods and services in the internal market. In EMU, however, a significant share of domestic output derives from so-called 'spatially fixed factors', such as real estate and heavy machinery, which are not affected by direct price competition (Maclennan *et al.* 1998). Moreover, regional economic adjustments based on real exchange differentials take a significant amount of time.

As first evidence from the past decade indicates, the relevant economic fundamentals in most euro area economies have tended to diverge. Looking at cross-country differences in the two crucial elements for the conduct of monetary policy – the inflation rate and the output gap – one can see that there were persistent differentials that generated at least some kind of redistributive effects. The ECB has published two main studies on inflation differentials (ECB 2003, 2005) and explicitly notes that 'inflation differentials in the euro area appear to be very persistent' (ECB 2005: 63). During much of the decade, member states such as Greece, Ireland, the Netherlands and Spain experienced significantly higher inflation rates than the euro area average. Most of them have also grown above potential. Of course, the situation of higher inflation has a dynamic effect of reducing the competitiveness of that country and therefore in principle in the long run works as an automatic stabilizer. Germany, by contrast, has had the lowest inflation and highest real interest rates, while remaining far below its potential growth rate. Again, low German prices would eventually be able to benefit the competitiveness of German products in the export markets even if not immediately. Overall, there is an intriguing positive relationship with a fit of roughly 0.5 between average deviations from euro area inflation and average deviations from the euro area output gap in the first years of EMU (Deroose *et al.* 2004: 10). The International Monetary Fund (IMF) (2004) also finds initial evidence for the primacy of the real interest rate effect over the real exchange rate effect.

The relationship between the real interest rate effect and the real exchange rate effect has crucial implications for the institutional set-up of EMU and also for the analysis of EMU's legitimacy (Enderlein 2006a). If the primacy of the real interest rate over the real exchange rate is a structural feature of EMU, as seems to be the case in the first decade of EMU, it is quite likely that in the euro area there will be a trend towards cyclical divergence instead of convergence. Ultimately, there could be a risk that EMU splits into two equally sized groups of countries, one with high growth and high inflation rates, the other with low growth and low inflation rates, with the ECB targeting a zero growth and zero inflation average in the middle. This scenario may become even more likely as new EU members join EMU. In such a context, the ECB's monetary policy would be inappropriate for all EMU members. As such, this would not generate insurmountable problems, however. As ECB President Duisenberg noted as early as September 1999: 'A single currency does not call for uniform wage developments or uniform economic or social policies in general. On the contrary – where national or regional economic developments are different, this should be reflected in different policy responses and wage developments' (ECB 1999). In other words, fiscal policy and wage-setting should be in charge of stabilizing the domestic business cycle, thus strengthening the role of domestic economic policies in EMU, rather than weakening them.

Most of the evidence suggests that EMU has triggered redistributive effects and that member state economic policies have responded with specific national answers (see Enderlein 2006b for a review of domestic adjustments). Rather than triggering further integration and synchronization of business cycles, EMU seems to have triggered diversion.

Redistribution as a consequence of welfare state adjustment

Would EMU be influencing member states' capacity to determine their own welfare state policies? Since EMU needs to be built on a strongly integrated internal market, national economic policies cannot freely choose their preferred domestic approach but have to adjust to significant regulatory pressure deriving from economic and monetary integration. Scharpf (2002: 648; italics in original) observes that 'compared to the repertoire of policy choices that was available two or three decades ago, European *legal* constraints have greatly reduced the capacity of national governments to influence growth and employment in the economies for whose performances they are politically accountable.'

Many authors who were writing on globalization and 'neo-liberalism' argued that the welfare state itself was at risk. The fear was that there would be a race to the bottom in terms of public expenditure on welfare states as a result of two mechanisms. First, competition between member states for investment would drive taxes down (thus generating fewer state revenues). Second, the same pressures would also drive social security premiums down so as to ensure that employers were not paying too much in non-wage costs that affected their cost structure. The result was a prediction that EMU would cause welfare state retrenchment (Leander and Guzzini 1997; Rhodes 1997). However, the creation of EMU has reduced the costs of servicing the debt. Interest rates on public debt have come down and effectively created more financial space for public spending.[1]

Tolga Bolukbasi (2007, 2009) suggests that although most of the literature supported the claim that EMU will lead to welfare retrenchment (and that this literature mostly felt this was a 'bad' development), the actual empirical studies of the amount of money spent on welfare state expenses throughout Europe in the past decade indicate that this amount has gone up rather than down. In other words, it is difficult to find support for the claim made by that literature. The debt servicing matter aside, it could, of course, very well be that the counterfactual (how much would governments have spent on welfare state expenditure *without EMU*?) could have been more. But the fact is that, despite EMU, welfare state expenditure did not go down. Also, the quality of expenditure and of the welfare state does not appear to have been reduced by all that much (if at all). There have been some changes in the allocation of funds in welfare states but some of those reallocations had to do with cost control in an environment that requires higher expenditure because of the ageing population, and so on. In other words, we cannot find support for the claim that EMU caused welfare state retrenchment in the sense that it undermined states' capacity to have a welfare state of their liking. What is, however, an effect of EMU is the fact that it is cheaper for governments to borrow money than it was before EMU.

Summing up, EMU has increased overall welfare; it has triggered redistributive effects via the real interest rate channel, but welfare state retrenchment has not taken place. What are the implications of this combination of effects? A monetary union has to strike a balance between considerations of union-wide efficiency and legitimacy (Sadeh *et al.* 2007). Obviously, that balance is more easily reached in an optimum currency area, where establishing a monetary union is a pure Pareto improvement and does not generate any redistributive implications. However, as soon as efficiency-increasing policies generate spill-overs of a redistributive nature, striking the balance between efficiency and legitimacy becomes more difficult (Eichengreen 1990).

3. EMU'S LEGITIMACY: WHAT HAVE WE LEARNED ABOUT THE DEMOCRATIC DEFICIT?

EMU's technical and institutional achievements are merely the necessary condition for its overall success. The sufficient condition implies a widespread acceptance of the implications triggered by EMU. Therefore, given the close functional links between different economic instruments, the spill-over effects discussed in the previous sections are likely to have an impact on EMU's legitimacy. If it was confirmed that business-cycle convergence is indeed tending to increase rather than decrease, the current EMU framework and its underlying provisions on legitimacy should be reassessed. In particular, new thought would have to be given to the future of the fiscal framework and to the possibility of preserving different social and employment models that currently coexist within the euro area.

The analysis of the 'democratic deficit' of EMU had started even before the euro was introduced and the ECB established (Jones 2002b; Verdun 1998). After a strong focus on the ECB itself, scholarly focus on legitimacy issues in EMU spread out to the institutional features of EMU as a whole (mainly discussing the question of the need for a *gouvernement économique* (Dyson 1994; Howarth 2001; Verdun 1996, 2000) before touching upon connected areas such as the Stability and Growth Pact (Collignon 2004; Heipertz and Verdun 2004, 2010; Howarth 2004; Savage and Verdun 2007), the open method of co-ordination and the Lisbon Strategy (Hodson and Maher 2001; Scharpf 2002), and the EU budget (Enderlein *et al.* 2005). We now briefly review the discussions on the ECB and the overall institutional framework.

The legitimacy of the ECB

In the early discussions on the design of the ECB, various authors argued that economic policy might fall victim to lack of speedy and effective co-ordination (Dyson 1994; Johnson 1994; Verdun 2000). Their argument was that with the creation of a supranational monetary authority but no transfer of sovereignty over fiscal policy, in case of difficulty, monetary policy could be easily conducted effectively, but not so fiscal policy.

The first ten years of EMU have shown the ECB to be very predictable about its policies. Many observers have taken the line that the ECB is 'secretive', 'slow', unnecessarily lacking 'flexibility' (Howarth and Loedel 2005). The point that the Governing Council of the ECB has tried to make, however, is that it needed to be predictable and that way build up credibility (De Haan *et al.* 2004). The overarching strategy to meet its mandate to preserve price stability was to anchor price expectations. As such, the ECB's assessment of its own legitimacy has been entirely on 'output legitimacy'. Looking at the assessment of the euro and the ECB's role in the first decade of EMU, the results are positive (Banducci *et al.* 2009).

Moreover, the intensity of the debates surrounding the ECB has significantly decreased in the course of the past decade. The main reason may be that the democratic structure underlying the ECB's role is being better understood: the ECB has been given a democratic mandate through democratically mandated procedures and bodies (national referenda, national parliaments, and indirectly through national government); the ECB statutes are part of the EU Treaty structure and thus signed by heads of state and government and ratified by parliaments. The mandate is clear, hierarchically structured and transparent. Monetary policy is geared towards the maintenance of price stability (the support of the general economic policies of the Community being only possible if the outcome is 'without prejudice to the objective of price stability', Treaty Establishing the European Community (TEC) Art. 105(1)) and thus leaves little room for policy discretion.

The above assessment confirms what Majone (1998) and others have shown: the ECB has been granted a mandate much like that of a constitutional court or an independent regulatory agency. The mandate can be changed if it is deemed inappropriate. Also, the ECB itself has developed a comprehensive system of channels of communication and practices of accountability (Jabko 2003).

In short, even if voices occasionally refer to the need for a *gouvernement économique* or changes to the ECB's mandate, no real discussion on this issue has emerged over the past decade. Numerous occasions, on which the statutes could have been changed (the Treaties of Amsterdam and Nice, the Treaty Establishing a Constitution for Europe and the Lisbon Treaty), did not even generate a discussion on the ECB, its mandate and statute.

The legitimacy of EMU's institutional design

When EMU was designed, it followed an incremental path of European economic integration that had been developing for decades. EMU firmed up the concrete basis that had been established during the 1980s through the European Monetary System (EMS), the single market project and incremental integration in various areas of policy-making. What it did not achieve, however, was to introduce a fully-fledged federal-like system. In the 1970s there had been various studies done about the need for fiscal federalism in the EU, such as the 1975 Tindemans Report and the 1977 MacDougall Report (Verdun 2000). In other words, by the late 1980s and early 1990s although the creation of a European System of Central Banks and a European Central Bank, modelled after the successful German central bank, the Bundesbank, was envisaged, the plan to create EMU in three stages did not envisage simultaneously the creation of a federal-like economic authority. In other words, the design of EMU was 'asymmetrical' (Verdun 1996, 2000).

This asymmetry did not produce a democratic deficit, however. There is now a solid common understanding of the nature of the present framework and its provisions on legitimacy. In the Maastricht Treaty, EMU is described as a rather rigid legal construction gearing at specific objectives, on which societal preferences have largely converged. Price stability and the soundness of fiscal policies are considered as the constitutive pillars of the framework and enshrined with comparatively great detail in the Treaty and primary legislation, thus enjoying significant isolation from direct policy input (Gormley and de Haan 1996). As stated above, the ECB's mandate is solidly anchored in the policy preferences of EMU participants (Kaltenthaler 2006). In a similar vein, the legal framework on fiscal policy co-ordination, as set out in the Stability and Growth Pact (SGP) and the Excessive Deficit Procedure (EDP), is focused on sustainability issues ('close to balance or in surplus', Council Regulations 1466/97 and 1467/97) rather than on welfare consequences of fiscal stances and their inter-temporal implications (e.g. Fatás and Mihov 2003). Many analyses also point to the normative origins of that approach as the emulation of the widely respected German case and its conceptual groundings in a certain understanding of economics (e.g. Dyson and Featherstone 1999; McNamara 1998).

The legitimacy of this framework clearly derives from the efficiency increases or welfare-enhancing components of EMU. In this perspective, monetary policy (often quoted together with competition policy) is interpreted as the area of economic governance that in basically every advanced industrial economy enjoys insulation from direct political contestation. Delegating this task to the European level should thus be considered as legitimate as keeping it in the national realm. In theoretical terms, the particular nature of monetary policy as a functionally clearly delimitated task geared towards the objective of price stability justifies the exclusive focus of legitimacy provisions on the output side (Verdun 1998), even though the typical problems deriving from such a principal–agent set-up are likely to arise (Elgie 2002). The ECB frequently uses this line of argumentation pointing out that it has been entrusted with the task of pursuing a commonly agreed goal that does not hamper member states' own policy choices (ECB 2001, 2002). Though member states are generally obliged to consider their economic policies as a 'matter of common concern' (TEC Article 107), they enjoy sufficient room for manoeuvre to follow citizens' policy inputs, thus complementing the output legitimacy dimension of monetary policy with an input dimension in the other areas.

Quite strikingly, this innovative design of structures of legitimacy has not translated into a 'democratic deficit' of EMU, even though the redistributive consequences of EMU are larger than expected (see above). Obviously, the issue of redistribution is likely to have an important impact on the question of the appropriate type of legitimacy. Pareto-improving policies can generally be legitimized on the basis of their result only ('output legitimacy'). Welfare distributing policies, on the other hand, either require a direct type of procedural legitimacy ('input legitimacy') or a very strong collective normative basis (often a common national identity) establishing the readiness of all participants to comply with the redistributive implications of an output-oriented type of policy (one example from national politics is unemployment insurance; in the European context one could think about fiscal federalism or redistribution via the EU budget).

In the EU, the degree of collective acceptance of possible redistributive implications of EMU is arguably quite low, in particular if one takes into account that such redistribution can hardly be justified as deriving from direct political input and thus bears the risk of being perceived as illegitimate. So it is puzzling to conclude that EMU's legitimacy seems to be solid, although redistributive effects are stronger than expected. If anything, this reconfirms the *sui generis* character of EMU and the difficulty of applying benchmarks from national contexts to the assessment of EMU.

3. EMU'S POWER STRUCTURE – IS FURTHER POLITICAL INTEGRATION NECESSARY?

EMU's institutional framework has also often been labelled as a *sui generis* construction. The puzzling results on the questions of redistribution and legitimacy ultimately also raise the question on the allocation of decision-taking powers in EMU and thus on the overall allocation of power. The claim by some observers that EMU had been built by utility-maximizing power-players (cf. Moravcsik 1998) implies that further political integration would either have to increase the power position of those actors or at least not take place at their expense. At the other extreme, one could have expected to see the emergence of truly European institutions and agenda-setters, slowly contributing to the emergence of a *gouvernement économique*. Neither of the two expectations proves right: after the first ten years of EMU, there is an abundance of views on how much political integration may be necessary to keep EMU sustainable in the long run; yet the system looks stable.

Assessing the overall institutional set-up of EMU, we have witnessed the consolidation of the EMU framework that, at the time it was conceived, many observers found odd, or unlikely to be stable (e.g. Cohen 1998: ch. 4; Feldstein 1997; McNamara 1998; McKay 1999). The peculiar mixture of national and European interests across formal, semi-formal and informal bodies and fora has seemed to work just fine (see Hodson 2009). The Eurogroup – the group of finance ministers from the euro area countries – meets before the Economic and Financial Affairs (Ecofin) Council meeting and seeks to co-ordinate fiscal policy in a rather secretive and very informal framework (there is not even a formal protocol). So the informal network has been strengthened, although many observers had feared that informal rules in EMU would lead to conflict.

At the European level, we have seen the ECB developing into an unexpectedly strong and autonomous European player, completely neglecting national concerns. The ECB has resisted criticism of its mandate, but has shown some flexibility in adjusting (and improving) its initial two-pillar strategy and has successfully responded to criticism on its provisions on transparency and accountability (Jabko 2003). At the same time, the ECB has been much less successful in strengthening its position as the worldwide voice of the euro. The external representation of EMU still looks as messy as a decade ago. The European Commission's role in supervising the institutional framework of EMU has been of mixed success. While it managed to keep the common fiscal framework pretty much alive (see below), it has certainly not managed to take on a leading autonomous co-ordinating role in economic policy-making. A ranking of the importance of the three key individuals in the management of the euro area would put the EU's Commissioner for Economic and Financial Affairs clearly behind the ECB President and the President of the Eurogroup.

Looking at fiscal policies, we have seen that the half-institutionalized frame-work that was so aggressively criticized might have crumbled, but did not fall apart. The French and German governments might have managed to interrupt the rules of the EDP of the SGP and buy themselves time. But ultimately, the discussions of November 2003 and the reform of 2005 had a surprisingly stabilizing effect on the overall framework. If anything, by 2007 it seemed that most countries had accepted the broader SGP regime and were incorporating in their daily business the medium-term objectives and the reference values for excessive deficits (Heipertz and Verdun 2010). Moreover, even the most critical observers must admit that financial markets cared much less about fiscal free-riding that many had assumed (Leblond 2006). Also, financial markets did not respond much to the fiscal profligacy of member states in the run-up to the SGP crisis of November 2003 or in its immediate aftermath. Moreover, fiscal free-riding and excessive deficits in the largest member states had no immediate impact on ECB monetary policy, despite the fear of a game of 'chicken' arising between fiscal and monetary policy authorities and vague ECB threats that it would (Howarth and Loedel 2005). Until the recent global financial crisis the yield spreads on euro-denominated government bonds of euro member states narrowed.

Yet another result emerges from the assessment of economic policy co-ordination. We have seen that EMU actually brought about a small renaissance of domestic economic policy-making rather than generating widespread co-ordination of economic policies in EMU (Enderlein 2006b). This room for manoeuvre was possible in part due to the safety-net provided by EMU; financial markets could no longer respond to these policies by targeting the country's exchange rate if economic policies were not in line with market expectation (as was the case in the early 1980s when there was a run on the French franc following the policies of Mitterrand; or the difficult position Denmark and Sweden are in today following the fall-out of the global financial market of autumn 2008). Indeed, EMU member states have experienced that there are good reasons to preserve a high degree of national autonomy in fiscal policy to act counter-cyclically in an asymmetric downturn (fiscal consolidation indeed took place during cyclical upswings). And wage-setting was chosen by several countries as an instrument to fight domestic inflation or to increase competitiveness within EMU (see Johnston and Hancké 2009; also Enderlein 2006b).

As a conclusion, and perhaps most surprisingly, this strange mixture of contradicting results on political integration has not led to an overall weakening of EMU. Most observers refer to EMU as a success, even though today's features of EMU probably do not correspond to what critics or proponents had in mind 10 to 15 years ago. So the assessment that EMU would become unstable without further institutional change in the area of political union or without more centralization of economic government did not seem to be a necessary condition, at least based on the experience of the first ten years of EMU.[2]

4. CONCLUSION AND OUTLOOK: EMU IN THE GLOBAL FINANCIAL CRISIS

The first decade of EMU has shown that the risks envisaged by critics did not materialize in any serious way. Yet EMU's success story does not follow the plot of a slick screenplay either. The first ten years have resulted in a strange mixture of outcomes, which do not correspond to any of the many causal chains identified by its critics. EMU is generating welfare distributing effects, yet its legitimacy is strong and the innovative or peculiar institutional framework is functioning quite well. Thus, we draw the main conclusion that EMU has strengthened its *sui generis* character and might continue to do so in the coming years. Having said this, the big question for the next decade is whether this peculiar mixture of outcomes will stay the same even in the context of the global financial crisis.

Looking at current developments, one can identify three main reasons why the financial crisis might negatively affect EMU's success story. First, the economic downturn could have an effect on EMU's legitimacy – accepting redistributive effects in good times is much easier than in bad times. Second, the rapidly worsening fiscal position of many euro area member countries could put significant strain on the common fiscal framework – ultimately, even a sovereign default in the euro area cannot be completely excluded. Having said that, to date, countries within EMU have fared better in the financial crisis than those outside. Third, national utility maximization might well resurface, giving rise to concepts that were about to disappear, such as protectionism, the support of domestic industries and the financial sector with subsidies, beggar-thy-neighbour wage and tax policies, and the like.

The financial crisis could also have positive effects. First, the ECB, the euro, EMU even with its fiscal regime, could emerge strengthened (Heipertz and Verdun 2010). Depending on how the crisis management continues, Europeans might look at EMU as a safety net in the crisis. Second, the EU's still chaotic framework of banking regulation and supervision could finally become more centralized, thus giving rise to further integration in financial markets (see Quaglia 2009). Such a move would definitely strengthen EMU. Third, the crisis could foster co-ordination of domestic economic policies. Even though the Franco-German dissent in the autumn of 2008 on how to react to the crisis referred back to the run-up to EMU, the widely acknowledged successes of the French Presidency of the EU in managing the crisis could give rise to calls for further integration and centralization.

EMU as a teenager looks very different to what we expected at its birth. But we are confident that it will meet the challenge of its teenage years. We have to acknowledge that the linkages between the economic mechanisms at work in EMU and the political setting, in which they are embedded, are still not as well understood as we would like. The 'sui generis question', i.e. the question as to whether a monetary union can operate successfully in the absence of a highly integrated political union, is still awaiting a clear answer. The financial crisis is the first major test of EMU's teenage years, but it is as much a challenge as an opportunity. If EMU manages to cope with this enormous challenge, it will likely have an easier life as an adult.

NOTES

* We thank David Howarth and Erik Jones for comments and criticisms on an earlier version of this article.
1 We are grateful to Erik Jones for reminding us of this point.
2 Of course, some observers argued that even though EMU was not designed according to the textbook, the specific European model might make it robust in the long run. Jones (2002a) argued that EMU's diversity was a strength and not a weakness and that efforts to centralize authority would be more destabilizing that stabilizing; Verdun (2000) argued that there was no support for further economic and political integration to accompany the creation of EMU in the late 1990s, and that a crisis would be needed to make any next steps politically desirable and acceptable. We will see what the future brings.

REFERENCES

Banducci, S.A., Karp, J.A. and Loedel, P.H. (2009) 'Economic interests and public support for the euro', *Journal of European Public Policy*, special issue on 'Ten Years of EMU', 16(4): 564–81.

Bolukbasi, H.T. (2007) 'Plus ça change . . .? The European social model between "economic governance" and "social Europe" from the Maastricht Treaty to the European Constitution', *Current Politics and Economics of Europe* 18(2): 149–79.

Bolukbasi, H.T. (2009) 'On consensus, constraint and choice: economic and monetary integration and Europe's welfare states', *Journal of European Public Policy*, special issue on 'Ten Years of EMU', 16(4): 527–44.

Bordo, M.D. and Jonung L. (2003) 'The future of EMU: what does history tell us?', in F.H. Capie and G.E. Wood (eds), *Monetary Unions: Theory, History, Public Choice*, London and New York: Routledge.

Cohen, B.J. (1998) *The Geography of Money*, Ithaca, NY: Cornell University Press.

Collignon, S. (2004) 'Is Europe going far enough? Reflections on the EU's economic governance', *Journal of European Public Policy* 11(5): 909–925.

Commission of the European Communities (1990) 'One money, one market', *European Economy*, No. 44.

Commission of the European Communities (1991) The economics of EMU. Background studies for *European Economy No. 44 – One Money One Market'*, *European Economy*, Special Edition No. 1.

De Haan, J., Ambtenbrink, F. and Waller, S. (2004) 'The transparency and credibility of the European Central Bank', *Journal of Common Market Studies* 42(4): 775–94.

Delors Report (1989) *Report on Economic and Monetary Union in the European Community*, Committee for the Study of Economic and Monetary Union, Luxembourg: Office for Official Publications of the European Communities.

Deroose, S., Langedijk, S. and Roeger, W. (2004) 'Reviewing adjustment dynamics in EMU: from overheating to overcooling', *European Commission Economic Paper*, No. 198.

Dyson, K.H.F. (1994) *Elusive Union: The Process of Economic and Monetary Union in Europe*, London and New York: Longman.

Dyson, K. and Featherstone, K. (1999) *The Road to Maastricht: Negotiating Economic and Monetary Union*, Oxford: Oxford University Press.

ECB (1999) The past and future of European integration: a central banker's perspective, Peer Jacobsen Lecture by Willem F. Duisenberg.

ECB (2001) 'The economic-policy framework in EMU', *ECB Monthly Bulletin*: 51–65.

ECB (2002) 'The accountability of the ECB', *ECB Monthly Bulletin*: 45–57.

ECB (2003) *Inflation Differentials in the Euro Area*, Frankfurt/Main: European Central Bank.

ECB (2005) 'Monetary policy and inflation differentials in a heterogeneous currency area', *ECB Monthly Bulletin*: 61–77.

Eichengreen, B. (1990) 'One money for Europe: lessons from the us currency union', *Economic Policy* 10, April.

Eichengreen, B. (1993) 'Is Europe an optimum currency area?', in S. Borner and H. Grubel (eds), *The European Community after 1992. Perspectives from the Outside*, London: Macmillan, pp. 138–61.

Eichengreen, B. (1995) 'Fiscal policy and EMU', in B. Eichengreen and J. Frieden (eds), *The Political Economy of European Monetary Unification*, Boulder, CO and Oxford: Westview Press, pp. 167–90.

Elgie, R. (2002) 'The politics of the European Central Bank: principal–agent theory and the democratic deficit', *Journal of European Public Policy* 9(2): 186–200.

Enderlein, H. (2006a) 'The euro and political union: do economic spillovers from monetary integration affect the legitimacy of EMU?', *Journal of European Public Policy* 13(7): 1133–46.

Enderlein, H. (2006b) 'Adjusting to EMU: the impact of monetary union on domestic fiscal and wage-setting institutions', *European Union Politics* 7(1): 113–40.

Enderlein, H., Lindner, J., Calvo-Gonzáles, O. and Ritter, R. (2005) *'The EU budget: how much scope for institutional reform?'*, ECB Occasional Paper Series *27*.

EU Commission (2008) *EMU@10 – successes and challenges after ten years of economic and monetary union;* http://ec.europa.eu/economy_finance/emu10/reports_en.htm

Fatás, A. and Mihov, I. (2003) 'The case for restricting fiscal policy discretion', *Quarterly Journal of Economics* 118(4): 1419–47.

Feldstein, M. (1997) 'EMU and international conflict', *Foreign Affairs,* November–December 76(6): 60–73.

Frankel, J.A. and Rose, A.K. (1998) 'The endogeneity of the optimum currency area criteria', *The Economic Journal* 108(449): 1009–25.

Gormley, L. and de Haan, J. (1996) 'The democratic deficit of the European Central Bank', *European Law Review* 21(1): 95–112.

Heipertz, M. and Verdun, A. (2004) 'The dog that would never bite? What we can learn from the origins of the Stability and Growth Pact', *Journal of European Public Policy* 11(5): 765–80.

Heipertz, M. and Verdun, A. (2010, forthcoming) *Ruling Europe: The Politics of the Stability and Growth Pact*, Cambridge: Cambridge University Press.

Hodson, D. (2009) 'EMU and political union: what, if anything, have we learned from the euro's first decade?', *Journal of European Public Policy,* special issue on 'Ten Years of EMU', 16(3): 508–26.

Hodson, D. and Maher, I. (2001) 'The open method as a new mode of governance: the case of soft economic policy co-ordination', *Journal of Common Market Studies* 39(4): 719–46.

Hodson, D. and Maher, I. (2002) 'Economic and monetary union: balancing credibility and legitimacy in an asymmetric policy-mix', *Journal of European Public Policy* 9(3): 391–407.

Howarth, D. (2001) *The French Road to European Monetary Union*, Basingstoke: Palgrave.

Howarth, D. (2004) 'Introduction' (special issue on European economic governmance and the Stability and Growth Pact) *Journal of European Public Policy* 11(5): 761–4.

Howarth, D. (2007) 'Making and breaking the rules: French policy on EU "gouvernement économique"', *Journal of European Public Policy* 14(7): 1061–78.

Howarth, D. and Loedel, P. (2005) *The European Central Bank*, 2nd edn, Basingstoke: Palgrave Macmillan.

IMF (2004) 'Has fiscal behavior changed under the European economic and monetary union?',, *World Economic Outlook*, September: 103–36.

Jabko, N. (2003) 'Democracy in the age of the euro', *Journal of European Public Policy* 10(5): 710–39.

Johnson, C. (1994) 'Fiscal and monetary policy in economic and monetary union', in A. Duff, J. Pinder and R. Pryce (eds), *Maastricht and Beyond. Building the European Union*, London and New York: Routledge, pp. 71–83.

Johnston, A. and Hancké, B. (2009) 'Wage inflation and labour unions in EMU', *Journal of European Public Policy,* special issue on 'Ten Years of EMU', 16(4): 601–22.

Jones, E. (2002a) *The Politics of Economic and Monetary Union: Integration and Idiosyncrasy*, Lanham, MD: Rowman & Littlefield.

Jones, E. (2002b) 'Macroeconomic preferences and Europe's democratic deficit', in A. Verdun (ed.), *The Euro: European Integration Theory and Economic and Monetary Union*, Lanham, MD: Rowman & Littlefield, pp. 145–64.

Kaltenthaler, K. (2006) *Policy-Making in the European Central Bank: The Masters of Europe's Money*, Lanham, MD: Rowman & Littlefield.

Kenen, P.B. (1969) 'The theory of optimum currency areas: an eclectic view', in R. Mundell and A. Swoboda (eds), *Monetary Problems of the International Economy*, Chicago: University of Chicago Press, pp. 41–60.

Krugman, P. (1993) 'Lessons of Massachusetts for EMU', in F. Giavazzi and F. Torres (eds), *The Transition to Economic and Monetary Union in Europe*, Cambridge: Cambridge University Press, pp. 241–61.

Leander, A. and Guzzini, S. (1997) 'European economic and monetary union and the crisis of social contracts', in P. Minkkinen and H. Patomäki (eds), *The Politics of Economic and Monetary Union*, Helsinki: The Finnish Institute of International Affairs.

Leblond, P. (2006) 'The political Stability and Growth Pact is dead: long live the economic Stability and Growth Pact', *Journal of Common Market Studies* 44(5): 969–90.

Maclennan, D., Muellbauer, J. and Stephens, M. (1998) 'Asymmetries in housing and financial market institutions and EMU', *Oxford Review of Economic Policy* 14(3): 54–80.

Majone, G. (1998) 'Europe's "democratic deficit": the question of standards', *European Law Journal* 4(1): 5–28.

McKay, D. (1999) 'The political sustainability of EMU', *British Journal of Political Science* 29: 463–85.

McKinnon, R. (1963) 'Optimum currency areas', *American Economic Review* 53: 717–25.

McNamara, K.R. (1998) *The Currency of Ideas: Monetary Politics in the European Union* Ithaca, NY: Cornell University Press.

Moravcsik, A. (1998) *The Choice for Europe: Social Purpose and State Power from Messina to Maastricht*, Ithaca, NY: Cornell University Press.

Mundell, R.A. (1961) 'A theory of optimum currency areas', *American Economic Review* 51: 509–17.

Padoa-Schioppa, T. (2004) *The Euro and Its Central Bank*, Cambridge, MA: The MIT Press.

Quaglia, L. (2009) 'Political science and the "Cinderellas" of economic and monetary union: payment services and clearing and settlement', *Journal of European Public Policy*, special issue on 'Ten Years of EMU', 16(4): 623–39.

Rhodes, M. (1997) 'The welfare state: internal challenges, external constraints', in M. Rhodes, P. Heywood and V. Wright (eds), *Developments in West European Politics*, London: Macmillan, pp. 57–74.

Risse, T., Engelmann-Martin, D., Knope, H.-J. and Roscher, K. (1999) 'To euro or not to euro: the EMU and identity politics in the European Union', *European Journal of International Relations* 5(2): 147–87.

Sachs, J.D. and Sala-i-Martín, X. (1992) 'Fiscal federalism and optimum currency areas: Evidence for Europe from the United States', in M. Canzoneri, V. Grilli and P.R. Masson (eds), *Establishing a Central Bank: Issues in Europe and Lessons from the US*, Cambridge: Cambridge University Press.

Sadeh, T. and Verdun, A. (2009) 'Explaining Europe's monetary union: a survey of the literature', *International Studies Review* 11(2), (June).

Sadeh, T., Jones, E. and Verdun, A. (2007) 'Legitimacy and efficiency: revitalizing EMU ahead of enlargement', *Review of International Political Economy* 14(5): 839–45.

Savage, J.D. and Verdun, A. (2007) 'Reforming Europe's stability and growth pact: Lessons from the American experience in macrobudgeting', *Review of International Political Economy* 14(5): 842–67.

Scharpf, F.W. (1999) *Governing Europe. Effective and Democratic?*, Oxford: Oxford University Press.

Scharpf, F.W. (2002) 'The European social model: coping with the challenges of diversity', *Journal of Common Market Studies* 40(4): 645–70.

Verdun, A. (1996) 'An "asymmetrical" economic and monetary union in the EU: perceptions of monetary authorities and social partners', *Journal of European Integration* 20(1): 59–81.

Verdun, A. (1998) 'The institutional design of EMU: a democratic deficit?', *Journal of Public Policy* 18(2): 107–32.

Verdun, A. (2000) *European Responses to Globalization and Financial Market Integration. Perceptions of EMU in Britain, France and Germany*, Basingstoke: Macmillan/ New York: St.Martin's Press.

Verdun, A. (2003) 'La nécessité d'un "gouvernement économique" dans une UEM asymétrique. Les préoccupations françaises sont-elles justifiées?', *Politique Européenne* 10: 11–32.

Verdun, A. and Christiansen, T. (2000) 'Policies, institutions and the euro: dilemmas of legitimacy', in C. Crouch (ed.), *After the Euro: Shaping Institutions for Governance in the Wake of European Monetary Union*, Oxford: Oxford University Press, pp. 162–78.

Verdun, A. and Christiansen, T. (2001) 'The legitimacy of the euro: an inverted process?', *Current Politics and Economics of Europe* 10(3): 265–88.

EMU and political union: what, if anything, have we learned from the euro's first decade?

Dermot Hodson

INTRODUCTION

The revival of plans for economic and monetary union (EMU) in the late 1980s gave rise to competing claims concerning the relationship between monetary and political integration in Europe. At one end of the spectrum, the Delors Committee, which had been asked by the European Council in 1988 to prepare a blueprint for EMU, rejected the existence of a link between these two streams of integration. A monetary union, its final report concluded, could 'continue to consist of individual nations with differing economic, social, cultural and political characteristics ... and autonomy in economic decision-making' (Committee for the Study of Economic and Monetary Union 1989: 17). At the other end of the spectrum, the British Chancellor Nigel Lawson insisted that EMU implied 'nothing less than European Government ... and political union, the United States of Europe' (quoted in Dyson 1994: 1). It is now ten years since eleven member states took the decision to adopt the euro, making the Delors Committee's vision of EMU a reality. What, if anything, have we learned over the last decade about the relationship between monetary and political integration in Europe?

This article offers a three-fold answer to this question. Firstly, euro area members have intensified the co-ordination of macroeconomic policies and structural reforms over the last ten years but EMU has not, as some predicted, created noticeable functional pressures for a further centralization of economic decision-making in the European Union (EU). Secondly, the last ten years have disappointed those who expected euro area members to press ahead with plans for political integration beyond the economic sphere. Thirdly, member states' reluctance to address fundamental questions about EMU's future during the negotiations of the Lisbon Treaty suggest that, if anything, the processes of monetary and political integration in Europe may be decoupling. Although it may be premature to declare the Delors Committee victor in the debate over EMU and political union, arguments that posit a strong relationship between the two projects appear, from the present juncture, to have been overstated.

The remainder of this article is divided into three main sections. Section I discusses different definitions of political union and explores two broad strands of argumentation concerning the relationship between monetary and political integration in the EU. Section II asks how well these arguments stood up during the first decade of the euro. Section III explores the Lisbon Treaty's limited focus on EMU and considers the possibility that monetary and political integration may be decoupling.

I. TWO ARGUMENTS ABOUT EMU AND POLITICAL UNION

The concept of political union is, as Padoa-Schioppa (2000: 166) notes, 'much less clear-cut, much more elusive, than it might appear at first sight'. Commentators who posit the existence of a relationship between EMU and political union rarely define the term 'political union' explicitly or spell out what they understand the causal relationship between monetary and political integration to be. To gain some analytic leverage on this issue, this section distinguishes between two broad strands of argumentation that have underpinned academic and policy debates. The first equates political integration with the centralization of economic decision-making in the EU, which it treats as a matter of functional necessity for the smooth functioning of EMU. The second focuses on the centralization of decision-making beyond the economic sphere and treats political union as a goal that euro area members will intentionally pursue.

The Hungarian economist Bela Balassa (1961) famously distinguished between the five stages of economic integration: (i) a free trade area in which tariffs and quantitative restrictions on commodities have been removed; (ii) a customs union which combines a free trade area with equalized tariffs *vis-à-vis* third parties; (iii) a common market in which barriers to the free movement of capital and labour are also eliminated; (iv) an economic union involving some degree of harmonization between national economic policies; and (v) a complete union characterized by the unification of monetary, fiscal, social and countercyclical policies under the control of a supranational authority. According to this classification, EMU is an advanced but incomplete stage of economic integration in so far as the Treaty Establishing the European Community (TEC) provides for the creation of a supranational monetary authority (Article 8 TEC) but recognizes member states' right to conduct their own economic policies (Article 98 TEC).

A recurring theme in scholarly and policy debates about EMU and political union is that EU policy-makers will find it necessary to take further steps towards a 'complete union' in order to reap the full benefits of the euro. Following Wolf (2002), this strand of argumentation is referred to as 'functionalist', since it echoes Mitrany's dictum that 'form follows function' (Mitrany 1943: 236). The terms neo-functionalism and intergovernmentalist are deliberately avoided here as those who treat political union as a functional necessity of EMU remain largely silent on the question of whether supranational institutions, subnational actors or national governments are the key drivers of integration.[1]

A number of reasons have been offered to support the claim that EMU necessitates political union thus defined. Tsoukalis (2005: 159) predicts that 'EMU is bound to have a centralising effect on economic policies' because the stabilization function of EMU 'should involve a continuous dialogue between the central bank and a European political institution responsible for economic policy'. This argument is reminiscent of the 1970 Werner Report, which, in addition to calling for integration in the monetary sphere, recommended the establishment of a supranational Centre of Decision for Economic Policy, which would act 'in accordance with the Community interest' and exercise 'a decisive influence over the general economic policy of the Community' (Werner 1970: 12).[2]

A variation on this argument suggests that EMU will necessitate the creation of a supranational budgetary instrument in the form of a euro area tax or system of transfer payments. There are two broad lines of support for this position. The first argues that a monetary union characterized by low factor mobility and comparatively sluggish product, labour and capital markets will have little choice but to create a supranational budgetary instrument to adjust to asymmetric economic shocks (see Goodhart and Smith 1993; Obstfeld and Peri 1998). An alternative justification suggests that a supranational budgetary instrument will be required to compensate the winners and losers from monetary integration and to address long-term growth and inflation differences in the euro area. This link between EMU and political union was emphasized by the McDougall Report (European Commission 1977) and, more recently, by De Grauwe (2006).

Another reason for thinking that EMU will necessarily lead to political union is that centralized decision-making in the economic sphere will be required to secure the legitimacy of monetary integration. This argument was famously employed by the Bundesbank President Karl Otto Pöhl, who suggested, in a paper he submitted to the Delors Committee, that '[a]lthough complete political union is not absolutely necessary for the establishment of a monetary union, the loss of national sovereignty in economic and monetary policy associated with it is so serious that it would probably be bearable only in the context of extremely close and irrevocable political integration' (Pöhl 1989: 136).

The idea that EMU should be embedded within a broader polity has its origins in coronation theory, an economic philosophy that is traditionally associated with Germany, reflecting the fact that the mark was adopted in 1879, eight years after political unification and 45 years after the establishment of the *Zollverein* (Maes 2004). The basic tenet of coronation theory is that a high degree of economic convergence coupled with measures to co-ordinate economic policies and promote solidarity with countries were required to ensure the sustainability of the single currency (Dyson and Featherstone 1999: 291).

For some scholars, the decision to centralize monetary policy in the euro area while leaving control of economic policy in the hands of member states could have grave consequences for the legitimacy of EMU. Dyson (1994) argues that '[i]n the absence of a European political order that promotes an effective identification with a single currency, by means of a range of common political symbols and channels for popular participation and influence, a depoliticized monetary policy lacks essential legitimacy' (Dyson 1994: 336). Verdun and Christiansen (2000: 178) warn that the failure of EMU's architects to embed the euro in a 'wider European polity' leaves the euro's legitimacy dangerously dependent on its perceived economic benefits and hence on short-term economic fluctuations.

Balassa's classification treats centralized economic decision-making as the end goal of European integration. The Dutch economist Willem Molle (2001: 18) offers an alternative taxonomy that gives greater attention to the possibility of integration beyond the economic sphere. He defines a 'full union' as a step beyond EMU, involving common policies in economic areas such as social security and income tax but also in non-economic areas such as judicial, foreign and security policy.

The idea that EMU might pave the way for political integration beyond the economic sphere is a longstanding one in debates about the dynamics of European integration. As early as 1950, the French economist Jacques Rueff is reported to have said that Europe would be unified through the creation of a single currency or not at all (quoted in Issing 2008: 8). This argument gathered force in advance of the single currency's launch with the scenario that euro area members might be willing to pursue additional forms of integration beyond the monetary and macroeconomic sphere being considered by some commentators to be an 'obvious possibility' (Wallace 1997: 232).

The most famous proponents of this argument were Wolfgang Schäuble and Karl Lamers, who linked membership of the European vanguard to participation in EMU. In their influential *Kerneuropa-Papier*, these authors called on EU member states who were on track to qualify for stage 3 of EMU to form an integrationist 'hard core' that would 'be recognizably more Community-spirited in their joint action that others, and launch common initiatives aimed at promoting the development of the Union' (Schäuble and Lamers 1994: 77).

This line of reasoning implies, as Andréani (2001: 15) puts it, that 'the inner core of countries participating in phase III of EMU would also be the countries most dedicated to political integration.' By adopting the single currency, euro area members have, in other words, revealed their willingness and ability to adopt a key plank of political union. The same group of countries should, it follows, be favourably disposed towards efforts to implement the remaining elements of political union. The term 'intentionalist', which is borrowed from Wolf (2002: 35), is used to describe this argument since it implies that political union follows EMU not out of necessity but because euro area members will voluntarily subscribe to this goal. Labels such as neo-functionalist, liberal-intergovernmentalist and constructivist are avoided here, since intentionalist arguments offer little insight into the mechanisms through which national preferences are generated.

In summary, the distinction drawn in this section between functionalist and intentionalist arguments is admittedly a simplistic one. Perhaps its most contentious assumption is to follow Balassa (1961) in equating political union with the centralization of decision-making at the EU level. As Pelkmans (2006: 9) points out in his powerful critique of Balassa's stages of economic integration, the validity of this assumption is questionable since existing political unions, such as the USA and Canada, are characterized by varying degrees of centralization in the economic and political sphere. This point is a valid one and it is taken up again in the conclusion. Nevertheless, the distinction between functionalism and intuitionalism is maintained on the grounds that it is sufficient to tease out what many (but not all) commentators mean when they argue that EMU will lead to political union. The next section switches focus from argument to evidence, asking whether there is any indication after a decade of the single currency to suggest that political union is a functional necessity for EMU or that euro area members are forging ahead with plans for ever closer union.

II. EMU AND POLITICAL UNION IN PRACTICE

The first decade of EMU provided a steep learning curve for European economic policy-makers. The ups and downs of the business cycle as well as developments in labour, housing and financial markets provided invaluable and sometimes harsh lessons in macroeconomic management and the link between structural reform and economic performance (see European Commission 2008). What, if anything, was learned during this period about the relationship between EMU and political union?

The European Council took a number of steps in advance of the euro's launch to reinforce macroeconomic policy co-ordination. The most important of these was the signature of the Stability and Growth Pact in 1999 with a view to speeding up and clarifying Article 104's excessive deficit procedure and promoting sound budgetary policies over the medium term. In the same year, the European Council agreed to establish (what became known as) the Eurogroup in response to concerns that EMU lacked an institutional forum in which the European Central Bank (ECB) and Finance Ministers could have an informal exchange of views on the economic policy mix.

EU policy-makers also implemented measures during this period to strengthen the co-ordination of supply-side reforms. The Luxembourg Process was launched in 1997 to give effect to the Amsterdam Treaty's provisions on the Employment

Guidelines. This was followed in 1998 by the Cardiff Process, a co-ordinated approach to product and capital market reforms, and in 1999 by the Cologne Process, which established a Macroeconomic Dialogue involving EU macroeconomic authorities and the Social Partners. These processes were streamlined under the Lisbon Strategy, an ambitious reform agenda launched in 2000 with the objective of making the EU the world's most competitive economy by 2010. The launch of the euro also intensified the EU's efforts to integrate financial markets and promote a convergence between national financial supervision practices through the adoption of the Financial Service Action Plan in May 1999.

Although the *function* of these policy initiatives – to plug the perceived gaps in the Maastricht Treaty's provisions for economic policy co-ordination – echoes the functionalist arguments reviewed in the previous section, the *form* they have taken does not. Attempts to strengthen economic policy co-ordination under EMU have steered well clear of encouraging a further centralization of economic policy, relying instead on new modes of policy-making that assign responsibility for policy formulation and implementation to member states rather than to supranational institutions (Hodson and Maher 2001).

The Stability and Growth Pact, though it gives the Commission a role in the surveillance of member states' budgetary policies, leaves the power of decision-making in the hands of national governments. The Eurogroup is a deliberative forum that keeps discussions between euro area Finance Ministers on a firmly intergovernmental footing (Puetter 2006). Likewise, the Lisbon Strategy places economic reform high on the EU's political agenda but it ultimately falls to member states to take responsibility for the design and implementation of specific policy initiatives. The EU's decentralized approach to financial market integration is embodied in the Lamfalussy Process, which, *inter alia*, fosters voluntary co-operation between officials from the European Commission and national supervisory authorities with a view to achieving the consistent and convergent implementation of EU directives in the securities, banking and insurance sectors (see Quaglia 2008).

If functionalist arguments are correct, then we would expect EMU to have paid a high price for member states' reluctance to relinquish control over their economic policies both in terms of the euro area's economic performance and with respect to the legitimacy of monetary integration. There is no conclusive evidence, thus far, to suggest that such a price has been paid even though EMU's decentralized system of governance encountered serious economic and political challenges during the euro's first decade.

In the budgetary sphere, the Stability and Growth Pact struggled to convince all euro area members to pursue sound budgetary positions over the medium term, most notably in France which, in contrast to Germany, has made limited progress in reducing cyclically adjusted net borrowing since the pronounced deterioration in the state of its public finances in the early years of EMU (see Figure 1). Nevertheless, the euro area, with its decentralized budgetary framework and informal approach to macroeconomic co-ordination, achieved a more significant and consistent reduction in cyclically adjusted

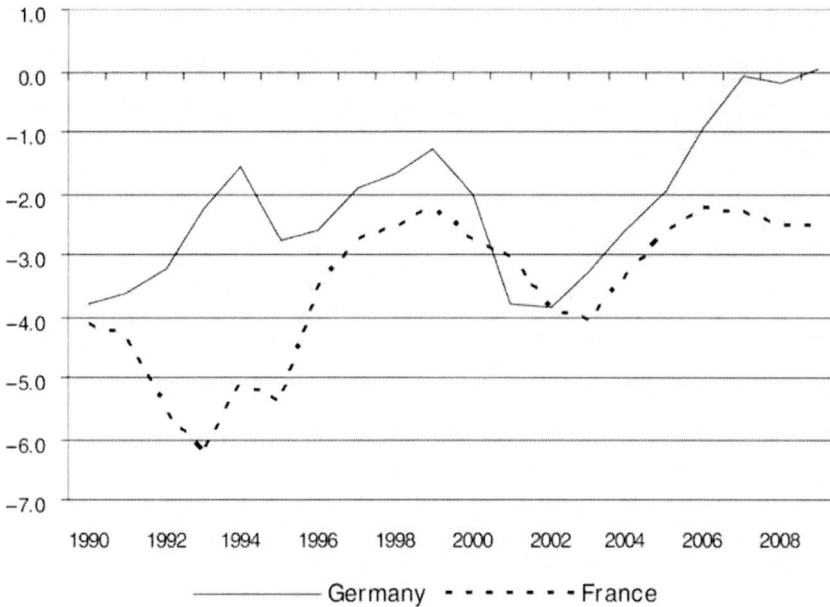

Figure 1 Cyclically adjusted general government balances (France and Germany, 1990–2008)
Source: OECD Economic Outlook.

borrowing during EMU's first decade than more centralized fiscal unions such as the UK and USA (see Figure 2).

After a decade of the euro the jury is still out on the question of whether EMU would benefit from the creation of a fiscal federation. Firstly, there are longstanding doubts about whether slow-moving centralized budgetary instruments can respond with sufficient rapidity to short-term economic shocks (Goodhart and Smith 1993: 420). Secondly, empirical estimates suggest that the redistributive effect of existing fiscal federations is far greater than their stabilization effect, i.e. they tend to compensate regions suffering from long-term economic disadvantage but have a limited impact on a region's capacity to adjust to short-term economic shocks (Fatás 1998). Thirdly, the debate about how a centralized budgetary mechanism could overcome the problems of adverse selection and moral hazard is ongoing (see Schelkle 2005; von Hagen and Wyplosz 2008).

In the structural domain, the Lisbon Strategy fell well short of its (original) aim to create the world's most competitive, dynamic knowledge-based economy by 2010 (Kok 2004). Analysis by Brandt et al. (2005) suggests, moreover, that although euro area members were among the Organization for Economic Co-operation and Development's (OECD's) most active structural reformers over the period 1994–2004, reform intensity in the euro area slackened following the launch of the euro in 1999. This finding raises serious doubts

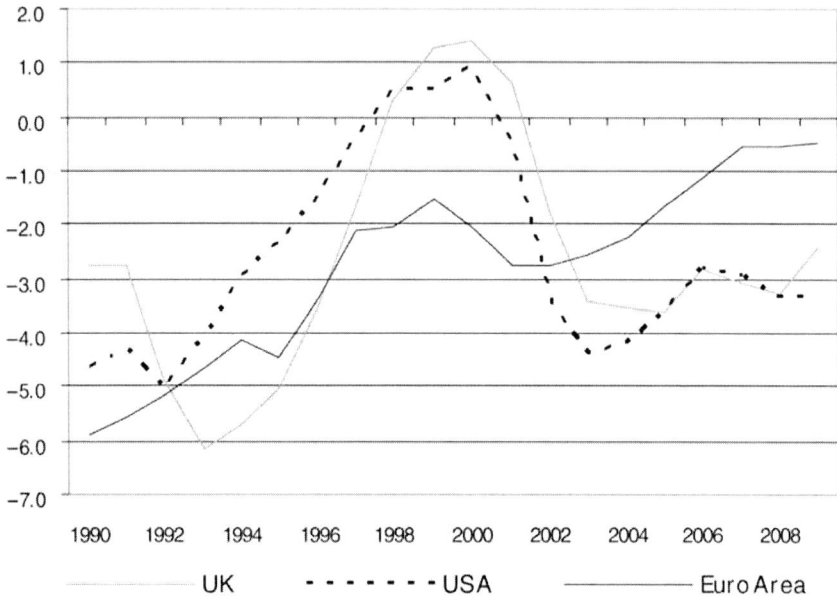

Figure 2 Cyclically adjusted general government balances (euro area 12, UK and USA, 1990–2008)
Source: OECD Economic Outlook.

about the ability of euro area members to adjust to asymmetric shocks, doubts which have been heightened by the persistence of cross-country inflation differences over the last decade (see Figure 3). Although concerns over macro-economic divergences within the euro area and the slow pace of adjustment have triggered debate about the sustainability of EMU (see Gros *et al.* 2005; European Commission 2006), these concerns do not in themselves justify a more centralized approach to structural reform in the EU. Imposing a common approach to economic reform could do more harm than good in member states that rely on different varieties of capitalism (see Hancké *et al.* 2007). There is also limited evidence thus far of significant positive cross-border spillover from product or labour reforms or negative spillover from a lack thereof (Tabellini and Wyplosz 2006).

   This situation has been strikingly different in the financial domain. The global turmoil that followed the collapse of the US subprime mortgage market in August 2007 confirmed the capacity for financial contagion within the EU and between the EU and the rest of the world. EU member states' initial response to this crisis included strengthening co-operation between national financial supervisors in the context of the Lamfalussy Process (ECOFIN Council 2008). It remains to be seen whether the crisis will pave the way for more radical changes, with some commentators calling for the creation of a centralized European System of Financial Supervisors (Lanoo 2008).

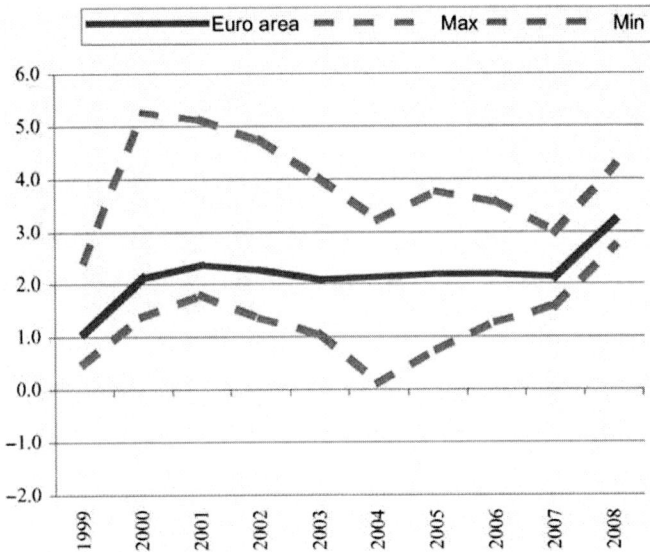

Figure 3 Cross-country inflation differences in the euro area (annual percentage change in the Harmonized Index of Consumer Prices, euro area 12, 1999–2008)
Note: Based on euro area 12. Max indicates the highest rate of inflation among euro area members in a given year while Min indicates the lowest.
Source: DG ECFIN AMECO.

Concerns over EMU's legitimacy did not dissipate during the first decade of the single currency. Although the Eurobarometer suggests that overall support for EMU remains strong and relatively stable among the general public, cross-country variation gives some cause for concern. Overall support for the single currency rose during EMU's first decade in some member states, most notably Ireland, Germany and Finland, but dropped significantly in others, most notably Italy and Greece (see Figure 4). These developments were consistent with warnings that EMU would be dangerously dependent on the perceived economic benefits of the single currency (Verdun and Christiansen 2000; Hodson and Maher 2002). As Deroose *et al.* (2007) suggest, those member states in which the perceived impact of the euro changeover on price rises was highest experienced the most significant loss in support for EMU, even though the official economic data estimate that the introduction of the single currency had a trivial impact on the rate of inflation.

Whether political union could help to address these concerns over the legitimacy of EMU remains a moot point. Firstly, it is uncertain whether a supranational economic authority could do anything to address misperceptions about the euro's impact on prices that the ECB as a supranational monetary authority cannot do already. Furthermore, the creation of a supranational economic authority could intensify concerns over EMU's legitimacy particularly if it gives the EU a greater role in taxation and expenditure decisions, domains in which

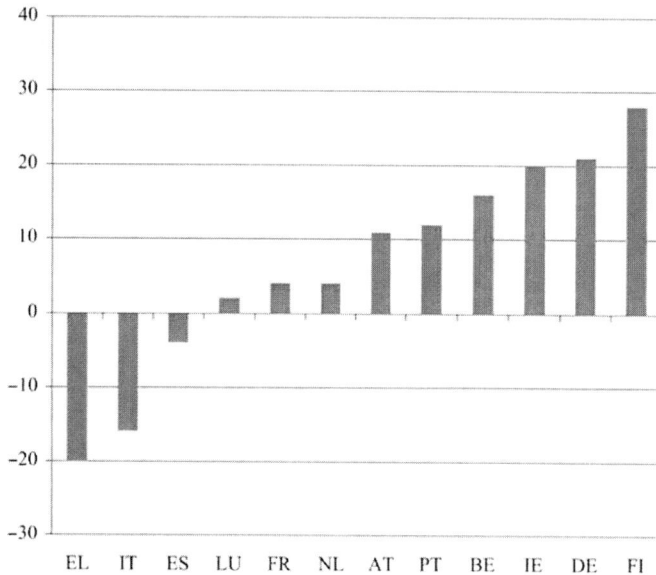

Figure 4 Swings in support for EMU (change in percentage of respondends expressing support for EMU, 1998–2007)
Source: Eurobarometer.

national governments continue to guard their sovereignty.[3] For its part, the European Commission has been reluctant to endorse functionalist arguments about the need for a further centralization of economic policy-making in the euro area. In its report on ten years of EMU, the Commission argues that a radical reform of EMU's institutional architecture is unwarranted at this juncture, calling instead for measures to strengthen existing 'institutions and structures' (European Commission 2008: 285). These measures include enhancing macroeconomic surveillance to take better account of, *inter alia*, cyclical variations and internal and external imbalances, consolidating the euro area's representation in international financial institutions and fora, and enhancing the role of the Eurogroup and its President (European Commission 2008: 245–93).

So much for the functionalist claims about the link between EMU and political union. Is there any evidence to support the intentionalist argument that euro area members would be more inclined to choose to pursue political integration beyond the sphere of economic policy? There were a number of high-profile calls during EMU's first decade for euro area members to act as a pro-integrationist vanguard. In April 2000, Valéry Giscard d'Estaing and Helmut Schmidt suggested that deeper political integration among euro area members was the 'only realistic option' for ever-closer union in Europe (Giscard d'Estaing and Schmidt 2000). Joschka Fischer, in a speech at Humboldt University in May 2000, allowed for the possibility of reinforced co-operation among other groups of member states but nonetheless suggested that euro area members should be allowed at move ahead with plans for a 'politico-economic union' (Fischer 2000).

The Belgian Prime Minister Guy Verhofstadt (2006) took several steps further in his book *The United States of Europe*, in which he presented his ideas for a two-tier system of integration in Europe. Under this plan, pro-integrationist countries would form a United States of Europe, committed to closer co-operation on economic, social, political, technological, judicial and security policies. The remaining member states would form a loosely affiliated Organization of European States. Membership of the United States of Europe would be restricted, in the first instance, to members of the euro because these countries have already demonstrated their European 'credentials' by giving up their national currencies.

In spite of the interventions of Giscard d'Estaing, Schmidt, Fischer, Verhofstadt and others, euro area members have not, thus far, demonstrated a willingness to press ahead with political integration beyond the economic sphere. The explanation may, in part, be a legal one since it is not entirely clear that euro area members would be permitted to invoke the Treaty's provisions on enhanced co-operation. For Duff (2005: 200), the fact that euro area monetary policy is an exclusive competence of the EU rules out the possibility of enhanced co-operation among euro area member states under Article 43 TEU. The same treaty article requires enhanced co-operation to be open to all EU member states, which suggests another reason why euro area members might not be permitted to go it alone with plans for deeper political integration.

Even if the Treaty's provisions on enhanced co-operation were more flexible, there are few signs that a political consensus exists among euro area members on the need for centralized decision-making beyond the economic sphere. The pro-spect of enhanced military co-operation between the members of the euro area, of example, would be complicated by the presence of three countries, Austria, Finland and Ireland, which practise a policy of *de-facto* or *de-jure* neutrality and by the absence of the UK and Poland, countries whose participation in military co-operation is generally regarded as indispensable. Ireland is also a laggard when it comes to co-operation in the area of justice and home affairs, having chosen to preserve its common travel arrangements with the United Kingdom rather than sign the Schengen Agreement.

Of course, membership of the euro area does not only depend on a member states' willingness to give up its currency but also on its ability to meet the Treaty's convergence criteria.[4] Under Article 121 TEC, it falls to the Commission, the ECB and, ultimately, the Council, meeting in the composition of the Heads of State or Government, to decide whether a member state has achieved a high degree of sustainable convergence. It follows that a member state that wishes to join the euro area may be denied entry, as was the case in May 2006 when Lithuania's application to join the euro area was refused on the grounds that its inflation rate was fractionally above the average of the EU's three best performers from the point of view of price stability.

In short, there is little evidence after the euro's first decade to support either functionalist or intentionalist claims about the link between EMU and political union. Political union has not thus far proved to be a necessary condition for a smooth functioning EMU. Although there has been no shortage of efforts to co-ordinate economic policies under EMU, such initiatives have, for the most part, confirmed rather than challenged member states' ascendancy in the economic domain. Likewise, euro area members have confounded those who expected them to be an integrationist vanguard, in part because of a lack of consensus concerning the future direction of EU policy-making.

III. ARE EMU AND POLITICAL UNION DECOUPLING?

The previous section found little evidence from the single currency's first decade to support claims that EMU would lead to political union out of either necessity or choice. The penultimate section of this article takes this argument one step further by proposing that the projects of monetary and political integration in the EU show tentative signs of decoupling after ten years of the euro. This claim is supported with reference to the treatment of EMU-related issues in the EU's latest round of treaty revisions.

The Lisbon Treaty, which was signed by the Heads of State or Government in December 2007, would introduce a number of significant modifications to the EU's institutional architecture. Among the most ambitious changes would be the creation of two new high-level posts: the President of the European Council and the High Representative for Foreign and Security Policy. The Treaty would also cap the size of the College of Commissioners, establish a new 'double-majority' voting system in the Council of Ministers, give national parliaments a greater say in EU legislation, and extend the Community Method to significant new areas of justice and home affairs.

The Lisbon Treaty's proposed changes to euro area economic governance are altogether more modest. Adopting the European Constitution's provisions on this issue largely unchanged, the Lisbon Treaty's most significant addition is Article 137 Treaty on the Functioning of the European Union (TFEU). This provision (along with an accompanying protocol) would give quasi-legal status to the Eurogroup and its President but it would stop well short of putting this forum on a par with the Economic and Financial Affairs (ECOFIN) Council. Other changes would strengthen the euro area specific dimension of the Broad Economic Policy Guidelines (Article 136 TFEU) and allow the Commission to issue a direct warning against member states that pursue economic policies that jeopardize the smooth functioning of EMU (Article 121 TFEU).

Although it is tempting to suggest that questions about the future of Europe and EMU were not coupled to begin with, this explanation would be misleading. Questions about EMU's future were ever-present in the debates about the future of Europe not only in Joschka Fischer's aforementioned speech to Humboldt University in May 2000 but also in the European Council's

December 2001 Laeken Declaration. Though the Laeken Declaration stopped short of endorsing Fischer's idea of a politico-economic union, the question of how to strengthen economic policy co-ordination was included among its long list of questions about the future of Europe (European Council 2001).

A more convincing explanation is that questions about EMU's future were, to all intents and purposes, put to one side during the negotiation of the Lisbon Treaty and the European Constitution. From the very outset of the European Convention, there were signs that a radical reconsideration of EMU's institutional architecture would not be up for discussion. The decision to appoint Klaus Hänsch, a distinguished former President of the European Parliament but a relative unknown in economic circles, to head the Convention's Working Group on Economic Governance suggested that the Praesidium's calls 'to consider improved economic co-ordination mechanisms in the context of monetary union' lacked conviction (Secretariat of the European Convention 2002). The Working Group on Economic Governance did not challenge EMU's institutional design, insisting in its final report to the Convention that the 'current structure whereby exclusive competence for monetary policy within the Eurozone lies with the Community, exercised by the ECB under powers conferred upon it by the existing Treaty, and competence for economic policy lies with the member states, should be maintained' (Hänsch 2002: 2).[5]

Timing may have been a factor in the European Convention's treatment of EMU-related issues. The Working Group on Economic Governance met during a period of heightened tension over the enforcement of the Stability and Growth Pact. The Convention presented its draft of the European Constitution in July 2003, a matter of months before the ECOFIN Council voted to leave disciplinary action against France and Germany 'in abeyance'. The Intergovernmental Conference (IGC) on the European Constitution presented its final draft of the Constitution in June 2004, a month before the European Court of Justice ruled on the Commission's challenge against ECOFIN's application of EMU's budgetary rules. Under such circumstances, there was little appetite among the members of the European Convention's Working Group on Economic Governance to become embroiled in the controversy over the Stability and Growth Pact by calling for radical reforms to EMU's institutional architecture.

EU Finance Ministers also discouraged the members of the European Convention from being too ambitious in their plans for strengthening economic policy co-ordination. As Puetter (2007) records, Jonny Åkerholm, the President of the Economic and Financial Committee, made it clear in his appearance before the Convention's Working Group on Economic Governance that EU Finance Ministers would oppose any plans to upgrade the Eurogroup to the status of a full Council formation and give the European Commission a stronger role in euro area economic governance. Under such circumstances, Hänsch recognized that the pursuit of radical changes to EMU's institutional architecture could have a destabilizing effect on the overall work of the Convention (Puetter 2007: 1308).

In the period of reflection that followed the referenda on the European Constitution in France and the Netherlands in mid-2005, some commentators called for future treaty revisions to play closer attention to the issue of economic governance. A vocal proponent of this position was Andrew Duff (2005: 200), who criticized the drafters of the original European Constitution (of which he was one) for failing 'to spell out clearly the economic policy objectives of the Lisbon agenda in terms of public and private investment, education, training and research – goals which, if disseminated, could not fail to appeal even to French and Dutch workers'. In the end, Duff's argument failed to gain political traction. The IGC, which was convened in July 2007, was content to 'cut and paste' the European Constitution's provisions on euro area economic governance into the Lisbon Treaty.

The desire to reach a rapid solution to the EU's constitutional crisis may have made the Lisbon Treaty's drafters reluctant to reopen the debate about euro area economic governance. So too did the resurgence of tensions between France and Germany over the need for a political counterweight to the ECB. Following a presidential campaign in which the ECB's focus on price stability was severely criticized, the eventual victor, Nicolas Sarkozy, called for a substantial reform of euro area economic governance in advance of the European Council in Brussels in June 2007 (Münchau 2007). Such plans were given short shrift by German Chancellor Angela Merkel, who expressed concerns that they could undermine the independence and credibility of the ECB (Benoit and Atkins 2007). Faced with such bickering between the Franco-German couple, the chances of making much headway on EMU-related issues in the IGC on the Lisbon Treaty were slim.

In short, the EU's most recent experience of treaty negotiations suggests that EMU is a pressure point rather than a focal point in discussions about the future course of European integration. Although questions about the necessity and desirability of further political integration in the euro area were among those that motivated the EU's reflections on the future of Europe, the debate about EMU's institutional architecture was effectively put to one side once the European Convention began work. Faced with political tensions over the enforcement of the Stability and Growth Pact and a lack of consensus between France and Germany on an alternative to the status quo, the Lisbon Treaty, like the European Constitution before it, effectively decoupled questions of monetary and political integration. The result is a set of treaty changes that would make significant headway in fields such as the common foreign and security policy and justice and home affairs while leaving the Maastricht Treaty's provisions on EMU largely untouched.

CONCLUSION

It may be premature, after a decade of the euro, to draw definitive conclusions about the relationship between monetary and political integration. But there is surely sufficient water under the bridge to revisit arguments that expect EMU to spur political union in some way, shape or form. This article has explored two such arguments, the first predicting that EMU will necessitate a further centralization of economic decision-making in the EU, and the second suggesting that euro area members will intentionally choose to forge ahead with plans for ever-closer union.

These arguments appear, with the benefit of hindsight, to have overstated the relationship between monetary and political integration in the EU. EMU has not created strong functional pressures for centralized economic policy-making. Member states have stepped up the co-ordination of budgetary policies and structural reforms over the last decade but the locus of economic decision-making remains firmly at the national level. The last ten years have also disappointed those who expected euro area members to create a European vanguard, in part because the countries sharing the euro lack a common vision concerning deeper political integration beyond the economic sphere.

As the euro enters its second decade, there are tentative signs that EMU and political union may be decoupling. Questions about the evolution of EMU, which had been central to the 'future of Europe' debate, were effectively put to one side by the members of the European Convention and both the drafters of the European Constitution and the Lisbon Treaty. As a result, the latest round of treaty revisions proposes modifications to euro area economic governance that would be minor when compared to the planned changes to the common foreign and security policy and justice and home affairs.

As the euro enters its second decade, the chief concern facing euro area policy-makers is not whether EMU will spur centralized decision-making but how its decentralized approach to economic policy-making can overcome the many challenges to its effectiveness and legitimacy highlighted in this article. This concern is, for better or for worse, reflected in the mandate of the González Group, which has been asked by the European Council to put forward ideas on 'strengthening and modernizing' the European economy by 2010 with the added proviso that such measures must be feasible 'within the framework set out in the Lisbon Treaty' (European Council 2008).

The analysis presented in this article has two wider implications for the study of EMU and the EU more generally. Firstly, the limited explanatory power of functionalist and institutionalist arguments raises the question of whether it is still meaningful to discuss the link between EMU and political union. If it must be salvaged, the concept of political union needs to be updated and further elucidated.[6] Secondly, the fact that EMU has survived thus far in its present institutionalist form raises important questions about the relationship between economic and political integration in the EU. For comparativists, the first ten years of the euro challenge traditional assumptions that centralized economic decision-making is a necessary step in the EU's evolution as a political system. For integration theorists, institutional developments in the EU following the introduction of the euro add fuel to the fire of debates about the importance of economics as a driver of integration in the political sphere.

ACKNOWLEDGEMENTS

An earlier version of this article was presented at a workshop at the Hertie School of Governance in Berlin in April 2008. Thanks to the participants at this workshop, especially Femke Van Esch and Dieter Wolf; the editors of this special edition, Henrik Enderlein and Amy Verdun; Ivo Maes and two anonymous referees for constructive comments. The usual disclaimer applies.

NOTES

1 There is, of course, a wealth of literature applying theories of European integration to understand the economic and political origins of EMU. See Verdun (2002) and Sadeh and Verdun (2009) for a summary.
2 The concept of *gouvernment économique* is put to one side in this discussion, as it is generally associated with calls for closer intergovernmental co-operation rather than a further centralization of economic policies at the EU level. See Howarth (2007) for a discussion of this point.
3 For an alternative viewpoint, see Collignon (2004), who calls for democratic government as a means of enhancing the efficiency and legitimacy of economic decision-making in the EU.
4 Only Denmark and the United Kingdom have formal opt-outs from EMU's third stage, but in practice member states can exercise a degree of discretion over their compliance with the convergence criteria. This is evident from the case of Sweden which violates the criteria on exchange-rate stability since the government has decided to remain outside the exchange rate mechanism (ERM II).
5 According to Norman (2005: 102), issues such as tax harmonization and social policy rather than the future of EMU dominated discussions in the Working Group on Economic Governance.
6 See Crowley (2006) for a recent attempt to do exactly this.

REFERENCES

Andréani, G. (2001) *What Future for Federalism?*, London: Centre for European Reform.
Balassa, B. (1961) *The Theory of Economic Integration*, London: Richard D. Irwin.
Benoit, B. and Atkins, R. (2007) 'Merkel rounds on Paris over euro and ECB', *Financial Times*, 11 July.
Brandt, N., Burniaux, J.M. and Duval, R. (2005) 'Assessing the OECD Jobs Strategy: Past Developments and Reforms', OECD Economics Department Working Papers 429, Paris: OECD.
Collignon, S. (2004) 'Is Europe going far enough? Reflections on the EU's economic governance', *Journal of European Public Policy* 11(5): 909–25.

Committee for the Study of Economic and Monetary Union (1989) 'Report on Economic and Monetary Union in the Community', Brussels: Committee for the Study of Economic and Monetary Union.

Crowley, P. (2006) 'Is there a logical integration sequence after EMU?', *Journal of Economic Integration* 21(1): 1–20.

De Grauwe, P. (2006) 'What have we learnt about monetary integration since the Maastricht Treaty?', *Journal of Common Market Studies* 44(4): 711–30.

Deroose, S., Hodson, D. and Kuhlmann, J. (2007) 'The legitimation of EMU: lessons from the early years of the euro', *Review of International Political Economy* 14(5): 800–19.

Duff, A. (2005) *The Struggle for Europe's Constitution*, London: UK Federal Trust.

Dyson, K. (1994) *Elusive Union: The Process of Economic and Monetary Union in Europe*, London: Longman Press.

Dyson, K. and Featherstone, K. (1999) *The Road to Maastricht: Negotiating Economic and Monetary Union*, Oxford: Oxford University Press.

ECOFIN Council (2008) '2866th Council Meeting – Economic and Financial Affairs', Press Release 8850/08, 14 May, Brussels: Council of Ministers.

European Commission (1977) 'Report of the Study Group on the Role of Public Finance in European Integration', Brussels: European Commission.

European Commission (2006) 'EU Economy Review', European Economy No. 6, Luxembourg: Office for Official Publications of the European Communities.

European Commission (2008) 'EMU@10: Successes and Challenges after 10 Years of Economic and Monetary Union', European Economy No. 2, Luxembourg: Office for the Official Publications of the European Communities.

European Council (2001) 'Laeken Declaration on the Future of the European Union', Annex 1, Conclusions of the European Council, SN 300/1/01 REV 1, 14–15 December, Brussels: European Council.

European Council (2008) 'Presidency Conclusion', Press Release 16616/1/07, 14 February, Brussels: European Council.

Fatás, A. (1998) 'Does EMU need a fiscal federation?', in D. Begg, J. von Hagen, C. Wyplosz and K.F. Zimmerman (eds), *EMU: Prospects and Challenges for the Euro*, Chichester: Wiley. Also in *Economic Policy: A European Forum* 26(4): 163–203

Fischer, J. (2000) 'From confederacy to federation – thoughts on the finality of European integration'. Speech at the Humboldt University in Berlin, 12 May 2000.

Giscard d'Estaing, V. and Schmidt, H. (2000) 'La leçon d'Europe', *Le Figaro*, 4 October.

Goodhart, C. and Smith, S. (1993) 'Stabilisation', in the Economics of Community Public Finance, European Economy, Reports and Studies 5: 417–56, Luxembourg: Office for the Official Publications of the European Communities.

Gros, D., Mayer, T. and Ubide, A. (2005) 'EMU at Risk', 7th Annual Report of the CEPS Macroeconomic Policy, Brussels: Centre for European Policy Studies.

Hancké, R., Rhodes, M. and Thatcher, M. (2007) *Beyond Varieties of Capitalism: Conflict, Contradictions, and Complementarities in the European Economy*, Oxford: Oxford University Press.

Hänsch, K. (2002) 'Final report of Working Group VI on Economic Governance', Report from the Chairman of Working Group VI on Economic Governance to the Members of the Convention, CONV 357/02, WG VI 17, Brussels: European Convention.

Hodson, D. and Maher, I. (2001) 'The open method as a new mode of governance: the case of soft economic policy co-ordination', *Journal of Common Market Studies* 39(4): 719–46.

Hodson, D. and Maher, I. (2002) 'Economic and monetary union: balancing credibility and legitimacy in an asymmetric policy mix', *Journal of European Public Policy* 9(3): 391–407.

Howarth, D.J. (2007) 'Making and breaking the rules: French policy on EU "gouvernment économique"', *Journal of European Public Policy* 14(7): 106–78.

Issing, O. (2008) 'The Euro – A Currency without a State', Centre for Financial Studies, Working Paper No. 2008/51, Center for Financial Studies, Goethe-University: Frankfurt am Main.

Kok, W. (2004) 'Facing the challenge The Lisbon strategy for growth and employment: Report from the High Level Group chaired by Wim Kok', Luxembourg: Office for the Official Publications of the European Communities.

Lanoo, K. (2008) 'Concrete Steps towards More Integrated Financial Oversight: The EU's Policy Response to the Crisis', Brussels: CEPS Task Force Report.

Maes, I. (2004) 'On the origins of the Franco-German EMU controversies', *European Journal of Law and Economics* 17(1): 21–39.

Mitrany, D. (1943) 'A Working Peace System: An Argument for the Functional Development of International Organisation', London: Royal Institute of International Affairs.

Molle, W. (2001) *The Economics of European Integration: Theory, Practice, Policy*, 4th edn, Aldershot: Dartmouth Publishing.

Münchau, W. (2007) 'Sarkozy's plans for the euro area are bad economic governance', *Financial Times*, 28 May.

Norman, P. (2005) *The Accidental Constitution: The Making of Europe's Constitutional Treaty*, Brussels: Eurocomment.

Obstfeld, M. and Peri, G. (1998) 'Regional non-adjustment and fiscal policy', in D. Begg, J. von Hagen, C. Wyplosz and K.F. Zimmerman (eds), *EMU: Prospects and Challenges for the Euro*, Chichester: Wiley. Also in *Economic Policy: A European Forum* 26(4): 205–59

Padoa-Schioppa, T. (2000) *The Road to Monetary Union in Europe: The Emperor, the Kings and the Genies*, Oxford: Oxford University Press.

Pelkmans, J. (2006) *European Integration: Methods and Economic Analysis*, 3rd edn, Harlow: Prentice-Hall.

Pöhl, K.O. (1989) 'The Further Development of the European Monetary System', Collection of Papers, Committee for the Study of Economic and Monetary Union, Brussels: Committee for the Study of Economic and Monetary Union.

Puetter, U. (2006) *The Eurogroup: How a Secretive Circle of Finance Ministers Shapes European Economic Governance*, Manchester: Manchester University Press.

Puetter, U. (2007) 'Intervening from outside: the role of EU finance ministers in the constitutional politics', *Journal of European Public Policy* 14(8): 1293–1310.

Quaglia, L. (2008) 'Committee governance in the financial sector', *Journal of European Integration* 30(3): 565–80.

Sadeh, T. and Verdun, A. (2009) 'Explaining Europe's economic and monetary union: a survey of the literature', *International Studies Review*, forthcoming.

Schäuble, W. and Lamers, K. (1994) 'Reflections on European foreign policy', document by the CDU/CSU Group in the German Bundestag, reprinted', in B.F. Nelsen, A.C.-G. Stubb (eds) (1998) *The European Union. Readings on the Theory and Practice of European Integration*, Basingstoke: Macmillan, pp. 71–81.

Schelkle, W. (2005) 'The political economy of fiscal policy co-ordination in EMU: from disciplinarian device to insurance arrangement', *Journal of Common Market Studies* 43(2): 371–91.

Secretariat of the European Convention (2002) 'Summary of Conclusions: Meeting of the Praesidium Brussels', 25 April, Brussels: European Convention.

Tabellini, G. and Wyplosz, C. (2006) 'Supply-side policy coordination in the European Union', *Swedish Economy Policy Review* 13(1): 101–56.

Tsoukalis, L. (2005) *What Kind of Europe?*, Oxford: Oxford University Press.

Verdun, A. (ed.) (2002) *The Euro: European Integration Theory and Economic and Monetary Union*, Lanham, MD: Rowman & Littlefield.

Verdun, A. and Christiansen, T. (2000) 'Policies, institutions and the Euro: dilemmas of legitimacy', in C. Crouch (ed.), *After the Euro: Shaping Institutions for Governance in the Wake of European Monetary Union*, Oxford: Oxford University Press, pp. 162–78.

Verhofstadt, G. (2006) *The United States of Europe*, London: Federal Trust.

Von Hagen, J. and Wyplosz, C. (2008) 'EMU's Decentralized System of Fiscal Policy', European Economy, Economic Paper No. 306, Luxembourg: Office for the Official Publications of the European Communities.

Wallace, H. (1997) 'Pan-European integration: a real or imagined community?', *Government and Opposition* 32(2): 215–33.

Werner, P. (1970) 'Report to the Council and the Commission on the Realisation by Stages of Economic and Monetary Union in the Community', Supplement to the Bulletin 11-1970 of the European Communities, Luxembourg: Office for the Official Publications of the European Communities.

Wolf, D. (2002) 'Neofunctionalism and intergovernmentalism amalgamated: the case of EMU', in A. Verdun (ed.), *The Euro: European Integration Theory and Economic and Monetary Union*, Lanham, MD: Rowman & Littlefield, pp. 29–49.

On consensus, constraint and choice: economic and monetary integration and Europe's welfare states

H. Tolga Bolukbasi

INTRODUCTION

This article aims to address what we have learned in the political economy literature on the relationship between economic and monetary union (EMU) and what constitutes the heart of the European social model – the welfare state. It concerns itself with the impact of 'the single most important and supra-national step in European integration on the single most important area still reserved to national politics' (Martin and Ross 2004: 17). From the early 1990s onwards, research reports on European welfare states referred to significant pressures stemming from EMU that severely constrained domestic social policies. In parallel, the literature on EMU pointed to serious ramifications for European welfare states. In fact, scholars of diverse persuasions were surprisingly in general agreement. Whether with anxiety or exultation, opponents and advocates of EMU expected that EMU would potentially downsize Europe's welfare states through imposing macroeconomic austerity in general and budgetary restraint in particular. According to the conventional wisdom of the time, the integration process would breed very strong pressures on domestic budgets to 'slim down' on the way to EMU membership and these would ultimately lead to the downsizing of welfare states. Additionally, it was often suggested that EMU would also provide governments with a trump-card that would serve to strengthen their hands in pruning their welfare states. Some scholars even went so far as to claim that this scenario of across-the-board retrenchment would spell the end of the European welfare state as we know it.

In fact, academics were not alone in their dire expectations regarding EMU's consequences; *everyone* expected that the euro would rapidly and radically undermine Europe's welfare states. In political debates, right-wing politicians cheered for the euro, as they hoped it would help them to get rid of the 'excessively generous', 'outdated' welfare states. Left-wing politicians, faced with what they saw as unremitting structural pressures, attempted to shift accountability to Maastricht by decrying helplessness in safeguarding their welfare states. In policy-making circles, social partners and technocrats expected EMU to downsize their national welfare states: monetary authorities and employers across the EU were keen on having such 'adjustment' take place through the 'market mechanism' by means of 'social dumping' and 'tax competition', whereas trade unions, anticipating all these, were hoping to build centralized, EU-level social policies to mitigate against these risks (Verdun 2000). Regarding public opinion, underlying the precipitous decline in public support for European integration in the 1990s was the reaction to EMU and its budgetary implications for the welfare state (Eichenberg and Dalton 2007). The euro was subsequently rejected by European citizens on different occasions for fear that it would bring an end to the welfare state as they knew it. In both the Danish and Swedish referenda on the euro of 2000 and 2003 respectively, the victorious 'no' camps capitalized on the prevailing conviction that EMU would threaten their welfare states. Later on, in the French referendum on the European Constitution, the 'no' camp mobilized the widespread fear that the Constitution, which they saw as based on 'too neoliberal' EMU, would compromise the French social model (Bolukbasi 2007).

Despite these scholarly and public convictions, new empirical evidence showed that while welfare states were in a constant process of transformation, these could not, even during the trials and tribulations of the convergence period, be characterized by downright retrenchment. After the convergence decade, scholars benefiting from hindsight and informed by new theoretical approaches increasingly emphasized the strength of socio-political impediments to retrenchment in explaining the perceived resilience of Europe's welfare states. Thus, as the most authoritative study representing the state-of-the-art on the impact of EMU on welfare states concludes, 'the European social model has proved more resilient in the face of these challenges than many actors and analysts had anticipated' (Martin and Ross 2004: 17; cf. Jenson and Pochet 2005).

In reviewing the literature on EMU's impact on Europe's welfare states this stock-taking exercise addresses the conspicuous gap between the ex ante convictions and theoretical scenarios of the convergence decade on the one hand, and the more recently revealed ex post facts on the welfare state on the other. It provides a reassessment of the theoretical expectations and empirical findings on the impact of economic and monetary integration on Europe's welfare states. The rest of this paper is structured as follows: first, it reviews commonplace claims in the political economy literature on how EMU reflects the primordial conversion to neoliberalism, presents the conventional hypothesis, and identifies the assumptions and predictions characterizing the theoretical literature of the 1990s. Second, it surveys the second wave of empirical literature that emphasizes the resilience of Europe's welfare states in the face of EMU-induced budgetary pressures by relying on quantitative studies on social expenditures and qualitative case studies on welfare reform. It shows why the theoretically expected scenario of radical welfare state retrenchment did not take place in spite of the structural pressures stemming from, and the discursive opportunities afforded by, EMU. It attempts to highlight the conditions under which reforms transpired and the role EMU played in these processes. This section also presents alternative strategies adopted for meeting the Maastricht targets, showing how EMU targets were achieved even in the absence of savings that would have otherwise been afforded by welfare reform. The article concludes by reassessing the hypothesis and assumptions underlying the conventional scenarios of the 1990s in light of the recent empirical findings and draws broad lessons for the discipline of political economy.

CONSENSUS ON EMU'S GOVERNANCE: NEOLIBERAL CONVERSION TO MACROECONOMIC DISCIPLINE

There exists a broad agreement in the political economy literature on the view that the EMU project represents the final stage in the process of institutionalization of neoliberalism across the EU. The origins of this process, however, remain contested among scholars. In explaining the emergence of the neoliberal policy consensus, some scholars emphasized the centrality of structural economic imperatives in their accounts (Sandholtz 1993; Moravcsik 1998). In the aftermath of the world economic crisis of the 1970s, it was claimed that a set of changes in the international political economy occurred in the structure of commodity and financial markets. Based on Mundell's 'unholy trinity', it was impossible to sustain free trade, capital mobility and stable exchange rates without renouncing independent domestic monetary policy. At the same time, a series of national policy failures made the neoliberal turn 'unavoidable' and shifted the policy agenda towards opportunities afforded by co-operation at the European level. Following the primordial convergence of domestic policy preferences among member states, collective conversion to macroeconomic discipline through EMU constituted the rational policy option for governments which were stripped of their abilities to govern. Underlying the choice for EMU were the 'structural economic interests' of governments abandoning Keynesian interventionism for neoliberal, anti-inflationary monetarism. Thus, the EMU intergovernmental bargain reflected the primordial consensus on neoliberal policies in a world of functional, structural 'necessities'.

In contrast to the structuralist accounts, other scholars emphasized the role of neoliberal policy ideas as causal factors behind a neoliberal EMU. The shift from 'embedded liberalism' towards 'competitive neoliberalism' was, for these scholars, 'socially constructed, or ideationally forged' rather than a rational response to structural constraints. Underlying this historic policy consensus were popular perceptions of policy failures discrediting traditional Keynesian policies. Here, monetarism provided a new policy paradigm to frame new economic policies for governments to control inflation, and the German model provided a template for success at a time when Europe was struggling with stagflation (McNamara 1998). Therefore, the neoliberal shift resulted more from the intellectual coherence, political resonance, and sheer availability of these ideas than from their objectively functional solutions to emerging structural problems (Parsons 2003). EMU, in this way, meant a paradigm shift from Keynesianism to monetarism through the workings of an 'epistemic community' of political, technocratic and financial élites in Europe (Verdun 1999; Dyson 1994).

Whether it was for structural necessities or ideational factors, political economists generally agreed that EMU institutionalized neoliberalism in general and monetarism in particular at the EU level. Scholars qualifying EMU this way ranged from political scientists working on the European Union EU (Dyson 1994, 2000; Hay *et al.* 1999; Hay 2000; Jenson and Pochet 2005; Leander and Guzzini 1997) to heterodox (political) economists (Arestis *et al.* 2001; Baimbridge *et al.* 1999; Grahl and Teague 1997; Teague 1998) to constructivists (Marcussen 2000; McNamara 1998; Verdun 2000) and to critical theorists and neo-Gramscians (Bieler 2003; Bieling 2001; Cafruny and Ryner 2007; Gill 1998; Wylie 2002). One lacuna in the literature stems from the ambiguity that generally surrounds these claims – seldom do scholars substantiate their claims regarding the nature of EMU and the terms 'neoliberal' and 'monetarist' were used liberally and interchangeably.[1]

For many, the project represents the application of standard monetarist principles to European macroeconomic governance, which, it seems, stems from the fact that EMU was informed by the new classical macroeconomic theory that emphasized the 'reputation of institutions' and the 'credibility of anti-inflationary commitments' which constitute the hallmarks of 'monetarism mark II'. Core elements of this strand of monetarism that are attributed to EMU in the literature include: (i) a resolute commitment to price stability as the principal objective of macroeconomic policy through a politically independent central banking system; (ii) the subordination of fiscal to monetary policy as reflected in the 'asymmetry' of 'E' (economic) and 'M' (monetary) in EMU; (iii) an understanding of inflation as a monetary phenomenon through exclusively emphasizing price stability; and (iv) the imposition of 'sound finances' targeting the public sector borrowing requirement (Arestis *et al.* 2001; Hay 2004). A functional link between the monetarist macroeconomic policy template and microeconomic neoliberal reforms is evoked whereby macroeconomic discipline brought by EMU would prove ineffective unless it is complemented by welfare reforms. When references to these microeconomic arguments are added to those of monetarism, political economy literature closes the circle between EMU and economic neoliberalism. Therefore, many saw EMU as representing a 'larger package of neoliberal marketization' (Martin and Ross 1999) institutionalizing what is variously characterized as 'default neoliberalism' (Hay 2000), 'subversive liberalism' (Rhodes 1998), or even a 'disciplinary neo-liberalism' (Gill 1998) having grave consequences for Europe's welfare states. Although these accounts describe the 1990s, the neoliberal consensus, it is claimed, is still alive and well (McNamara 2006).

EXPECTED IMPACT: EMU AS *THE* CONSTRAINT ON WELFARE STATES[2]

The pioneering study on the potential impact of EMU on social protection was conducted by Iain Begg and his colleagues for the European Parliament (Begg *et al.* 1994) who hypothesized a combined effect of two chain reactions with negative and positive consequences for welfare states. When the literature on the issue grew, surveys on the scholarly positions distinguished between those who had foreseen that monetary integration would lead to welfare retrenchment ('pessimists') and others who contended that EMU would in fact support Europe's welfare states ('optimists') (Pakaslahti 1998; Pochet and Vanhercke 1999). In this growing literature, however, pessimistic scenarios gained currency as the convergence process loomed large in the 1990s.

Earlier accounts: ex ante expectations of EMU's impact on welfare states

Although it was easy to find alarm or delight in the literature on EMU's social consequences and while they were expressed in broad and complicated contexts in a varied literature, scholars of diverse persuasions were generally in agreement on one point: both *Euro-philes* and *Euro-sceptics* predicted that EMU would lead to across-the-board downsizing of Europe's welfare states through imposing macroeconomic austerity in general and budgetary restraint in particular.[3]

Within the *Euro-sceptic* group, some scholars argued that, given the high level of budget deficits and public debt during the early 1990s, the convergence process would necessitate radical fiscal retrenchment for EMU membership. Since social security programmes are largely publicly funded and they constitute a big ticket item in total outlays, restricting deficit and debt levels would lead to diminishing resources for welfare states, forcing sizeable cutbacks (Scharpf 2000; Teague 1998). Other scholars added that EMU, by bringing about a recessionary 'macro-economic policy regime', would put unremitting pressures on total output and employment. Falling incomes would lead to declining revenues out of which social expenditures are largely financed. Accordingly, facing tighter budget constraints, governments would retrench social spending (Begg and Nectoux 1995; Burkitt and Baimbridge 1995; Grahl and Teague 1997; Leibfried 2000). Still others added that by making social benefit costs more transparent across the euro-zone, EMU would lead to a 'race-to-the-bottom' in social provision by putting producers in high social protection jurisdictions in a disadvantaged position *vis-à-vis* their competitors from locations with lower social standards. In order not to lose competitiveness, governments would be forced to introduce drastic cutbacks in social security programmes (Leander and Guzzini 1997; Martin and Ross 1999; Rhodes 1997). In these narratives, scholars predicted that EMU, by constituting 'the most serious attack mounted on the welfare state during the post-war period' (Burkitt and Baimbridge 1995: 110), would 'spell the death-knell' of the European model of society (Martin and Ross 1999: 171) or that it would become 'the altar upon which the European social model is ultimately sacrificed' (Hay 2000: 521) resulting in 'the end of the national welfare state as we know it' (Leibfried 2000: 49).

Echoing the expectations of Euro-sceptics, Euro-philes viewed EMU as breeding inexorable structural correctives on Europe's welfare states. Emanating mainly from international organizations such as the Organization for Economic Co-operation and Development (OECD) and the International Monetary Fund (IMF) (Kopits 1997; Visco 1999), these accounts were phrased in a euphemistic language with EMU 'inviting' structural reforms. These experts expected that fiscal rectitude imposed by economic and monetary integration would result in the 'rightsizing' of Europe's welfare states because, if not, fiscal discipline required for EMU would prove ineffective.

In contrast to these influential accounts, others contended that EMU might even lead to the expansion of social protection. Official sources viewed EMU as a new macroeconomic policy framework creating a more stable macroeconomic environment. Such stability would boost economic activity and with output and incomes rising, public revenues would increase, creating a larger pool for financing the welfare state (Calon *et al.* 1992).

Structural constraints and discursive opportunities

Conceptualized in these ways, scholars viewed EMU as *the* source of domestic change. In order to analyse the mechanisms of change, Dyson (2002: 24) suggested that we need to 'clarify the relationship between EMU as a material phenomenon, associated with changes in markets and in policy mechanisms, and EMU as a discursive construction'. The existing literature seems to have done this implicitly. First, underlying these accounts was the common expectation that EMU would breed a host of *coercive, structural constraints* on Europe's welfare states to 'slim down' on the way to euro-entry through the workings of the Excessive Deficit Procedure and the Stability and Growth Pact.[4] These budgetary pressures would ultimately lead to the downsizing of Europe's welfare states through the 'cost-containment' strategy by 'tying the hands' of policy-makers or 'strapping them to the mast' (Dyson *et al.* 1995).

In fact, to the extent that exogenous factors are attributed with causal power in driving welfare state change, the literature sees EMU to be *the* external constraint on contemporary social security systems. Although the relative explanatory powers of EMU and globalization can only be demonstrated by empirical investigation, conventional accounts concur that EMU represents 'a far more immediate and pressing constraint on expansive and inclusive welfare provision' than any other external constraint (Hay *et al.* 1999: 6; see also Baimbridge *et al.* 1999; Grahl and Teague 1997; Gill 1998; Hay 2000; Rhodes 1998).

Second, many political economists expected that EMU would provide governments with a trump-card, strengthening their hands in pursuing policies otherwise unpalatable, such as highly unpopular welfare reforms. Scholars expected that policy-makers (especially conservative politicians) would use EMU as a *discursive instrument* in justifying their reform efforts. It seemed that while EMU brought with it a problem, it also provided the best solution to this problem – using EMU as a *vincolo esterno*: the external discipline imposed by monetary integration on public balances would have provided policy-makers with an argument for an 'external link' in implementing unpopular policies (Dyson and Featherstone 1996; Pierson 2001; Verdun 2000). Ross (2000: 107) caricatures typical arguments that policy-makers resort to when reforming welfare states: 'we have to change because Europe and the coming of the euro obliges us to – we are all in this boat together and if we don't get into EMU we will suffer.'

Underlying the literature there is a common hypothesis and set of assumptions. The conventional hypothesis that unites political economists in opposite camps is that EMU would radically downsize/rightsize Europe's welfare states by imposing macroeconomic austerity in an environment of weakening policy instruments. The widely shared assumptions include the following: (i) the fiscal consolidation strategy that member states were to pursue would be exclusively expenditure-based with no 'degrees of freedom' in the politics of economic policy choice; (ii) although there was no provision in the convergence criteria that compelled budget cuts to be concentrated on welfare state expenditures, given the centrality of social spending within the public budgets, the tight fiscal restraint would lead to disproportionately higher cutbacks in social expenditures; and (iii) EMU is an omnipotent instrument for both meeting fiscal targets through what came to be called the 'Maastricht effect' and for facilitating large-scale welfare reform through 'technocratic empowerment' and/or 'strengthening of the executive'.

EMPIRICAL OUTCOMES: POLITICAL ECONOMY OF CHOICE IN DOMESTIC WELFARE REFORM

While the literature has yet to amass detailed empirical studies demonstrating 'how EMU as a causal factor produces change in welfare states' (Verdun 2005: 1125), recent empirical studies reporting on welfare state trajectories call into question the validity of the underlying hypothesis and assumptions of earlier studies. The literature has increasingly moved away from ex ante apocalyptic predictions characterizing much of the earlier theoretical accounts

towards ex post empirical studies that are less apprehensive of EMU's consequences for Europe's welfare states.[5] The reasons underlying this change are
rooted in the following developments in the field: first, new statistical evidence
covering social spending in the 1990s that became available in the early 2000s
revealed that the convergence decade had been characterized much less by
retrenchment than originally proposed. Second, while some scholars initially
overlooked or dismissed the newly available quantitative evidence, recent qualitative case studies on reform processes and outcomes covering the 1990s corroborated more or less what the expenditure trajectories showed and pointed to
incremental forms of welfare state change instead of radical retrenchment.
Finally, recognizing the surprising resilience of welfare states in 'standing up
to EMU', scholars were compelled by the insights of new theoretical accounts
that became influential in the late 1990s. Most prominent among these was
Pierson's (2001) 'new politics' of the welfare state emphasizing socio-political
impediments to radical welfare retrenchment.

The striking gap between the ex ante theoretical scenarios of the convergence
decade and the more recently revealed ex post facts on the welfare state trajectories provokes the following questions: why was there no radical retrenchment
despite structural pressures stemming from the Maastricht timetable and ideational tools afforded by the *vincolo esterno*? What were the intervening factors
that mediated the relationship between EMU and welfare reform trajectories?
If there had been no systematic retrenchment, does this imply that no reform
happened at all? Under what conditions did these reforms happen and what
was the role of EMU in these processes? If EMU had not afforded sizeable
savings through welfare reform, how was EMU convergence possible? What
alternative strategies were used for meeting the Maastricht targets? Before
turning to these questions, the next section reviews the second wave of
studies presenting new empirical evidence on the welfare reform outcome
during the 1990s.

More recent accounts: ex post findings from quantitative and case studies

The more recent wave of empirical literature relies on evidence based on quantitative indicators of social expenditures and qualitative case studies of domestic
welfare reforms. The earlier literature flatly predicted radical cutbacks in aggregate social expenditures on the road to EMU as part and parcel of a 'cost-
containment' strategy. Since EMU was expected to impose fiscal austerity in
terms of public expenditures, scholars claimed that curtailing the level of total
social expenditures would constitute *an immediate aim in itself* for policy-
makers as part of the budgetary strategy for EMU eligibility. Contrary to
these scenarios, however, numerous studies show that there has been no
systematic and significant social expenditure retreat on the road to EMU.[6]
The evidence based on the OECD's *Social Expenditure Database* suggests
that, although the rate of growth of social spending had declined, welfare
states remained largely stable during the 1990s among EMU candidates – a

finding overwhelmingly at odds with the earlier expectations. In particular, social spending remained relatively stable in the face of ever-declining total public outlays triggered by EMU austerity (Rhodes 2002; Pochet 2006; Bolukbasi, forthcoming). These findings are corroborated by other empirical studies relying on EUROSTAT's ESSPROS methodology (Pochet and Vanhercke 1999; Bolukbasi 2006). Interestingly, these studies also suggest that welfare effort in EMU candidates behaved no differently from those in the non-EMU countries, as there seems no marked, systematic difference with respect to social spending trajectories among EMU and non-EMU countries.

These quantitative findings are broadly consistent with qualitative case studies on the impact of EMU on welfare reforms (Featherstone *et al.* 2001 on Greece; Ferrera and Gualmini 2004 on Italy; Radaelli 2002 on Italy; contributions in Martin and Ross 2004 on Italy, Belgium, France, Germany, Spain and the Netherlands; Bolukbasi, forthcoming on Belgium, Greece and Italy). These studies show that in budgetary policy and politics, structural pressures and discursive opportunities of EMU appear to have led governments to achieve dramatic fiscal turnarounds especially in member states with parlous fiscal balances.[7] At the same time, confirming earlier expectations, all governments that came to power in the 1990s intended to retrench their welfare states. As reflected in their pre-election campaigns, party programmes, declarations, and in everyday political discourse, governments were determined to meet the Maastricht criteria 'at all costs'. They pointed to welfare programmes as *the* cause of mounting fiscal burdens that could preclude euro-entry. When governments attempted to reform welfare programmes, however, the literature suggests that their reform capacities were effectively demarcated by an alliance of entrenched interests: broad-based, powerful coalition blocs including unions, interest groups, traditionally 'protected groups', professional groups, opposition parties in parliament, coalition partners in the government, and even cabinet ministers. The convergence period is marred by successive episodes of mass mobilization of unions against pension reforms which ended up being diluted at best. Opposition parties (or even political parties forming ruling coalitions) reined back governments from pushing far-reaching reforms or completely blocked radical cutbacks. The working and middle classes took to the streets in protest against reform plans to scale down pension programmes. Thus, in the words of Martin and Ross (2004: 15), the 'political constellations' characterized by 'strong and slowly changing cleavage patterns, rooted in evolving deep social structures and organized by parties with their respective ideological orientations in the context of distinct and durable state traditions ... coupled with new constituencies built up around components of social models' explain the 'persistence' of Europe's welfare states. Consequently, in some cases, reform initiatives were shelved and proposals never saw the light of day. In others, governments' ambitions were scaled down, resulting in reforms which were much more modest than had originally been planned. Interestingly, even when reforms were passed, they did not raise significant savings that would accrue to state coffers during the Maastricht horizon due to two main reasons:

first, reforms that were enacted were done so only after their impact had been postponed to the future once bills faced opposition, and, second, in many instances, governments postponed the implementation of reform measures enacted by previous governments when faced with political resistance. In fact, in some cases, governments had to expand welfare benefits in order to appease unrest that would otherwise threaten not only the fiscal consolidation process but also the life of these governments.

Variables mediating the relationship between EMU and welfare states

By producing analytical narratives of reform, the above case studies also help us to unpack the relationship between EMU and welfare states by pointing to domestic political variables that 'refract the pressures generated by EMU in directions that preserve high degrees of social protection and labour rights' (Martin and Ross 2004: 3). While the intervening variables that mediate this relationship are not explicitly identified in the literature, recent research provides us with significant clues as to the factors underlying welfare states' resilience. As an emerging approach that became fashionable in the 2000s, the 'new politics' literature drew our attention to societal forces intent on maintaining the status quo in welfare reform processes. These forces include the broad electoral support for existing welfare programmes rendering cutbacks politically unpopular and the rigidity of welfare state institutions stemming from their path-dependent development and the institutional veto points that are able to obstruct reform. In fact, most case studies on EMU's social consequences seem to have been inspired by the 'new politics' literature in explaining the political economy of welfare reform in the run up to EMU. With respect to electoral politics, even the otherwise omnipotent *vincolo esterno* in the political game of blame avoidance has not been useful enough for policy-makers to enact radical reforms because, as the foregoing discussion shows, these proved almost always politically treacherous. Regarding path dependence in the institutional pillars of welfare states, even the strongest of structural pressures, such as those emanating from EMU, have not been effective in clawing back what was popularly perceived as 'acquired rights' by both traditionally 'protected groups' and by middle and working classes as client groups. Additionally, since European welfare states are generally characterized by mature pay-as-you-go pension systems, they are structurally 'locked-in' despite powerful pressures such as EMU; the current labour force would have to finance the past commitments to the current retirees while simultaneously building up a capital stock for their own retirement. Path dependence also helps to explain why governments were forced to allow for 'grandfathering clauses' that rendered reforms much less incisive. At the same time, with respect to the centrality of veto players, the case studies identify many actors whose agreement is necessary for a change of the status quo, such as strong upper houses that inhibit reform.

Welfare reform processes depicted in the case studies also suggest that the socio-political forces that shaped the 'old politics' of welfare state expansion still remain powerful obstacles for the process of reforming welfare states. First, regarding the role of unions, the findings point to cases where unions and groups mobilized under union leadership still shape the politics of retrenchment in European welfare states, putting radical reform beyond the grasp of governments, even when faced with impending budgetary constraints. Second, concerning left-labour power, although the above findings may seem to suggest that the influence of 'partisan politics' is fading because all political parties – left, right and centre – have attempted radical reform on the road to EMU, the left has in fact approached and acted on reforms in markedly different ways, drawing our attention to the continuous importance of social democratic forces as defenders of the welfare state. At the same time, leftist parties have played a critical leadership role in processes of welfare reform, confirming the 'Nixon-goes-to-China' hypothesis. All of these insights point to the central findings that there was always room for political leadership, and more importantly political choice, in the politics of retrenchment, and that EMU's impact on domestic welfare states was highly contingent on many factors that are effectively shaped, if not determined, by domestic political constellations.

Under what conditions has EMU helped reform?

The case studies suggest that a scenario of across-the-board, radical retrenchment seems to have been averted. This does not mean, however, that welfare states did not undergo any transformation. In fact, the 1990s and early 2000s saw a series of reforms, mostly incremental in nature, introducing changes in parameters.[8] To be sure, EMU has not determined the content of these reforms, but it has determined their direction and timing (Featherstone 2004).

First, as an instrument of 'blame buffering' in processes of reform, the *vincolo esterno* shifted the responsibility on to politicians when technocratic experts, as credible neutral arbiters, professed that reform was necessary. This was possible, however, almost exclusively when reforms were presented as a means to 'preserve' welfare programmes and render them 'sustainable' through 'containing runaway spending'. Second, in cases of acute domestic financial crises, EMU helped governments to put their financial houses in order through allowing extraordinary measures, some of which included welfare reform. The *vincolo esterno* helped especially under circumstances where the technocratic veil legitimized any political decision to reform welfare programmes. Third, popular support for European integration seems to have prevailed over popular support for welfare programmes in certain instances of reform. The important caveat here is that it did so only to the extent that the proposed reforms remained modest. Fourth, consensual policy-making played a significant role in reform on the road to the single currency. Significant reforms were successfully passed when their negotiations culminated in social pacts, quite often among different political parties, and almost always with social partners. While these pacts have contained cutbacks in welfare benefits in some cases, they allowed for incisive reforms in some others. Fifth, EMU's impending constraints helped reformers when they resorted to co-optation and compensation methods. Submission by social partners to reform were usually based on *quid pro quos* whereby governments introduced new programmes or expanded existing benefits (such as minimum social allowances) in exchange for reduced benefits in another policy area when governments had to push for general austerity programmes. Sixth, EMU helped governments to rely on information asymmetries and obfuscation techniques which were rendered possible through the cloak of Maastricht 'targets'. It did so by directing cuts at politically weak, unorganized groups and by making cuts less visible through what may be referred to as 'politics of stealth'. Finally, EMU helped policy-makers to pursue 'sustainable finances' when 'cost containment' was not an option in reform. In most Bismarckian countries, when governments faced opposition to benefit retrenchment, they could increase social security contributions instead in order to meet the Maastricht criteria. These reforms prioritized actuarial principles by strengthening the link between contributions and benefits in social insurance schemes, thereby bolstering their Bismarckian basis. By facilitating regime-specific change in this way, EMU convergence pressures gave way to largely path-dependent welfare reforms.

Achieving Maastricht without major savings from welfare retrenchment: the politics of 'Plan B'

The literature shows that even the heavily indebted countries have managed to reverse their budgetary plight on the road to EMU. If EMU had not helped to secure large savings in welfare state budgets, how was budgetary convergence even possible when it seemed hopeless to many even a year or two before the Maastricht deadline? During the convergence process, when successive attempts at welfare reform failed to produce cost savings, governments resorted to alternative fiscal strategies to comply with the criteria. These strategies included raising fiscal and non-fiscal revenues, reducing non-social expenditures, and in some cases, resorting to creative accounting.

First, perhaps the most striking aspect of the transition period was the strong emphasis on raising public revenues. Many governments introduced tax reforms and took other measures such as improving tax compliance, broadening tax bases, and updating tax administrations. Through these measures, tax burdens hit record levels in EMU candidates which already had the highest rates among OECD members. Regarding non-tax measures, most EMU candidates have put the family jewels up for sale in major privatization programmes, which proved perhaps the most convenient instrument that did not necessitate relying on politically difficult social security cutbacks and unpopular tax increases.[9] Interestingly, privatization receipts dropped markedly when EMU entry was guaranteed, which suggests that most, if not all, were EMU induced. Additionally, some EMU candidates received sizeable transfers from the EU, which, in part, made possible an upward trend in social expenditures even when the candidates were facing EMU pressures.

Second, although their fiscal consolidation strategies mainly relied on rising revenues, governments repeatedly announced that they would have to undertake spending restraint for EMU convergence. With the scaling back of many initiatives, however, welfare reforms failed to produce significant savings towards the consolidation effort. To the extent that deficit reductions were realized through curtailing total outlays, these mainly centred on *non-social* expenditures through a de-emphasis on industrial policy, reduced subsidies, declining defence expenditures, and declining spending on other items (such as general public services) leaving considerable leeway for welfare state portfolios. The convergence period saw remarkable increases in the shares of social spending within total outlays, implying a striking shift away from non-social priorities towards social priorities. At the same time, the economic growth performance of the EMU candidates brought about extra political breathing space during the second half of the 1990s when member states were striving to qualify for EMU.

CONSENSUS, CONSTRAINT AND CHOICE: BRINGING POLITICS BACK INTO STUDYING EMU'S CONSEQUENCES FOR EUROPE'S WELFARE STATES

What do these empirical cases have to say about the scholarly literature on EMU's impact? The earlier expectations of political economists were largely confirmed with respect to the emergence of structural pressures on domestic public budgets and the opening of windows of opportunity in budgetary policy and politics. At the same time, EMU seems to have forced all governments to make significant attempts at retrenching their welfare states during the 1990s and perhaps even after. However, recent studies suggest two sets of problems.

First, the earlier literature placed an exclusive focus on the incentive structures and the goals of policy-makers which were conceived as either downright constrained or effectively strengthened by EMU. By *overestimating* the power of EMU as a *structural constraint* on welfare states, these studies overlooked the fact that governments could resort to alternative means of spending restraint and/or raising revenues, thereby diverting fiscal pressures on welfare budgets. Scholars also *overestimated* the power of EMU as a *discursive opportunity* in bringing about welfare reform. Although the *vincolo esterno* helped governments in pursuing euro-entry, rendering incisive tax reforms palatable, when governments attempted to cut back welfare programmes, the otherwise omnipotent 'external link' largely failed to deliver large-scale reform.

The second set of problems lies in the recent revelation that earlier work largely *underestimated* the *power of resistance* to retrenchment initiatives by societal forces including organized labour, traditionally 'protected groups', opposition parties, and even dissenting members of the ruling party. Earlier studies also *underestimated* the policy-makers' *room to manoeuvre*, particularly in budgetary policies. Governments sought alternative means of fiscal consolidation when they felt that the welfare reform option had been foreclosed by effective opposition.

They embarked on fiscal strategies other than retrenching welfare when they sensed that acting otherwise could have adverse electoral consequences.

This brings us to the next question: what are the lessons that political economists may draw from studying the relationship between EMU and domestic welfare reforms? EMU has been an ideal test case in understanding the interplay between the economics of constraint and the politics of reform. The discipline of political economy has benefited from the empirical studies in at least two ways: first, with respect to the *empirical landscape*, the impact of EMU – regardless of how neoliberal in nature and principles it may be – has not turned out to be as dramatic as expected. Recent empirical studies show that the transition stage and the early years of EMU are characterized much less by welfare state retrenchment than by stability. The very survival of European welfare states in the face of the most dramatic EMU pressures compels us to be more modest with respect to our sweeping generalizations and encourage more 'cautious and tentative' conclusions (cf. Martin and Ross 2004: 3) contingent on variables that we generally treat as extraneous in overblown scenarios. Although the jury is still out over the future impact of EMU, a scenario of across-the-board retrenchment seems most unlikely in the foreseeable future.

Second, with respect to our *theoretical preoccupations*, these studies draw our attention to the centrality of the political economy of reform in mitigating retrenchment pressures on welfare states. The degree of freedom in these processes – even under stringent external constraints – is largely determined not only by the willingness of policy-makers to bring about reform but also by the level of commitment to welfare state goals that each society holds and the strength of the coalition of its societal actors aligned against reforms. The extent to which pressures may be modified, muted or even fully mitigated by counter-tendencies was, therefore, contingent on the very *politics* of reform. Whether pressures are successfully resisted, enthusiastically embraced, or taken advantage of discursively depends on domestic political institutions and choices. We should therefore not simply write off reform outcomes even when we have to acknowledge the severity of constraints imposed and the remarkable political opportunities provided by EMU for retrenchment engineers; political economists should beware of deterministic scenarios and foregone conclusions and always allow for political contingency in their analyses. In a way, what the empirical studies collectively amount to is a call – albeit not with explicit intent in most cases – to bring politics back into the study of economic constraints and their social consequences.

ACKNOWLEDGEMENTS

I would like to thank Amy Verdun for her editorial guidance and three anonymous referees for their very useful comments on an earlier draft of this article.

NOTES

1 In these accounts, while economists usually refer to 'monetarism' in analysing EMU's structure and the process of EMU, political scientists generally choose 'neoliberalism' in describing the policies and politics associated with EMU.
2 The term 'welfare state' is not conceptualized uniformly in the literature as there remain variations in meaning in usages by different scholars. These range from narrowly defined state benefits and services protecting citizens from labour market risks to broader conceptualizations encompassing mechanisms of social protection against and redistribution of market mechanisms and outcomes.
3 In this survey Euro-sceptics and Euro-philes are taken to represent scholars who are critical and approving of EMU respectively, but only regarding its alleged consequences for Europe's welfare states. For example, the term Euro-sceptic here does not necessarily imply a general scepticism towards EMU or the EU in general.
4 In fact, the power of the structural constraint has subsided with the securing of EMU membership. The Stability and Growth Pact, after subsequent revisions, does not constitute as strong a pressure as in the case of the convergence criteria.
5 For example, Rhodes (1997), who pioneered a Euro-sceptical account earlier, moved towards a more Euro-phile position (Rhodes 2002).
6 While there were some cases where an indicator based on social expenditures had declined during the convergence process, in some of these cases there was an alternative measure of spending that suggests an absence of cutbacks (Bolukbasi, forthcoming).
7 Many empirical studies documented the 'Maastricht effect' in member states' budgetary behaviours. However, Hallerberg (2004) shows that the impact of EMU on budgetary politics and policy was not uniform across EMU candidates: for example, whereas the Treaty may explain policy changes in southern Europe, others in Scandinavia carried out reforms for reasons that had little to do with EMU.
8 Acknowledging the fact that the 1990s were in fact less characterized by wholesale 'retrenchment', scholars have described changes in welfare states by other terms such as 'recasting', 'restructuring' or 'recalibration'.
9 Although privatization receipts were, in principle, not to be counted towards reducing the deficit, many instances of doing so were subsequently approved by EUROSTAT (Savage 2005).

REFERENCES

Arestis, P., Brown, P. and Sawyer, M. (2001) *The Euro*, Cheltenham: Edward Elgar.
Baimbridge, M., Burkitt, B. and Whyman, P. (1999) 'Convergence criteria and EMU membership: theory and evidence', *Journal of European Integration* 21(4): 281–305.
Begg, I. and Nectoux, F. (1995) 'Social protection and economic union', *Journal of European Social Policy* 5(4): 285–302.
Begg, I. *et al.* (1994) *The Social Consequences of Economic and Monetary Union: Final Report*, Luxembourg: European Parliament, Social Affairs Series.
Bieler, A. (2003) 'Labour, neo-liberalism and the conflict over economic and monetary union: a comparative analysis of British and German trade unions', *German Politics* 12(2): 24–44.

Bieling, H.J. (2001) 'European constitutionalism and industrial relations', in A. Bieler and A.D. Morton (eds), *Social Forces in the Making of the New Europe*, Basingstoke: Palgrave, pp. 93–114.

Bolukbasi, H.T. (2006) 'Would monetary integration with the United States threaten the Canadian social model? Insights from European monetary unification', *Current Politics and Economics of Europe* 17(2): 313–49.

Bolukbasi, H.T. (2007) '*Plus ça change* ... ? The European social model between "economic governance" and "social Europe" from the Maastricht Treaty to the European Constitution', *Current Politics and Economics of Europe* 18(2): 149–79.

Bolukbasi, H.T. (forthcoming) *Euros and European Welfare States*, Toronto: University of Toronto Press.

Burkitt, B. and Baimbridge, M. (1995) 'The Maastricht Treaty's impact on the welfare state', *Critical Social Policy* 14(3): 100–11.

Cafruny, A.W. and Ryner, J.M. (2007) 'Monetary union and the transatlantic and social dimensions of Europe's crisis', *New Political Economy* 12(2): 141–65.

Calon, A., Frey, L., Lindley, R., Lyon-Caen, A., Markmann, H. and Perez-Diaz, V. (1992) *The Social Aspect of Economic and Monetary Union*, Brussels: European Parliament.

Dyson, K. (1994) *Elusive Union*, London: Routledge.

Dyson, K. (2000) 'EMU as Europeanization: convergence, diversity, and contingency', *Journal of Common Market Studies* 38(4): 645–66.

Dyson, K. (2002) 'Introduction: EMU as integration, Europeanization, and convergence', in K. Dyson (ed.), *European States and the Euro*, Oxford: Oxford University Press, pp. 1–27.

Dyson, K. and Featherstone, K. (1996) 'Italy and EMU as a "vincolo esterno": empowering technocrats, transforming the state', *South European Society and Politics* 1(2): 270–92.

Dyson, K., Featherstone, K. and Michalopoulos, G. (1995) 'Strapped to the mast: EC central bankers between global financial markets and regional integration', *Journal of European Public Policy* 2(3): 465–87.

Eichenberg, R.C. and Dalton, R.J. (2007) 'Post-Maastricht blues: the transformation of citizen support for European integration, 1973–2004', *Acta Politica* 47: 128–52.

Featherstone, K. (2004) 'The political dynamics of external empowerment', in A. Martin and G. Ross (eds), *Euros and Europeans*, Cambridge: Cambridge University Press, pp. 226–47.

Featherstone, K., Kazamias, G. and Papadimitriou, D. (2001) 'The limits of external empowerment: EMU, technocracy and reform of the Greek pension system', *Political Studies* 49: 462–80.

Ferrera, M. and Gualmini, E. (2004) *Rescued by Europe?*, Amsterdam: Amsterdam University Press.

Gill, S. (1998) 'European governance and the new constitutionalism: economic and monetary union and alternatives to disciplinary neoliberalism in Europe', *New Political Economy* 3(1): 4–25.

Grahl, J. and Teague, P. (1997) 'Is the European social model fragmenting?', *New Political Economy* 2(3): 405–26.

Hallerberg, M. (2004) *Domestic Budgets in a United Europe*, Ithaca, NY: Cornell University Press.

Hay, C. (2000) 'Contemporary capitalism, globalization, regionalization and the persistence of national variation', *Review of International Studies* 26: 509–31.

Hay, C. (2004) 'The normalizing role of rationalist assumptions in the institutional embedding of neoliberalism', *Economy and Society* 33(4): 500–27.

Hay, C., Watson, M. and Wincott, D. (1999) 'Globalization, European integration and the persistence of European social models', One Europe or Several Working Paper, 3/99.

Jenson, J. and Pochet, P. (2005) 'Employment and social policy since Maastricht: standing up to the European monetary union', in R. Fishman and A. Messima (eds), *The Year of the Euro*, Notre Dame, IND: University of Notre Dame Press.

Kopits, G. (1997) 'Are Europe's social security finances compatible with EMU?' *IMF Papers on Policy Analysis and Assessment*, Washington, DC: IMF.

Leander, A. and Guzzini, S. (1997) 'European economic and monetary union and the crisis of social contracts', in P. Minkkinen and H. Patomaki (eds), *The Politics of Economic and Monetary Union*, Helsinki: The Finnish Institute of International Affairs.

Leibfried, S. (2000) 'National welfare states, European integration and globalization: a perspective for the next century', *Social Policy and Administration* 34(1): 44–63.

Marcussen, M. (2000) *Ideas and Elites: The Social Construction of Economic and Monetary Union*, Aalborg: Aalborg University Press.

Martin, A. and Ross, G. (1999) 'Europe's monetary union: creating a democratic deficit?', *Current History* April: 171–6.

Martin, A. and Ross, G. (2004) *Euros and Europeans*, Cambridge: Cambridge University Press.

McNamara, K. (1998) *Currency of Ideas*, Ithaca, NY: Cornell University Press.

McNamara, K. (2006) 'Economic governance, ideas and EMU: what currency does policy consensus have today?', *Journal of Common Market Studies* 44(4): 803–21.

Moravcsik, A. (1998) *The Choice for Europe*, Ithaca, NY: Cornell University Press.

Pakaslahti, J. (1998) 'EMU and social protection in the European Union', in P. Pochet and B. Vanhercke (eds), *Social Challenges of Economic and Monetary Union*, Brussels: European Interuniversity Press.

Parsons, C. (2003) *A Certain Idea of Europe*, Ithaca, NY: Cornell University Press.

Pierson, P. (2001) 'Post-industrial pressures on the mature welfare states', in P. Pierson (ed.), *The New Politics of the Welfare State*, Oxford: Oxford University Press.

Pochet, P. (2006). 'Influence of European integration on national social policy reforms'. Presented at the conference on 'A Long Goodbye to Bismarck?', Centre for European Studies, Harvard University, 16–17 June 2006.

Pochet, P. and Vanhercke, B. (1999) 'The challenges of economic and monetary union to social protection', in J. Saari (ed.), *Financing Social Protection in Europe*, Helsinki: Ministry of Social Affairs and Health Publications, No. 21.

Radaelli, C. (2002) 'The Italian state and the euro: institutions, discourse, and policy regimes', in K. Dyson (ed.), *European States and the Euro*, Oxford: Oxford University Press, pp. 212–37.

Rhodes, M. (1997) 'The welfare state: internal challenges, external constraints', in M. Rhodes, P. Heywood and V. Wright (eds), *Developments in West European Politics*, London: Macmillan.

Rhodes, M. (1998) '"Subversive liberalism": market integration, globalization and West European welfare states', in W.D. Coleman and G.R.D. Underhill (eds), *Regionalism and Global Economic Integration*, London: Routledge, pp. 99–121.

Rhodes, M. (2002) 'Why EMU is – or may be – good for European welfare states', in K. Dyson (ed.), *European States and the Euro*, Oxford: Oxford University Press, pp. 304–33.

Ross, G. (2000) 'The euro and European social policies', in D.J. Kotlowski (ed.), *The European Union: From Jean Monnet to the Euro*, Athens, OH: Ohio University Press.

Sandholtz, W. (1993) 'Choosing union: monetary politics and Maastricht', *International Organization* 47: 1–39.

Savage, J.D. (2005) *Making the EMU*, Oxford: Oxford University Press.

Scharpf, F.W. (2000) 'The viability of advanced welfare states in the international economy: vulnerabilities and options', *Journal of European Public Policy* 7(2): 190–228.

Teague, P. (1998) 'Monetary union and social Europe', *Journal of European Social Policy* 8(2): 117–37.

Verdun, A. (1999) 'The role of the Delors Committee in the creation of EMU: an epistemic community?', *Journal of European Public Policy* 6(2): 308–28.

Verdun, A. (2000) *European Responses to Globalization and Financial Integration*, New York: St Martin's Press.

Verdun, A. (2005) 'Review of *Euros and Europeans*', *West European Politics* 28(5): 1124–5.

Visco, I. (1999) 'Should economic policies be coordinated for EMU?', *The OECD Observer*, January: 215.

Wylie, L. (2002) 'EMU: a neoliberal construction', in A. Verdun (ed.), *The Euro: European Integration Theory and Economic and Monetary Union*, Oxford: Rowman & Littlefield.

EMU's diverging micro foundations: a study of governments' preferences and the sustainability of EMU

Tal Sadeh

1. INTRODUCTION

In the aftermath of the rejection of the European Constitution in referendums in France and the Netherlands in May and June 2005 respectively, there was talk of the imminent collapse of the euro zone. An Italian politician suggested that Italy should abandon the euro, Europe's single currency, and reintroduce the lira. In Germany there were signs that over half of the country's citizens wanted the Deutschmark back, and the government openly criticized the euro as a cause of low growth. Lucas Papademos, Vice-President of the European Central Bank (ECB), seemed to support some of these criticisms when he suggested that the euro zone had lowered growth in Europe and might collapse in the future.

Strong criticism of the single currency is relatively new to the academic and political mainstream in continental Europe. However, British and American commentators have long emphasized the diverse economic fortunes of the member states of the euro zone (*The Economist* 2006: 33; Tilford 2006).

Some economists, such as Paul De Grauwe, suggested that economic and monetary union (EMU) would fail if its institutional structure remained unchanged (*Financial Times* 2005). Amid this criticism, might EMU indeed fail?

The purpose of this study is to find out whether the governments of European Union (EU) member states have, since the launch of EMU, become less committed to policies and values that are compatible with a sustainable currency union in Europe. Previous empirical studies relevant to the sustainability of EMU have focused on evidence for divergence in the performance of European economies. Policy studies mostly focused on a single aspect of EMU (for example, Franco-German relations) or on a small subset of the member states. Other studies focused on public opinion surveys to detect trends in the level of support for the single currency among the citizens of Europe (for references to these studies, see Sadeh and Verdun 2009).

This study takes advantage of recent developments in the study of party politics that enable an analysis of the intentions of coalition governments in EU member states with regard to a variety of policies and issue-areas. These intentions are to be distinguished from actual government policies, which are formulated against material (budget), domestic (interest groups) and international or transnational constraints. Such a government orientation analysis has never before been carried out in the context of the debate on EMU's sustainability. This study is important because the policy orientation of parties and the governments that they form is part of the 'plumbing', or transmission mechanism, through which voter preferences affect national policies. This study is also innovative in that it attempts to move from single country studies, common in the existing literature, into a larger dataset.

The remainder of this article is structured as follows. The next section discusses the concept of EMU sustainability, and identifies the types of policies (on the part of member state governments) that can be judged as contributing to the sustainability of EMU.

The third section presents operational measures for government intentions with regard to these EMU-helpful policies, based on a dataset of the pre-2004 EU member states from 1990 to 2006. These measures should not be interpreted as an attempt to comprehensively operationalize the sustainability of EMU in the sense of producing ultimate and objective measures of it. That could be a worthy project, but it would greatly exceed the scope of this study.

The fourth section runs statistical tests on these measures and the fifth section provides conclusions. It argues that, while the member states of the euro zone have in recent years converged in support of macroeconomic policies that are important for a sustainable EMU, they have also become more divergent about the imperative microeconomic policies, and their scepticism with regard to the authority of EU institutions has become more consensual. This may challenge the sustainability of EMU.

2. THE SUSTAINABILITY OF EMU AND GOVERNMENTS' POLICIES

2.1 The sustainability of EMU

The term 'sustainability' is mostly associated with the work of Cohen (2000), who argues that great power politics explains currency unions more than any institutional design or economic cost–benefit analysis. The sustainability of a currency union (in terms of the member states' compliance with their commitments, and the preservation of membership) depends on the presence of a locally dominant state, willing and able to use its influence to ensure monetary co-operation. Failing this, the sustainability of a currency union depends on sharing a strong sense of political community among the member states.

Institutional arrangements matter too, according to Cohen, because they can raise defection costs and maintain international co-operation even when national interests change. Specifically, institutional centralization increases exit costs (Cohen 1998). Furthermore, compliance with commitments is greater in the presence of a broad network of institutional linkages sufficient to make the loss of national autonomy tolerable to each partner (Cohen 2000). However, Cohen argues that in the end institutional factors do not determine the fate of currency unions.

Finally, Cohen maintains that, while economic factors can support a currency union, they are neither sufficient nor necessary for its sustainability. There are many historical examples of economically inefficient currency unions that survive for many years, or currency unions that at least potentially seem to have great economic merit but founder over political differences.

This understanding of sustainability is difficult to use in the case of EMU. As argued below, EMU lacks some of the structural features central to Cohen's interpretation of the concept, namely a dominant power. Nevertheless, Europe's common currency has survived for ten years and there are no real signs of its impending demise.

Indeed, EMU enjoys the backing of highly developed institutions, as well as deep economic integration among the member states. Europe's single market ensures robust flows of goods, services, capital and labour among the member states. It would seem unreasonable to suggest that an economic cost–benefit analysis is completely irrelevant to EMU's sustainability. Of course, a costly EMU may yet be sustainable, but as its costs increase at the margin it must be getting somewhat less sustainable. In other words, rather than adopt Cohen's assertion of the absolute dominance of international structure in determining sustainability, this paper assumes that a trade-off exists among a few factors.

For example, other things being constant, higher economic costs in a currency union must be compensated for by an even greater dominant power, a greater sense of political community among the member states, or stronger institutions. Perhaps a little more community spirit can go a long way in compensating EMU for high economic costs, but the precise 'exchange rate' between these factors is hard to measure or ascertain even in a very crude manner.

Thus, this study adopts a nuanced version of Cohen's interpretation of the sustainability concept. Henceforth, sustainability is understood as resting on three legs, without judging which is more important than the other: the structural leg (the distribution of power among member states, and the extent to which they form a political community), the institutional leg, and the economic leg.

2.2 The structural leg of EMU sustainability

The structural leg of EMU's sustainability consists of the distribution of power among its member states, as well as the extent to which they form a political community. EMU is clearly not dominated by any hegemonic power. Specifically, while some argue that Germany has dominated earlier stages of the European monetary integration process,[1] there is no evidence that Germany sought to 'lead' or to purposely influence other monetary authorities (Maes and Verdun 2005). Germany definitely did not act as a lender of last resort, nor is it clear that it was a source of liquidity for Europe (Gros and Thygesen 1998: 169–74). Germany never possessed the power to actually coerce EU member states into accepting these rules, or to independently punish those who break the rules (McNamara 1998: 26–7).

As for a sense of community among the member states, this inevitably involves the formation of some kind of common collective identity. Risse *et al.* (1999) indeed argue that in important member states collective identities were dominant in shaping the discourse regarding EMU. While Germany's identity led it to opt for the single currency, Britain's Atlantic orientation pulled it away from the euro. However, Helleiner (2002) argues that, over time, membership in the single currency may weaken national identities and foster a pan-European identity, and Dyson (2002) understands EMU as a process of Europeanization. These studies underscore the potential relationship between a European common identity and membership in the euro zone. Thus, if a strong community spirit is important to the sustainability of EMU, a sustainable single currency is expected to be associated with strong support among the member state governments for the EU project in general.

A common collective identity rests on shared beliefs among the member states. Indeed, many scholars emphasized the central role of ideas in the establishment of EMU. Ideas affect policy by providing either road maps (prescriptions for action), or focal points, adopted when actors perceive a need to co-operate but face a multitude of co-operative solutions (Goldstein and Keohane 1993). Woods (1995) suggests that ideas contribute to the formation of a collective identity by attributing blame to some 'other' entity, providing an appealing vision of future benefits, creating effective group identities, and rationalizing actions already taken.

Based on these studies, Dyson (1994), Marcussen (2000) and Verdun (2000) explain that EMU was made possible as a result of the rise of neo-liberal ideas, particularly the 'sound money' idea. EMU is a system of causal beliefs providing both a road map and a focal point for co-operation. Similarly, McNamara (2006) explains EMU in terms of a continental ideological shift away from the Keynesian paradigm (see also Young 2002). The pooling of monetary policy was made possible by a growing consensus among the member states that Keynesian policies have failed and that neo-liberal policies, which were adopted in Germany, were the key to lower rates of inflation and unemployment, as well as higher growth rates.[2] Thus, a sustainable single currency is expected to be associated with strong support among the member states for neo-liberal ideas and weak support for Keynesian ideas.

2.3 The institutional leg of EMU sustainability

The institutionalist approach argues that high defection costs from monetary regimes ensure international co-operation even when national interests change. Indeed, EMU is embedded in a network of international compromises spanning many issue-areas (Martin 1993). These issue-linkages should increase defection costs because they give a long-term dimension to obligations (Watson 2004).

Some argue that in practice the wider political and social institutions of the EU are not sufficiently developed (Crouch 2000). For example, Europe lacks a common economic government (Begg 2002). Cohen (1998) has suggested that EMU's institutions are too decentralized, thus reducing exit costs and making EMU less sustainable. A minority of scholars are concerned that excessively strong EU institutions might produce a counter-reaction to the detriment of EMU,[3] but according to the bulk of the literature a sustainable single currency should be associated with support among the member state governments for strong centralized EU institutions.

2.4 The economic leg of EMU sustainability

Economists view currency unions as a means to greater efficiency and prosperity for participating member states. Currency unions can enhance trade and income by reducing the exchange rate trade barrier, at the expense of independent macroeconomic policies. Thus, currency unions would be efficient among major trade partners with co-ordinated business cycles, open economies, flexible prices, high labour mobility and financial market integration (the so-called optimum currency criteria – see Artis 2002; Tavlas 1993). Economists argue that inefficient currency unions may be unsustainable in the long run.

Economic studies of EMU have lead to mixed conclusions. Eichengreen (1997) and Sadeh (2005, 2006) find that many EU member states are not efficient candidates of a single currency (see also Artis 2003). In contrast, De Grauwe and Lavrač (1999), Frieden (1996, 1998) and Steinherr (1994) are less critical.

Whatever the judgement on the readiness of the member states to adopt the single currency, EU leaders, and especially the Barroso Commission, have accepted that completing the single market and ensuring the four freedoms is important to mitigate international strains within it. This explains, at least partly, their emphasis on the Lisbon Agenda. Thus, a sustainable single currency is expected to be associated with strong support among the member states for market reforms that enable the four freedoms and rapid adjustment to external shocks, and help to make EMU more efficient and profitable.[4]

To summarize, the discussion in this section highlights a number of government policies at the member state level that can make EMU more sustainable. A sustainable EMU is expected to be associated with support among its member states for the EU project in general and for neo-liberal ideas in particular. The member states are also expected to support strong centralized EU institutions, as well as market-oriented reforms that would make their common market more flexible and efficient.

3. MEASURING GOVERNMENT POLICY ORIENTATION

3.1 Dataset

This study uses a pooled time-series cross-sectional monthly dataset, including the pre-2004 15 EU member states over the period 1990–2006. Most of the 12 member states which joined the EU after 2004 experienced great turmoil in their party politics during the 1990s, and including them in the dataset might distort results. At any rate, except for the three member states which adopted the euro after 2007, most of the newcomers are regarded as being a long way from adopting it.

The dataset's period begins in 1990, when the first stage of EMU began, as prescribed by the Delors Report. The period 1990–2006 conveniently divides between nine pre-euro years and eight post-euro years. This allows analysis of the evolution of the above sustainability criteria over time, and whether indeed recent intentions of national governments enhance the sustainability of EMU more than at the start of the process.

All the operational measures of government intentions used below are indices of the bias of each member state's government in favour of a particular value or policy. Each index ranges from 1 for extreme positive bias (i.e. the government is highly in favour of this value or policy) to 0 for extreme negative bias. The government's stance on a particular value or policy is that of the political party in government. If there is more than one party in a coalition government, the government's index value is an average of the separate index values of all coalition partners, weighted by their seats in parliament.

The information on the policy bias of parties in this study is based on two sources. The first is the Comparative Manifesto Project (CMP) produced by Budge *et al.* (2001) and Klingemann *et al.* (2006). The CMP counts text mentions in party manifestos that relate positively (or negatively) to particular policies. For each analysed policy it then divides its text count by the overall number of text mentions in the manifesto. The greater this ratio, the more supportive (or unsupportive) of the policy the party is understood to be.

The index of the bias of each party calculated here adjusts the original CMP value to the relative importance in the manifesto of the general group of policies and values to which the particular policy belongs. This is done, as explained in greater detail below, by dividing the original CMP value by the sum of CMP values of all text mentions that relate to the general policy group. The purpose of this standardization is to eliminate a potential bias on the indices that may stem from different weights that whole issue-areas may have in different party manifestos.[5]

The CMP text analysis is repeated for the manifesto of each party in each country ahead of each election campaign. Here, the various values which the CMP reports are assumed to be constant between elections. This means that the index values of governments change only in the wake of new elections or a change in the party composition of the ruling coalition.

Another important database of party policies is provided by Benoit and Laver (2006). This is based on an expert survey of political parties in 47 countries, including many non-European ones. For every country a set of Substantive Policy Dimensions (SPDs) is covered, including the economy, society, decentralization of decision-making, the environment, and other issues of local relevance. For each SPD, each party is placed by a group of experts on two scales: a position scale, reporting how favourable the party is to the specific value or policy, and a scale of the SPD's importance to the party.

The index of the bias of each party calculated here adjusts the position value of the relevant SPD to its importance value. This is done by first rescaling the position and importance values of each SPD from 0 (least favourable position, or of least importance) to 1 (most favourable position, of greatest importance). Next, the difference between the rescaled position value and 0.5 (the mid-point of its new scale) is multiplied by the rescaled level of importance, and this product is added to 0.5. Thus, the adjusted position values tend to cluster around 0.5 and can reach (low or high) extreme values only if the original position value of the relevant SPD is extreme and the SPD is very important to the party concerned.

The survey was conducted in 2002–03 and provides a snapshot of party positions at the time. For the purpose of this study the values that the Benoit and Laver survey reports are applied for the entire 1990–2006 period. This means that the index values of governments calculated here change only if and when the party composition of the ruling coalition changes. The remainder of this section details how the various indices are constructed. The next section analyses their evolution over time.

3.2 Government policy intentions in the structural leg

One indicator, based on the CMP, is used as a proxy for the level of support for the EU project in general. PROEU calculates the balance between favourable and unfavourable mentions of the EU in general, the desirability of expanding the EU[6] and/or of increasing its competence, and the desirability of remaining a member state. This indicator is adjusted, as explained above, by dividing the difference between two original CMP values, one for and one against the EU, by the sum of these two CMP values. Rising values in this indicator are expected to contribute to the sustainability of EMU.

Five indicators are used as proxies for the level of support among the member states for general neo-liberal ideas. One (referred to as CUT-TAX) is based on Benoit and Laver's study and is an index of the extent to which a government promotes cutting public services in order to cut taxes. Rising values in this indicator are expected to contribute to the sustainability of EMU.

The other four indicators are based on the CMP, and are adjusted, as explained above, to the relative importance of the group of economic policies and values:

- ENTERPRISE: Favourable mentions of free enterprise capitalism, superiority of individual enterprise over state and control systems, private property rights, personal enterprise and initiative, and the need for unhampered individual enterprises.
- ORTHODOXY: Favourable mentions of the need for traditional economic orthodoxy, reduction of budget deficits, retrenchment in crisis, thrift and savings, support for traditional economic institutions such as stock market and banking system, and support for strong currency.
- WELFARE: Positive references to the need to introduce, maintain or expand any social service or social security scheme, and support for social services such as health service or social housing.
- KEYNESIAN: Positive references to demand-oriented economic policy, economic policy devoted to the reduction of depressions, increasing private demand by increasing public demand, and increasing social expenditures.

Rising values in ENTERPRISE and ORTHODOXY, and diminishing values in WELFARE and KEYNESIAN are expected to contribute to EMU's sustainability.

3.3 Government policy intentions in the institutional leg

Two indicators are used as proxies for the level of support for strong centralized EU institutions (based on Benoit and Laver's study):

- EU-AUTHORITY: Government favours increasing the range of areas in which the EU has authority and can set policy.[7]
- EU-ACCOUNTABILITY: Government favours greater accountability of EU institutions, rather than national institutions, to citizens.

Rising values in each of these indicators are expected to contribute to EMU's sustainability.

3.4 Government policy intentions in the economic leg

Five indicators are used as proxies for the level of support among the member states for market-oriented reforms. One indicator (DEREGULATION) is based on Benoit and Laver's study, and four others (COMPETITION, PLANNING, CONTROL, and CORPORATISM) on the CMP. All four CMP-based indicators are adjusted, as explained above, to the relative importance of the group of economic policies and values.

- DEREGULATION: Government promotes deregulation of markets at every opportunity.
- COMPETITION: Favourable mentions of the need for regulations designed to make private enterprises work better, actions against monopolies and trusts and in defence of consumer and small business, and encouraging economic competition.
- PLANNING: Favourable mentions of long-standing economic planning of a consultative or indicative nature, and the need for governments to create such a plan.
- CONTROL: Favourable mentions of the general need for direct government control of the economy, control over prices, wages and rents, and state intervention in the economic system.
- CORPORATISM: Favourable mentions of the need for the collaboration of employers and trade union organizations in overall economic planning and direction through the medium of tripartite bodies of government, employers and trade unions.

Rising values in DEREGULATION and COMPETITION, and diminishing values in PLANNING, CONTROL and CORPORATISM, are expected to contribute to EMU's sustainability.

4. EVIDENCE OF GOVERNMENT POLICY ORIENTATION AND THE SUSTAINABILITY OF EMU

The previous section developed 14 operational measures of government policy orientation expected to contribute or hamper EMU's sustainability. Comparing the values of the indices, developed above, in different member states and at different times could indicate whether national governments have, over time, become more committed to policies and values compatible with a sustainable EMU, and whether member states inside the euro zone are more committed to such policies than member states outside it.

Table 1 reports two average values for each index: one for the group of member states which have adopted the euro since 1999 (2001 for Greece), and the other for all other cases. These other cases include all member states before 1999 as well as member states that did not participate in the euro zone in 1999–2006. Since few of the EU-15 member states remained outside the euro zone, this 'other cases' column is dominated by the zone's member states, and reflects mostly temporal changes in the values of their indicators. The third column from the right in this table calculates the difference between these means (the 'other cases' value is subtracted from the euro zone value). The fourth column presents the same values as a percentage of the mean value for the variable over the entire sample (this mean is not reported in the table). The table also reports t tests and p values for the null hypothesis that the difference in the means is zero. The signs by the variables' names indicate the direction of the difference in

Table 1 Comparing government policy orientation inside and outside the euro zone

Variable	Mean in euro zone ('ins')	Mean among 'others'	Diff. in means (euro zone minus others)	Diff. in means (in % of sample mean)	t test	p
Government policy intentions in the structural leg:						
PROEU (+)§	0.895	0.878	0.017**	1.9	2.35	0.019
CUT-TAX (+)†	0.563	0.529	0.035***	7.6	7.80	0
ENTERPRISE (+)§	0.926	0.920	0.005	0.5	1.61	0.108
ORTHODOXY (+)§	0.934	0.846	0.088***	10.0	15.08	0
WELFARE (−)§	0.291	0.292	−0.001	−0.3	0.27	0.787
KEYNESIAN (−)§	0.010	0.014	−0.004*	−32.8	1.90	0.058
Government policy intentions in the institutional leg:						
EU-AUTHORITY (+)†	0.546	0.549	−0.003	−0.5	0.80	0.427
EU-ACCOUNTABILITY (+)†	0.427	0.430	−0.003	−0.7	0.43	0.667
Government policy intentions in the economic leg:						
DEREGULATION (+)†	0.529	0.510	0.019***	3.9	4.31	0
COMPETITION (+)§	0.094	0.073	0.021***	26.1	8.18	0
PLANNING (−)§	0.025	0.021	0.004*	17.9	1.94	0.052
CONTROL (−)§	0.028	0.039	−0.012***	−34.0	3.16	0.002
CORPORATISM (−)§	0.016	0.022	−0.005***	−25.3	2.94	0.003

Notes: The signs by the variables' names indicate the direction of the difference in their average values, if member states inside the Euro zone are more compatible with a sustainable EMU than member states outside it.
§Based on the Comparative Manifesto Project (CMP).
†Based on Benoit and Laver (2006).
*$0.05 < p \leq 0.10$. **$0.01 < p \leq 0.05$. ***$p \leq 0.01$.

the means, if member states inside the euro zone are more compatible with a sustainable EMU than member states outside it.

The results reported in Table 1 show that in two indices in the structural leg of EMU's sustainability (free enterprise and the welfare state) there is on average no significant difference between the governments of member states participating in the euro zone ('ins') and the governments of those either outside it or before it was established ('others'). However, the governments of member states participating in the euro zone are on average a little more favourable to the EU in general, suggesting that they may enjoy a somewhat stronger sense of community among them.

In addition, neo-liberal ideas seem to be promoted a little more strongly by euro zone governments. This is evident in their slightly greater emphasis on cutting taxes and on following macroeconomic orthodoxy (restraining budget deficits and emphasizing price stability). There may also be a lower emphasis on Keynesian ideas inside the euro zone, but the difference in the means here is of relatively weak statistical significance.

In the institutional leg of EMU's sustainability, Table 1 shows no significant difference between member states in the euro zone, and either member states outside of it or before it was established. In the economic leg, Table 1 shows that there is generally a greater bias in favour of market-oriented reforms in member states participating in the euro zone than in 'others'. The governments of the participating countries are on average significantly more favourable to the deregulation of markets and to ensuring competition in business, and are significantly less favourable to government control of the markets and to consultations with trade unions (CORPORATISM). However, when it comes to the need for governments to draw national economic plans, the difference between the two groups of countries is less significant, and actually shows that the insiders are more favourable to planning than the 'others'.

While the differences between the two groups of countries seem to be low in terms of absolute values in many of the variables, the fourth column in Table 1 shows that relative to the sample's average level some of them (mostly in the economic leg) are sizeable. In contrast, the low substantive significance of the differences between 'ins' and 'others' in many of the structural and institutional variables means that, should the 'others' join the euro zone, its sustainability would not truly be in jeopardy.

Table 2 examines the degree of convergence among the member states in their policy orientation. This is important because EMU is a multilateral project. A sense of community must be shared among the member states. Institutions must be supported by more than just a few enthusiastic member states if they are to function. And economic reform would be more effective if carried out in all member states. Thus, for each variable a standard deviation of national values was calculated in each monthly observation. The means reported in Table 2 are averages of these monthly values of the cross-section standard deviation. A sustainable EMU is associated with greater convergence (lower standard deviation) around a value conducive to a sustainable EMU. This is reflected in a combination of a negative sign for the difference in means in Table 2 and the appropriate sign in Table 1.

In the structural leg the member states of the euro zone are much more converged than those outside the euro zone, especially in PROEU, ENTERPRISE and ORTHODOXY. This finding lends support to the assertion that the 'ins' are as a group more devoted to the EU and its monetary project. While some of the 'others' may share some of these beliefs, the relatively high average values reported for them in Table 1 disguise great divergences among them. In the institutional leg Table 2 shows again that euro zone member states are no more supportive of the EU's institutions than the other member states. In the economic leg it seems that, given their low values in Table 1, the 'others' are (or were before 1999) more converged in their scepticism about economic reform.

As noted above, Benoit and Laver's expert surveys of party policies may not be relevant for the 1990s. Had their survey been extended to the 1990s, entries for the four indicators based on their survey in the 'others' columns of Tables 1 and 2 might change, but since these are averages any change is likely to be

Table 2 Comparing convergence in government policy orientation inside and outside the euro zone

Variable	Mean of std. in euro zone	Mean of std. among others	Diff. in means (euro zone minus others)	t test	p
Government policy intentions in the structural leg:					
PROEU[§]	0.123	0.228	−0.105***	2.35	0.019
CUT-TAX[†]	0.115	0.118	−0.003	7.80	0
ENTERPRISE[§]	0.065	0.087	−0.022***	1.61	0.108
ORTHODOXY[§]	0.045	0.204	−0.160***	15.08	0
WELFARE[§]	0.112	0.111	0.001	0.27	0.787
KEYNESIAN[§]	0.028	0.027	0.002	1.90	0.058
Government policy intentions in the institutional leg:					
EU-AUTHORITY[†]	0.097	0.090	0.008***	0.80	0.427
EU-ACCOUNTABILITY[†]	0.214	0.132	0.083***	0.43	0.667
Government policy intentions in the economic leg:					
DEREGULATION[†]	0.125	0.096	0.029***	4.31	0
COMPETITION[§]	0.061	0.056	0.005**	8.18	0
PLANNING[§]	0.053	0.029	0.024***	1.94	0.052
CONTROL[§]	0.059	0.058	0.001	3.16	0.002
CORPORATISM[§]	0.020	0.036	−0.016***	2.94	0.003

Note: The means reported in this table are averages of the monthly values of the cross-section standard deviation.
§Based on the Comparative Manifesto Project (CMP).
†Based on Benoit and Laver (2006).
*$0.05 < p \leq 0.10$. **$0.01 < p \leq 0.05$. ***$p \leq 0.01$.

mute, as changes in one country often offset changes in another. A significant change can only occur if it is more or less uniform across countries.

This could be the case if European left-wing parties edged to the centre in the 1990s. In that case in Table 1 the difference between 'ins' and 'others' in CUT-TAX and DEREGULATION would probably disappear. If the left was more in favour of EU institutions in the 1990s (seen as protecting workers from globalization) than later, higher average values of 'others' are likely in the institutional leg too, but a significant difference between the two columns is unlikely. In Table 2 a similar continental shift would leave cross-sectional divergence roughly unchanged (depending on cross-sectional differences in left-wing terms of office). In any case, all four indicators fail to support the notion of a sustainable EMU in Tables 1 and 2 and adjustments to them are unlikely to change the conclusions of the paper.

Tables 1 and 2 provide an aggregate picture of the sustainability of EMU inside and outside the euro zone. As explained above, the tests that they report mostly reflect changes in the indicators over time. However, a more accurate measure of the trends in these indicators could be helpful. Table 3 analyses

Table 3 Government policy orientation over time

	1990–2006 Entire data set		1999–2006 Euro zone	
	Indicator value 1	Cross-section divergence 2	Indicator value 3	Cross-section divergence 4
Government policy intentions in the structural leg:				
PROEU§ (+; −)	−0.029 (0.114)	−0.306*** (0.000)	−0.042 (0.191)	0.839*** (0.000)
CUT-TAX† (+; −)	−0.023* (0.099)	0.384*** (0.000)	0.159 (0.103)	−0.390*** (0.000)
ENTERPRISE§ (+; −)	0.090*** (0.000)	−0.628*** (0.000)	0.125*** (0.000)	−0.724*** (0.000)
ORTHODOXY§ (+; −)	0.029 (0.125)	−0.032 (0.650)	0.242*** (0.000)	−0.716*** (0.000)
WELFARE§ (−; −)	0.040** (0.032)	−0.808*** (0.000)	0.298*** (0.000)	0.459*** (0.000)
KEYNESIAN§ (−; −)	−0.064*** (0.001)	−0.325*** (0.000)	−0.191*** (0.000)	−0.873*** (0.000)
Government policy intentions in the institutional leg:				
EU-AUTHORITY† (+; −)	0.036** (0.044)	−0.780*** (0.000)	−0.065** (0.028)	0.070 (0.497)
EU-ACCOUNTABILITY† (+; −)	0.020 (0.265)	−0.389*** (0.000)	−0.025 (0.412)	−0.684*** (0.000)
Government policy intentions in the economic leg:				
DEREGULATION† (+; −)	−0.029 (0.104)	−0.185*** (0.008)	0.000 (0.998)	0.449*** (0.000)
COMPETITION§ (+; −)	0.069*** (0.000)	−0.052 (0.461)	−0.050 (0.115)	−0.867*** (0.000)
PLANNING§ (−; −)	0.042** (0.023)	0.274*** (0.000)	0.296*** (0.000)	0.931*** (0.000)
CONTROL§ (−; −)	−0.135*** (0.000)	−0.636*** (0.000)	0.040 (0.211)	−0.121 (0.241)
CORPORATISM§ (−; −)	−0.019 (0.316)	−0.173** (0.013)	0.029 (0.361)	−0.726*** (0.000)

Notes: Entries in columns 1 and 3 are correlation coefficients between the indicator and the time variable. Entries in columns 2 and 4 are correlation coefficients between the indicator's cross-sectional standard deviation and the time variable. The signs by the indicators' names indicate the combined directions of change that are expected to contribute to EMU's sustainability. The first sign relates to the indicator's value, the second sign to its divergence. Values in parentheses are the *p* values for the null hypothesis that the correlation coefficient is 0.
§Based on the Comparative Manifesto Project (CMP).
†Based on Benoit and Laver (2006).
*$0.05 < p \le 0.10$. **$0.01 < p \le 0.05$. ***$p \le 0.01$.

the entire dataset in columns 1 and 2 and a subset of euro zone member states only (since 1999) in columns 3 and 4. The table reports the correlation coefficient of each indicator with the time variable in columns 1 and 3. Thus a positive coefficient shows a tendency of the sustainability indicator to increase in time, and a negative coefficient means that the measure is diminishing with time. In columns 2 and 4 the table reports the correlation coefficient of the cross-sectional standard deviation of each indicator with the time variable. A positive coefficient shows a tendency of increasing divergence among the member states over time, and a negative coefficient means that the member states are converging. The closer the various coefficients in Table 3 are to 1 (or − 1), the more the processes that they represent are continuous; the closer they are to 0, the more the processes are erratic. Note that these coefficients say nothing about the speed of the processes (i.e. how much the indicator and its cross-sectional divergence have changed). Table 3 also reports (in parentheses) the p values for the null hypothesis that the correlation coefficient is 0.

In column 1 changes in the values of all indicators are barely noticeable. The coefficients of the cross-sectional divergence are larger (column 2) and show consistent convergence of all national governments in all indicators except CUT-TAX, ORTHODOXY, COMPETITION and PLANNING. This is generally consistent with a sustainable EMU, except in the case of DEREGULATION and the indicators in the institutional leg, which do not seem to have changed much, and have high average values (see Table 1). However, these three indicators may incorrectly measure party and government policies in the 1990s (see above).

Since 1999 column 3 shows consistent improvement in some indicators among member states of the euro zone only in the structural leg. Free enterprise and macroeconomic orthodoxy have been gaining small additional support inside the euro zone (see Figure 1) and Keynesian ideas have likewise fallen a little

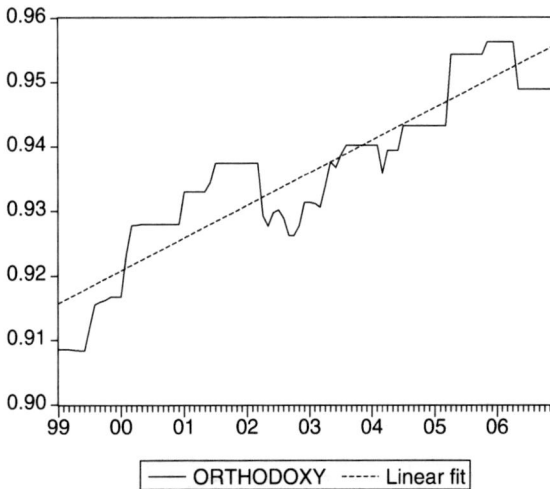

Figure 1 Support among euro zone governments for low defecit and strong currency

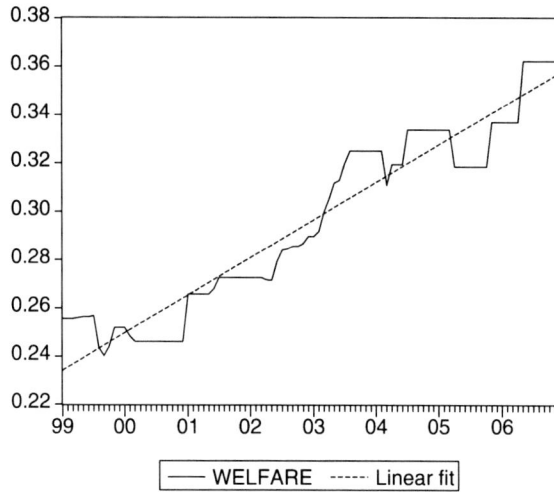

Figure 2 Support among euro zone governments for social security and social services

out of favour. In contrast, the welfare state has become more prominent in manifestos of governing parties inside the euro zone (Figure 2). This can be explained by the political and practical need to cushion society from the shocks that economic policy no longer tries to mitigate, but it does not strengthen the neo-liberal ideas upon which EMU is based. There is also a small but consistent increase in support for state planning in the economic leg (Figure 3).

Column 4 returns stronger results, which are consistent with a sustainable EMU in the cases of ENTERPRISE, ORTHODOXY, KEYNESIAN and CORPORATISM, but inconsistent with a sustainable EMU in the cases of CUT-TAX,

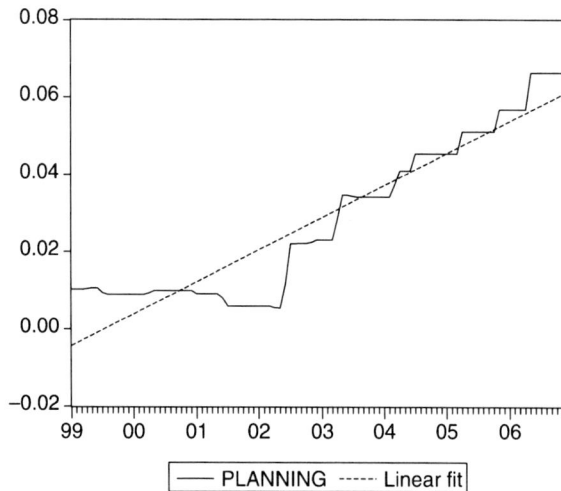

Figure 3 Support among euro zone governments for national economic planning

EU-ACCOUNTABILITY and COMPETITION (because they converge on unenthu-siastic levels of support), as well as PROEU, WELFARE, DEREGULATION and PLANNING.

The conclusion from columns 3 and 4 is that in the euro zone there is growing and especially converging support for some neo-liberal ideas that underscore EMU, but support is also growing for social cushioning mechanisms, and the member states are diverging in their support for economic reforms and conver-ging on their lacklustre support for EU institutions.

5. CONCLUSIONS

The sustainability of EMU can be understood to rest on three 'legs'. In the structural leg, the consolidation of the member states into a political community should make EMU more sustainable. This is served by support for the EU project in general and for neo-liberal ideas about the role of government in society and in the economy. In the institutional leg, EMU should be embedded in a network of international compromises spanning many issue-areas. These issue-linkages increase defection costs particularly because they give a long-term dimension to obligations. Thus, strong EU institutions should contribute to EMU's sustainability. In the economic leg, EMU would be more economi-cally efficient and profitable, and more flexible to adjust to external shock, the more the markets among its member states are liberalized and ensure the free flows of goods, services, capital and labour.

In order to find whether the governments of EU member states favour policies that contribute to the sustainability of EMU, this study uses a pooled time-series cross-sectional monthly dataset, including the pre-2004 15 EU member states over the period 1990–2006. This study uses 13 operational measures of the intentions of governments with regard to policies and issue-areas that affect the sustainability of EMU.

The results of this study show that governments of member states in the euro zone ('ins') share core beliefs and a sense of community slightly more when com-pared to themselves before 1999, and that governments of member states outside the zone ('outs') less sceptic about economic reforms. However, governments of the 'ins' are no more supportive of the EU's institutions than the 'others' are.

The results also show a minute strengthening of the commitment to some neo-liberal ideas among governments of member states of the euro zone, but support is also growing for social cushioning mechanisms and the member states are diverging in their support for economic reforms and converging on their lacklustre support for EU institutions. The lack of improvement in govern-ment attitudes towards EU institutions and towards market reforms is poten-tially unhelpful to EMU's sustainability. The reason for this is that defection costs may not rise and the ability of the member states to adjust to external shocks, and improve EMU's efficiency and profitability, may not improve.

Of course, these findings are important only to the extent that the intentions of governments are predictive of actual policies. This may not always be the case, if governments cannot dictate their policies, but rather formulate them in a political bargaining process with other domestic and transnational actors. In addition, the indicators used in this study may not accurately measure the intentions of governments. Party manifestos may be outdated, and even when they are updated their revision is often patchy, involving potential duplicity and incoherence. Decision-makers may try to pursue somewhat different goals from those explicitly mentioned in a manifesto, if it is an intra-party compromise with which they are unhappy. In addition, expert surveys of party policies may lack objectivity. Those used in this study may not be relevant for the 1990s.

Nevertheless, this study provides important insights into the potential vulnerability of EMU to changes in relevant government positions. While the member states of the euro zone have in recent years converged in support of macroeconomic policies that are important for a sustainable EMU, they have also become more divergent about the imperative microeconomic policies, and their scepticism with regard to the authority of EU institutions has become more consensual. This may explain the difficulties in implementing the Lisbon Agenda, and it may challenge the sustainability of EMU.

ACKNOWLEDGEMENTS

The author acknowledges helpful comments from the editors as well as other contributors to this special issue. The author also acknowledges the excellent research assistance provided by Idit Kra-Oz, and the support of the Leonard Davis Institute for International Relations at the Hebrew University of Jerusalem.

NOTES

1 See, for example, Bajo-Rubio and Montáves-Garcés (2002).
2 For example, see Cameron (1995) on French policy preferences.
3 See Howarth and Loedel (2005); Kaufmann (1995); McNamara and Jones (1996).
4 Jones (2002) argues that the diversity of member states does not impede EMU, because its costs and benefits are associated more with cross-border cleavages than with individual member states.
5 This adjustment follows the spirit of the suggestion made in Benoit and Laver (2007).
6 References to EU relevant policies are counted separately when they appear in an EU favourable context and in an EU sceptic context. Thus, for example, enlargement with the intention of weakening the EU or impeding its integration is counted as an EU sceptic reference.

7 EU-AUTHORITY can be interpreted as a specific case of PROEU, because greater authority for EU institutions is similar to greater competence, which is one of the elements of PROEU. Nevertheless, the overlap between these variables is small ($r = 0.15$).

REFERENCES

Artis, M.J. (2002) 'Currency interdependence: what economics has to say', *Journal of Public Policy* 22(2): 111–18.

Artis, M.J. (2003) 'Reflections on the optimal currency area (OCA) criteria in the light of EMU', *International Journal of Finance and Economics* 8(4): 297–307.

Bajo-Rubio, O. and Montáves-Garcés, M.D. (2002) 'Was there monetary autonomy in Europe on the eve of EMU? The German dominance hypothesis re-examined', *Journal of Applied Economics* 5(2): 185–207.

Begg, I. (ed.) (2002) *Europe: Government and Money. Running EMU: The Challenge of Policy Coordination*, London: Federal Trust.

Benoit, K. and Laver, M. (2006) *Party Policy in Modern Democracies*, London: Routledge.

Benoit, K. and Laver, M. (2007) 'Estimating party policy positions: comparing expert surveys and hand-coded content analysis', *Electoral Studies* 26(1): 90–107.

Budge, I., Klingemann, H.D., Volkens, A., Bara, J. and Tanenbaum, E. (2001) *Mapping Policy Preferences – Estimates for Parties, Electors, and Governments 1945–1998*, Oxford: Oxford University Press.

Cameron, D. (1995) 'From Barre to Balladur: economic policy in the era of the EMS', in G. Flynn (ed.), *Remaking the Hexagon: The New France in the New Europe*, Boulder, CO: Westview Press, pp. 117–57.

Cohen, B. (1998) *The Geography of Money*, Ithaca, NY: Cornell University Press.

Cohen, B. (2000) 'Beyond EMU: the problem of sustainability', in B. Eichengreen and J. Frieden (eds), *The Political Economy of European Monetary Unification*, 2nd edn, Boulder, CO: Westview Press, pp. 179–204.

Crouch, C. (ed.) (2000) *After the Euro: Shaping Institutions for Governance in the Wake of Monetary Union*, Oxford: Oxford University Press.

De Grauwe, P. and Lavrač, V. (1999) *Inclusion of Central European Countries in the European Monetary Union*, Boston: Kluwer.

Dyson, K. (1994) *Elusive Union: The Process of Economic and Monetary Union in Europe*, London: Longman.

Dyson, K. (2002) *European States and the Euro: Europeanization, Variation and Convergence*, Oxford: Oxford University Press.

The Economist (2006) Stormier weather ahead, 16 June.

Eichengreen, B. (1997) *European Monetary Unification: Theory, Practice and Analysis*, Cambridge, MA: MIT Press.

Frieden, J. (1996) 'The impact of goods and capital market integration on European monetary politics', *Comparative Political Studies* 29(2): 193–222.

Frieden, J. (1998) 'The euro: who wins? Who loses?', *Foreign Policy* 112: 25–40.

Goldstein, J. and Keohane, R. (eds) (1993) *Ideas and Foreign Policy – Beliefs, Institutions, and Political Change*, London: Cornell University Press.

Gros, D. and Thygesen, N. (1998) *European Monetary Integration*, 2nd edn, Harlow: Longman.

Helleiner, E. (2002) 'One money, one people? Political identities and the euro', in P. Crowley (ed.), *Before and Beyond EMU: Historical Lessons and Future Prospects*, London: Routledge, pp. 183–202.

Howarth, D. and Loedel, P. (2005) *The European Central Bank: The New European Leviathan*, 2nd edn, Basingstoke: Palgrave.

Jones, E. (2002) *The Politics of Economic and Monetary Union: Integration and Idiosyncrasy*, Lanham, MD: Rowman & Littlefield.

Kaufmann, H. (1995) 'The importance of being independent: central bank independence and the European system of central banks', in C. Rhodes and S. Mazey (eds), *The State of the European Union: Building a European Polity?*, Boulder, CO: Lynne Rienner, pp. 267–92.

Klingemann, H.D., Volkens, A., Bara, J., Budge, I. and McDonald, M. (2006) *Mapping Policy Preferences II – Estimates for Parties, Electors, and Governments in Eastern Europe, European Union and OECD 1990–2003*, Oxford: Oxford University Press.

Maes, I. and Verdun, A. (2005) 'The role of medium-sized countries in the creation of EMU: the cases of Belgium and the Netherlands', *Journal of Common Market Studies* 43(2): 27–48.

Marcussen, M. (2000) *Ideas and Elites: The Social Construction of Economic and Monetary Union*, Vilborg: Aalborg University Press.

Martin, L. (1993) 'International and domestic institutions in the EMU process', *Economics and Politics* 5(2): 125–44.

McNamara, K. (1998) *The Currency of Ideas – Monetary Politics in the European Union*, London: Cornell University Press.

McNamara, K. (2006) 'Economic governance, ideas and EMU: what currency does policy consensus have today?', *Journal of Common Market Studies* 44(4): 803–21.

McNamara, K. and Jones, E. (1996) 'The clash of institutions: Germany in European monetary affairs', *German Politics and Society* 14(3): 5–30.

Risse, T., Engelmann-Martin, D., Knopf, H.J. and Roscher, K. (1999) 'To euro or not to euro? The EMU and identity politics in the European Union', *European Journal of International Relations* 5(2): 147–87.

Sadeh, T. (2005) 'Who can adjust to the euro?', *The World Economy* 28(11): 1651–78.

Sadeh, T. (2006) *Sustaining European Monetary Union: Confronting the Cost of Diversity*, Boulder, CO: Lynne Rienner.

Sadeh, T. and Verdun, A. (2009) 'Explaining Europe's monetary union – a Survey of the literature', *International Studies Review* 11(2).

Steinherr, A. (ed.) (1994) *Thirty Years of European Monetary Integration from the Werner Plan to EMU*, London: Longman.

Tavlas, G. (1993) 'The "new" theory of optimum currency areas', *The World Economy* 16(6): 663–85.

Tilford, S. (2006) 'Will the eurozone crack?', *Centre for European Reform*, Working Paper.

Verdun, A. (2000) *European Responses to Globalization and Financial Market Integration. Perceptions of Economic and Monetary Union in Britain, France and Germany*, Basingstoke: Palgrave.

Watson, A. (2004) 'Economic and monetary union: of currencies and clubs', *Journal of European Integration* 26(1): 25–39.

Woods, N. (1995) 'Economic ideas and international relations: beyond rational neglect', *International Studies Quarterly* 39(2): 161–80.

Young, B. (2002) 'On collision course: the European Central Bank, monetary policy, and the Nordic welfare model', *International Feminist Journal of Politics* 4(3): 295–314.

Economic interests and public support for the euro

Susan A. Banducci, Jeffrey A. Karp and Peter H. Loedel

INTRODUCTION

With the European monetary union (EMU) celebrating its tenth anniversary in 2009, the euro has now settled into the minds and markets of more than half of the 27 European Union (EU) member states. After a somewhat rocky start in terms of its value, the common currency, which was first introduced into circulation in 12 member states in 2002, has strongly rebounded to be considered a viable alternative global reserve currency and competitor to the US dollar. Despite continued British reservations about its own membership, the eurozone has expanded eastward to include Slovenia in 2007 and Slovakia in 2009, and southward in 2008 to include Malta and Cyprus. Additional central and eastern European member states look to join in the near future (Estonia, the Czech Republic, and Hungary) or within the next five years.

Despite this rapid embracing of the euro, the mood within the EU has not been quite as robust. The rejection of the referendums on the European Constitution in France and in the Netherlands in 2005 highlighted divisions over the future of Europe. Further efforts to address the perceived democratic deficit in the EU through the Reform Treaty were complicated by the Irish rejection of the Lisbon Treaty in 2008. In addition, a cloudy or mixed economic outlook for the eurozone economy suggests difficult times ahead for the EU project.

This paper examines how the economic impact of the common currency has influenced support for the euro. Despite a surface level 'strength' to the euro project, we hypothesize that concerns about a loss in purchasing power may have weakened support for the euro. We focus on the extent to which these economic concerns as opposed to other explanations structure support for the common currency.

CHANGING ECONOMIC CONDITIONS AND EURO SUPPORT

The frequent use of referendums on European integration underscores the importance of public opinion to the success of the European project. A review of the literature reveals a range of theories that might help to understand the relationship between public opinion and European common currency. Explanations for public support for European integration can be grouped, generally, into utilitarian and identity theories. The utilitarian perspective relies on self-interested explanations of political attitudes and suggests that citizens are more likely to support integration if it results in a net benefit to the national economy or their own pocketbook (Eichenberg and Dalton 1993; Gabel 1998; Gabel and Palmer 1995; Anderson and Reichert 1995). Given its economic implications, it is reasonable to expect opinions about the euro to be shaped by economic self-interest and that, consequently, those who have the capacity and resources to benefit from monetary union will be more supportive (Karp and Bowler 2006). Even prior to adoption, previous studies found considerable empirical support for these claims in shaping attitudes about the common currency (Gabel and Hix 2005; Kaltenthaler and Anderson 2001; Banducci et al. 2003).

One of the more obvious economic consequences associated with the introduction of the new currency is its impact on purchasing power. Prior to the introduction of the common currency, high inflation was associated with higher levels of support for the euro (Banducci et al. 2003), suggesting that citizens expected the European Central Bank (ECB) to bring about stability and lower inflation. If these expectations are not met then support for the euro should decrease.

Although the adoption of the euro promised to bring stability in the long term, fears that price rises would accompany the introduction of the euro were widespread. A 2001 Eurobarometer revealed that two-thirds of European citizens feared cheating on prices once the euro came into circulation.[1] According to Eurostat (2003), these fears appear to have been unwarranted. The official rate of inflation within the eurozone remained at 2.3 per cent in 2002, the same as in 2001. Nevertheless, it did acknowledge in its report that price rises were evident in the service sector, such as restaurants and cafés, hairdressers, and recreational and sporting services. Consumers may have been more sensitive to these increases as they are likely to place greater weight on price changes of frequently purchased goods than on less frequently purchased goods (Angeloni et al. 2006: 369; Dziuda and Mastrobuoni 2007).

The introduction of the euro also coincided with a strengthening US dollar which may have affected support. The exchange rate, in particular, is not only an indicator of purchasing power but also has important symbolic value. While economists may suggest that a weak currency may have certain advantages, a strong currency can be seen by citizens as a symbol of economic strength (Hobolt and Leblond 2009; Banducci *et al.* 2003). When the euro first traded on world currency markets in 1999, its initial value was set at close to 1.20 dollars per euro. The new currency soon depreciated in value against other major currencies. In the first 16 months, the value of the euro plunged more than 20 per cent against the US dollar. The euro continued to depreciate, dropping to a low of 0.84 euros against the US dollar in 2002. At the time, economists feared that the euro's decline would raise the price of imports, reduce the standard of living and contribute to inflationary pressure. By 2003, the trend had reversed and the euro steadily gained in value, reaching its launch value by mid-year. By the end of 2007, the euro had reached a peak of 1.50 euros against the dollar.

Another economic indicator that may play a role in shaping attitudes about the common currency is a country's budget deficit. Prior to the adoption of the common currency, convergence criteria required countries to reduce their debt which produced a 'squeeze effect' for countries with loose fiscal policy (Gärtner 1997). An analysis of public support for the euro prior to its adoption, using individual level data, found that support for the euro was lower where debt decreased (Banducci *et al.* 2003: 698). The lack of support associated with a reduction in debt can be interpreted as a negative reaction to austerity measures or squeeze produced by tighter fiscal policy. These austerity measures still exist as a result of the Stability Pact of 1995 and the ongoing surveillance of government macroeconomic policy by the European Commission and the ECB. While some eurozone members have slipped in terms of adhering strictly to the guidelines, such as the 3 per cent target for annual deficits, eurozone members have largely continued to maintain the stability focus required by the Pact. Moreover, the ECB has upheld a tough policy line demanding that eurozone members maintain fiscal austerity. The ECB's decision not to follow the lead of other central banks to lower interest rates until October 2008, despite a spreading fear of economic downturn across Europe (triggered in large part by economic slowdown in the United States), is a reflection of its tough stand on inflation and its concern about how government spending might negatively impact the Bank's targets.

Finally, previous studies have also suggested that other indicators of economic stability, such as low unemployment, are a key byproduct of economic union and the monetary policy of the ECB. Citizens are expected to prefer stability in employment brought about through monetary union. Past research has demonstrated that higher unemployment leads to increased support for a common currency although the effect is not consistent across model specifications (Kaltenthaler and Anderson 2001).

While these economic concerns may shape public support, they may nonetheless feature less prominently than other factors. Some have suggested that feelings of national identity and pride (Gabel and Hix 2005; Risse 2003) or feelings of political community (Jupille and Leblang 2007) exert a more powerful influence. Indeed, the creation of territorial currencies was viewed by policy-makers as a way to strengthen national identities (Helleiner 2003). Those familiar with the story of Germany's decision to join EMU (see, for example, Loedel 1999; Risse 2003) know that the German public's attachment to the Deutschmark weighed heavily on the political decision to join EMU. In a survey in Austria prior to the euro's adoption, Meier and Kirchler (1998) found that extreme attitudes about the euro were linked to individuals' preoccupation with national identity. The adoption of the common currency has meant a fundamental shift in the role of the nation state, and we expect that those with strong national identities will be less supportive while those with a strong European identity will be more supportive.

THE PUBLIC'S REACTION TO THE CHANGEOVER

A qualitative study conducted shortly after the introduction of the new currency in May 2002 gauged citizens' reactions to the new currency, based on in-depth interviews with at-risk groups (the elderly and socio-economically disadvantaged) and a control group of 'average citizens' (European Commission 2002). Based on spontaneous reactions to the euro, citizens' attitudes reflect positive experiences, both expected and unexpected, as well as some expressions of uncertainty about the effect of the euro on prices. Positive expressions encompassed both instrumental benefits as well as symbolic benefits. Interviewees pointed to the [unexpected ease of the transition to the new currency, the increased ease in travel as well as the contribution of the common currency to economic stability. Other respondents' comments that 'I feel closer to other countries', and 'In sharing the same single currency I feel more connected with the rest of Europe', illustrate the ability of the currency to bring Europeans together and build a sense of shared identity (European Commission 2002: 8).] There was, however, some nostalgia among the elderly participants for the old currencies such as the French franc or the Greek drachma ('the oldest currency in the world').

Negative reactions to the currency centred on the feeling that prices had risen considerably with the introduction of the euro. The sentiment that purchasing power had been reduced was expressed across all categories of individuals and in all countries, being particularly true in the Netherlands and Germany (European Commission 2002: 20). Generally, people expressed the feelings that their money was not 'lasting as long', 'buying as much' or 'going as far' as before. The source of the increase in prices was identified as rounding up and businesses taking advantage of the change in currency to raise prices. One Dutch respondent said, 'There's no doubt that prices have gone up … people have taken advantage of it', with another adding, 'Prices have been rounded up just about everywhere' (European Commission 2002: 21).

Clearly, as is noted in the qualitative research conducted directly after the introduction of the euro currency, European citizens are concerned about price increases. These concerns were echoed in a Flash Eurobarometer conducted in May 2002. While a majority of respondents found the benefits of cheaper and easier travel and easier price comparison noteworthy, many citizens were still convinced that the introduction of the euro would still increase prices (especially in the removal of small denominations from their own national currencies). More pointedly, respondents widely believe that the euro has had a negative effect on prices. Over 80 per cent of all citizens believe that the euro has added to the increases in prices.

The sensitivity of the public to the price mechanism could also be the result of a majority of citizens still calculating prices based as much on old national currencies or a mix of national currencies and the euro. For example, 69 per cent of respondents still calculate prices on national currencies compared to 29 per cent when making exceptional purchases (buying a car or house). Even small purchases are still calculated either in national currencies or a mix of the euro and national currencies by 44 per cent of the population. Finally, a majority (59 per cent) of respondents suggest that they are either buying less out of fear of spending too much or buying more because they have difficulty realizing how much they have spent. In short, citizens' measures of how the euro is affecting their price calculations and the cost of goods are still high. An even more recent study of public opinion completed by the European Commission finds an almost even match between citizens' concerns with unemployment and inflation (27 per cent to 26 per cent respectively).[2] More strikingly, citizens' concerns with inflation have risen 8 per cent since early 2007. Furthermore, in Slovenia, which introduced the euro in 2007, 63 per cent of respondents noted inflationary concerns. This represents an increase of 45 per cent compared to the previous year. Clearly, citizen perceptions of the euro's inflationary impact appear to be quite strong.

The public's perception of price increases does not necessarily reflect the view coming from the ECB. The ECB uses a quantitative definition of price stability. The first measure is a reference value for the growth rate of a broad monetary aggregate (namely, M3: the stock of notes and coins in circulation, the value of bank current accounts, and deposit or interest-bearing accounts). The ECB's own measures of the growth of M3 since 2002 indicate some concern about uncertainty and volatility, sometimes rising outside the ranges desired by the ECB. However, in general, this more technical definition and the management of it have not generally caused the ECB to shift interest rates (Howarth and Loedel 2005). More important is the second measure, the Harmonized Index of Consumer Prices (HICP). The HICP for the euro area is based on national HICPs, which follow the same methodology in all euro area countries (European Central Bank 2008). The HICP covers monetary expenditures on final consumption by households in the euro area. An examination of this measure of 'inflation' indicates that the eurozone HICP ranged, on an annual rate of change, between 1.5 and 2.75 during the period 2002–2007.

There was a more recent surge to over 3 per cent in the last months of 2007 and early 2008, but nothing to indicate any dramatic 'surge' in prices, either after the introduction of the euro in 2002 or over the next five years. Moreover, interest rates have remained within a fairly narrow range throughout the time frame since the euro's introduction in 2002.[3]

UNDERSTANDING CHANGES IN SUPPORT FOR THE EURO

To examine public support for the euro, we rely on data from the Eurobarometer, which is conducted on behalf of the European Commission and regularly surveys citizens in each of the member states about their opinions on European matters. We aggregate for each member state year responses to a question about whether an individual was for or against a 'European monetary union with one single currency, the euro'.[4] Figure 1 displays the proportion of respondents in each member state who said they were in favour of a single currency from 2000–2007. The 15 EU member states are grouped by region and whether they are enthusiastic or sceptical about EU membership.

Although monetary policy has been relatively stable, support for the euro has varied considerably since its introduction. Clearly, outside the eurozone mass opinion is more negative than within the eurozone. The euro note's introduction in 2002 appears to have lifted support somewhat outside the eurozone but the overall level of support has remained relatively stable since 2002. The largest increase in support is evident in those countries within the eurozone that could be characterized as 'eurosceptic'. In both Austria and Finland, where a majority on average do not support European membership across the time period, there was an approximate 20 per cent increase in support for the

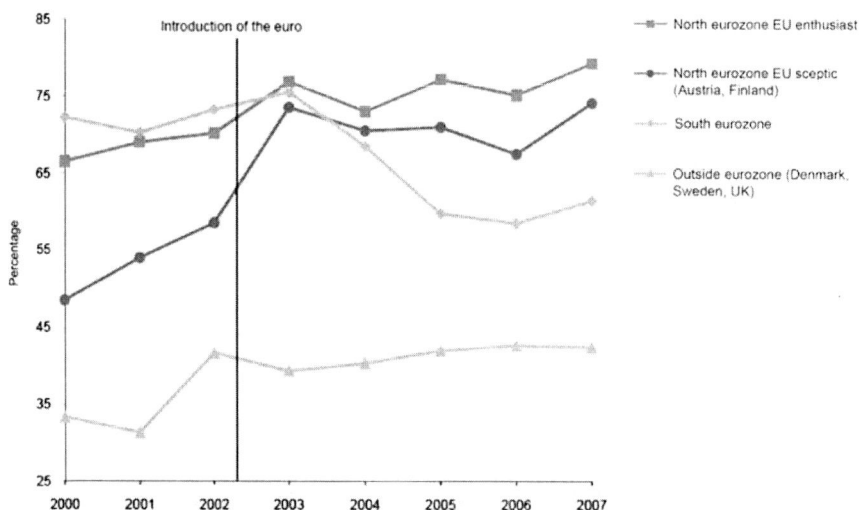

Figure 1 Changes in support for the euro (2000–2007)

euro between 2000 and 2003. The apparent euphoria surrounding the introduction of the euro continued through 2007. The overall level of support in
Finland and Austria now approximates that of the more enthusiastic EU
members in the north. Unexpected, however, is the loss of support in the
southern member states (Greece, Spain, Portugal and Italy). Support for the
euro has declined sharply in these states, from an average of three-quarters to
two-thirds support. It should be noted that despite the sharper decline,
support remains well above 50 per cent. In comparison, support in the northern
member states continues to rise.

The trends in Figure 1 indicate that support for the euro has shifted substantially over time. These changes have occurred primarily within the euro zone
and appear to be independent of support for EU membership. While support
increased in the eurosceptic countries, support decreased substantially in the
south which was initially more enthusiastic about the euro than anywhere else
in the EU. To determine whether these changes can be attributed to economic
influences, we undertake a multivariate analysis using pooled public opinion
and economic data from the 15 member states. We chose to start the time
series data in a year prior to the introduction of bank notes to capture any
shifts in opinion that accompanied the changeover.[5] Several indicators are
used to assess the impact of economic factors on euro support. We use the
inflation level as an indication of price stability, as measured by the annual
rate of change in the HICP. The effective range is limited given the convergence
criteria. Nevertheless, inflation does vary across space and time between 0.8 and
5.1. The change in the exchange rate against the US dollar is used to measure
changes in the value of the euro. As the euro increases in value against the
US dollar, support should increase. To capture the impact on fiscal policy,
the level of deficit (or surplus as a percentage of gross domestic product
(GDP) is used to represent any 'squeeze' in government spending which is
the result of meeting convergence criteria (see Banducci et al. 2003). We
include the rate of unemployment as another indicator of economic stability.[6]

In the model, we also use the lagged level of euro support and control for the
level of general EU support measured by the proportion of respondents who say
that EU membership is a good thing. We also control for GDP.[7] These controls
provide a fairly robust test for the effects of economic conditions on aggregate
support for the euro.

Given that the data are pooled time-series cross-sections (TSCS), statistical
issues arise which make estimation using ordinary least squares (OLS) problematic (Stimson 1985; Beck and Katz 1995). A common technique to deal
with the problem is to adjust for autocorrelation by using panel corrected standard errors (PCSE) (see Beck and Katz 1995). However, this fix only addresses
the problem of autocorrelation (if it exists) within the TSCS and does not take
into account heterogeneity either in intercepts or slopes across the panel units or
give full consideration to modelling dynamics (see Wilson and Butler 2007 on
these points). Following specification tests for autocorrelation and unit-time
effects (a fixed effects model), we find no significant autocorrelation but

significant unit-time effects. Therefore, we use a fixed effects model to estimate how economic factors influence euro support.[8] We estimate a model using data across all original 15 member states and then compare this to a model using only countries inside the eurozone. Table 1 shows the results from a fixed effects pooled cross-sectional model.

Our initial test of the model shows that the most important economic indicators are the change in the exchange rate and the level of inflation. Our indicator of the squeeze effect – the deficit – does not have a significant impact on euro support nor does unemployment either inside the eurozone or across all member states. This result is inconsistent with earlier findings prior to the introduction of the currency (see Gärtner 1997, for example). However, it does reflect some of the findings from individual-level analysis where objective economic indicators were found to have little impact (see Gabel and Whitten 1997, for example).

Although the qualitative studies after the introduction of the euro suggest that citizens may have blamed the euro for high prices, the coefficient for inflation,

Table 1 Economic conditions and support for the euro (2001–2007)

	15 original member states	Inside eurozone
Lagged euro support	0.44**	0.56**
	(0.08)	(0.09)
Inflation	−1.64[a]	−0.78
	(0.97)	(1.03)
Deficit/Surplus (as % GDP)	0.05	−0.70
	(0.45)	(0.55)
Unemployment	0.31	0.76
	(0.72)	(0.77)
Exchange rate change	0.27**	0.35**
	(0.09)	(0.10)
GDP	−0.02	0.02
	(0.20)	(0.21)
EU membership a good thing	0.51**	0.51**
	(0.11)	(0.13)
Euro in circulation	−4.13[a]	−4.91*
	(2.35)	(2.40)
Constant	11.43	−1.73
	(9.59)	(11.99)
N	105	84
R^2		
Within	0.74	0.58
Between	0.50	0.58
	0.80	0.65

Notes: Exchange rate is the change in the euro exchange against the US dollar.
    Standard errors are in parenthesis.
** $p < 0.01$; * $p < 0.05$; [a] $p < 0.10$.

while in the expected direction, is not statistically significant in the fixed effects model within the eurozone. Across all 15 member states, higher inflation appears to have a negative impact on levels of euro support. A 1 per cent increase in inflation is predicted to lower euro support by over 1.6 per cent, whereas we see no significant effect of inflation inside the eurozone.[9] This lack of evidence for the objective indicator of inflation effects on euro support does not square with the evidence from the focus groups or surveys in the post-introduction period.

While inflation does not appear to have affected support within the eurozone, the change in the exchange rate of the euro does appear to have a strong impact. The results suggest that a stronger euro (relative to the US dollar) boosts support which is consistent with other research showing that citizens are more reluctant to give up their national currency when it is strong (Banducci *et al.* 2003). Given the increase in the value of the euro over time, we were concerned that the exchange rate, as it varies only across time and not across countries, might be acting as a proxy for time. However, including a trend variable in the model along with the exchange rate does not alter the results. Furthermore, the trend variable, when included on its own in the model, is not significant. Therefore, we are confident that we are picking up effects of the exchange rate.

Finally, general levels of EU support are tied to more specific support for EU monetary policy in the form of the euro. A 1 per cent increase in general EU support increases euro support by a half of a percentage point. By controlling for general support, we have provided a more robust test of the effect of various economic indicators on the euro. The results indicate that the strength of the euro against the US dollar has affected public support more so than inflation, independent of general feelings about the EU. It should be noted that our aggregate model does not explicitly compare cultural explanations for euro support except in suggesting that general support is linked to specific support. In the individual level analysis that follows, we investigate more thoroughly the role of identity in structuring support for the euro.

A MODEL OF EURO SUPPORT

While the results presented so far suggest that some economic factors influence overall support, it is not clear how economic perceptions structure support. Nor is it clear how these factors weigh against other factors that are believed to play an important role in shaping individual opinions. In models of economic voting, perceptions of economic conditions weigh more heavily in decision-making than do the actual economic indicators (see, for example, Lewis-Beck 1988). Gabel and Whitten (1997), when investigating why Eichenberg and Dalton (1993) found little evidence of economic indicators influencing support for European integration, posit that perceptions of economic conditions rather than objective indicators may be more relevant. For example, the actual inflation rate may not have an impact because citizens perceive inflation to be much higher than it actually is. Likewise, even if we find little evidence that objective economic indicators matter in explaining euro support, we nonetheless may expect perceptions of the economy to influence variations in support for the euro. Namely, a belief that prices (or inflation) are high will decrease support for the euro. Furthermore, in the post-introduction phase, evaluations of national economic performance should increase support. However, we expect that these economic indicators will be tempered by general EU support and feelings of European and national identity. Overall, we expect that general EU support and a stronger European identity will boost euro support while strong national identity should decrease support. We also expect that outside the eurozone, where citizens do not have the day-to-day experience with the euro and may not link it to inflation, opinion will be structured more by attitudes about the EU, general support and identity. To the extent that domestic economic conditions matter, the stronger the economy, the less likely that citizens will agree that the euro is necessary.

To examine these questions, we rely on data from Eurobarometer 67.2, conducted in April–May 2007. The expansion of the EU to 27 member states as of 2007 provides a more diverse set of countries that includes ten new members that are former communist countries. An analysis based on data from 2007 also provides a sufficient amount of time since the changeover to gauge how the euro has settled into the minds of Europeans. Note that, at the time of the survey, the euro traded at a record high against the US dollar (1.35). We use the same question that was reported in the aggregate analysis to measure support. Therefore, the descriptive statistics show the proportion of respondents who say they are 'for' the euro.

As Figure 2 shows, there is considerable variation among EU member states, both within and across the eurozone.[10] Support is lowest in the UK, with fewer than 30 per cent in support of the euro, and strongest in Slovenia, the newest member, with over nine in ten supporting the euro. As reflected earlier in Figure 1, support is generally lower outside the eurozone. Within the eurozone, support is lowest in the southern member states. Overall, with the exception of Greece, over 50 per cent of respondents within the eurozone support the euro.

The 2007 survey includes several items that provide for a test of the euro's economic impact. These include an item asking respondents to identify the current inflation rate. Reflecting a substantial degree of ambivalence, just over half the sample (51 per cent) were not able to provide an estimate. Within the eurozone, 22 per cent estimated the inflation rate to be between 2 and 5 per cent while 12 per cent estimated it to be above 5 per cent. Outside the eurozone, citizens were more likely to estimate a higher rate; 25 per cent estimated a rate above 5 per cent. Because we are interested in how perceptions of prices influence support for the euro, we are not concerned about the fact that many respondents could not estimate the rate or provide a correct estimate. Of all economic concepts, citizens do seem to have the greatest understanding of and knowledge about inflation (Walstad 1997). Another economic item asks

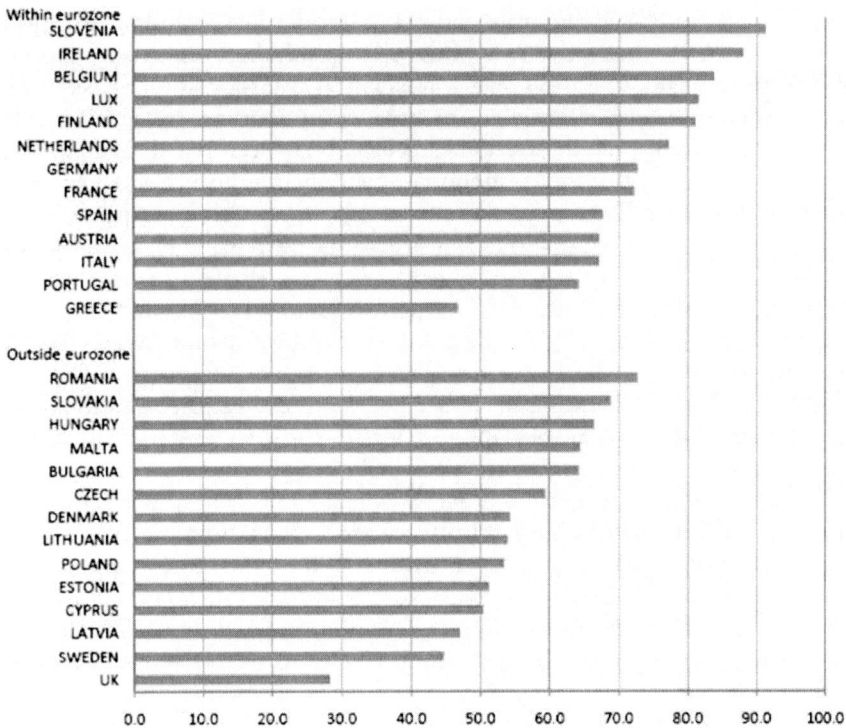

Figure 2 Support for the euro across the EU (2007)
Source: Eurobarometer 67.2 (Spring 2007).

respondents to assess the current situation of the national economy ranging from very good (+2) to very bad (−2). Those without an opinion are placed in the middle of the scale (0). Again, we expect that those who perceive inflation to be high or the national economy to be bad will be less supportive of the euro. However, outside the eurozone, inflation and a poor economic performance of the national government will lead to greater support for the euro.

To assess the impact of identity, an item measuring the strength of attachment to country and to the EU is used where those responding that they are 'very attached' are coded as a '1', while others are coded as '0'. One variable then indicates attachment to the EU and the other to the individual's country. As outlined earlier, identity has played an increasingly important role in the analysis of public support for the EU. However, given the symbolic importance of currencies, we would expect that national identity would be linked to less support for the euro while European identity leads to greater support for the euro.

To control for general support for the EU, we rely as above on the item that measures whether citizens believe their country's membership is a 'good thing' or a 'bad thing', which ranges from +1 to −1. Ambivalent responses are placed in the middle of the scale and coded as '0'. The inclusion of general support for the EU raises the issue of the relationship between general support of institutions and that of specific policies. Most models of general EU support suggest that utilitarian concerns and identity play key roles in structuring attitudes about European integration. Yet, it is also conceivable that support for specific policies, such as the common currency, may influence levels of more general support. While our main interest is in modelling support for a common currency, we must also take into account the possibility of a reciprocal relationship. This endogeneity is consistent with models that suggest that governmental policy performance underlies political support (Evans and Whitefield 1995; Mischler and Rose 2001). Therefore, we tested a structural model allowing the causal arrows to run both ways between euro support and general support for EU membership. While the results indicate support for a reciprocal relationship, the estimates for our main variables of interest do not change significantly. Therefore, we treat support for EU membership as an exogenous variable.[11]

Education is measured by the age at which a citizen stopped full-time education. Those with a high level of education are classified as ending their education in their 20s, while those with a medium level of education are those ending their education between 16–19 years of age. The comparison group are students and those ending their education before the age of 16. We also include dummy variables for citizens who are out of the labour force and are either unemployed or full-time students. Age and gender are included in the model as controls. As with the aggregate analysis, the dependent variable is based on those who are 'for' 'a European Monetary Union with one single currency, the euro'. Those who are against or those who are ambivalent are placed in the residual category. Given that we have different expectations about the effects of these variables on euro support where the euro has been introduced, we estimate two separate models for countries within and outside the eurozone. The results are presented in Table 2.

RESULTS

There is clear evidence that economic evaluations structure support for the euro within the eurozone. Those with positive assessments of the national economy are far more likely to support the euro than those who are pessimistic. Concerns about high inflation rates also appear to dampen support for the euro. Those who believe that inflation exceeds 5 per cent or those who are unsure about the rate are less likely to support the euro than those who believe that the inflation rate is less than 2 per cent. These results provide evidence that concern about rising prices dampens support for the euro. However, the effects of inflation do not appear to be as substantial as one might expect; the change in probability in support for the euro between those who perceive inflation as high compared to those who perceive it as low is just 6 per cent. We expected a positive effect of inflation outside the eurozone, but high inflation has a negative impact. Generally, outside the eurozone, the economic

Table 2 Explaning support for the euro

	Eurozone			Outside eurozone		
	Coef.	Robust S.E.	Min-Max	Coef.	Robust S.E.	Min-Max
National economic performance	0.35**	(0.09)	0.25	0.06	(0.07)	0.06
Perceived inflation rate 5%+	−0.36**	(0.13)	0.07	−0.35*	(0.15)	0.09
Perceived inflation rate 2–5%	−0.15	(0.11)	0.03	−0.19	(0.13)	0.05
Perceived inflation unknown	−0.39**	(0.11)	0.07	−0.52**	(0.13)	0.13
Unemployed	−0.15**	(0.06)	0.02	−0.08	(0.06)	0.02
National identity	0.03	(0.12)	0.01	−0.26**	(0.07)	0.06
EU identity	0.74**	(0.14)	0.11	0.85**	(0.10)	0.20
EU membership a good thing	0.94**	(0.06)	0.38	0.94**	(0.05)	0.44
Female	−0.25**	(0.06)	0.04	−0.35**	(0.06)	0.09
Age (in 10s)	−0.05	(0.34)	0.01	−0.48*	(0.21)	0.10
Student	0.92**	(0.12)	0.13	0.29*	(0.14)	0.07
Medium education	0.57**	(0.09)	0.09	0.24	(0.09)	0.06
High education	0.90**	(0.12)	0.14	0.42**	(0.11)	0.10
New entrant	1.34**	(0.13)	0.16	0.78**	(0.22)	0.19
Constant	−0.51**	(0.17)		0.09	(0.21)	
Number of countries	13			14		
n	13,140			13,273		
Cragg-Uhler(Nagelkerke) R^2	0.29			0.22		

Notes: Robust standard errors are clustered by country; Min-Max refers to the maximum change in probabability (i.e. first difference). ** $p < 0.01$; * $p < 0.05$.
Source: Eurobarometer 67.2 (Spring 2007).

effects on the euro are not at all clear. National economic performance has no influence on euro support but inflation does. Additionally, those who are unemployed are less supportive of the euro. These differences strongly suggest that citizens within the eurozone are linking economic performance to the euro while other factors may be at play outside the eurozone.

Outside the eurozone, there is little evidence that economic factors influence support. Evaluations of economic performance have no influence, while perceived inflation has a negative rather than a positive effect. In comparison, identity appears to play a greater role in euro support. Outside the eurozone, both national and EU identity are significant and in the expected direction. While national identity reduces support, attachments to the EU exert a more powerful influence on support for the euro. EU identity is also a factor within the eurozone while national identity appears to have no influence. Clearly, experience with the currency produces a different structure to euro support. Economic evaluations are important inside the eurozone while identity plays a more important role outside the eurozone.

Finally, attitudes about EU membership exert a powerful influence. A citizen who believes his or her country's membership is a good thing has a probability of supporting the euro that is 44 per cent greater than a citizen outside the euro zone who believes that his or her country's membership is a bad thing. While we note that the performance of the euro may lead to more generalized support for the EU, controlling for general support should provide a robust test of how economic perceptions and identity influence euro support. We also note that previous findings prior to the introduction of the euro, are consistent with the view that general attitudes about European integration structure specific support for the euro. The remaining variables are largely consistent across both models. Education has a positive, though somewhat weaker, influence outside the eurozone.

CONCLUSIONS: EUROPEAN INTEGRATION AND THE EUROPEAN CENTRAL BANK

Previous studies have found considerable empirical support for the impact of economic factors and identity on euro support. These studies relied on data that were either collected prior to the euro's introduction, when the currency remained an abstract concept, or outside of the euro zone, where the currency has not been adopted. In this paper we examined support for the common currency after the introduction of notes and coins in 2002. Whereas we find considerable evidence that euro support is responsive to economic conditions – both national inflation rates and the overall strength of the currency – we also find that identity and general EU support can boost support for the euro. Therefore, when the currency is strong and general EU support is high, there will be considerable support for the common currency.

Of the primary economic indicators, inflation was expected to have a strong negative impact on support for the euro. The official inflation rate, however, appears to be only weakly related to support across both time and space. Nevertheless, the results from the individual analysis suggest that citizens may have perceptions of inflation that do not necessarily coincide with the actual indicators. This may result from the tendency of citizens to be more sensitive to price changes of certain goods which may have increased in price. The results suggest that these perceptions do in fact influence support for the common currency. The magnitude of these effects, however, is not as great as more general assessments of economic performance, which appear to have a substantial impact on support.

Closely related, the prestige of the euro among the public will depend on how effectively the ECB can deal with various crises – from external shocks due to US dollar instability, internal shocks within certain regions, and the ongoing question of high unemployment in some parts of the eurozone. Monetary policy decisions affect member states differently due to different national economic cycles (despite some convergence) and differently structured economies. Given the lack of financial transfer payments to compensate those parts of the eurozone suffering from asymmetrical shocks, limited labour mobility and the strong constraints placed on the use of national fiscal instruments, the ECB's response to these shocks will be of considerable importance.

The long-term record may suggest that the ECB has done an effective job in moulding a broad level of public support for EMU which, in turn, has bolstered support for the European project. Thus the future of EMU rests on a solid institutional foundation. In general, citizens of the EU provide the political foundation or legitimacy for European integration. The evidence seems to suggest that the ECB has overcome, at least on one level, this legitimacy question. Those citizens who express their support for the euro thus provide the basis of support for the larger EU project. Thus, support for the euro project, managed effectively by the ECB, will support the larger public's attitudes toward the further integration of the EU. Indeed, nearly 70 per cent of EU citizens indicated strong support for an important role of the ECB in the life of the EU (Eurobarometer 2004, No. 61). It would seem then that the ECB and the euro are powerful foundations for the future of EU integration.

ACKNOWLEDGEMENTS

The authors would like to thank the four anonymous reviewers, the special issue editors and the participants at the conference 'Ten Years of the European Monetary Union' at the Hertie School of Governance, Berlin, for their helpful comments on earlier versions of this article.

NOTES

1 The flash Eurobarometer 98/2 asked, 'I am going to read you four statements concerning the replacement of the [NATIONAL CURRENCIES] by the euro in daily life. Could you tell me if you agree or disagree [with the following] 'You're afraid of abuses and cheating on prices.'
2 Eurobarometer 68, *Public Opinion in the European Union*, September–November 2007.
3 For example, the main refinancing rate has ranged from a low of 2 per cent to 4.25 per cent.
4 This question does not focus on EU competencies such as which level of government, EU or national, should handle monetary policy but instead gauges direct evaluations of the monetary union and primes respondents to focus directly on the currency.

5 Changes in question wording precluded any comparisons prior to 2000.
6 We estimated models using three different transformations of inflation and debt: actual level of debt, change in debt and deviation from the average debt across the eurozone average. All transformations yielded similar results. However, using the deviation from the eurozone average proved to be the most robust indicator across the different estimates of the model.
7 We also tested the 'gap' in GDP, the difference between potential outputs and actual outputs (potential GDP – actual GDP). However, this economic indicator was not significant in any of the models tested so we have opted not to report its effects in Table 1.
8 We compared results from models estimated using fixed effects, panel corrected standard errors, autoregressive (ARIMA) and random effects. Comparison across the models suggests that a fixed effects model is appropriate. A Hausman test comparing the fixed and random effects models indicated that the null hypothesis of equivalent coefficients across the models could not be rejected suggesting significant correlation between the unobserved random effects on the independent variables. Therefore, the random effects model, which has the same coefficient estimates as the PCSE models, is rejected in favour of the fixed effects model.
9 We examined the correlation between inflation and euro support in the three countries outside the eurozone: Denmark, Sweden and the UK. We expected high inflation in these countries to be accompanied by support for the euro following the expectation that those outside the eurozone would see some benefit (reducing inflation) in transferring monetary authority to the ECB. We found that in the UK there was indeed a strong positive correlation between inflation and euro support (r = 0.79). As inflation increased, the proportion of citizens willing to give up sovereignty over the national currency also increased. However, the correlation was strong and negative in both Denmark (r = −0.48) and Sweden (r = −0.68). While outside the eurozone, the economies of these countries are closely linked with those in the eurozone such that the UK, of all the original 15 member states, may be considered the only country outside the eurozone. Perhaps citizens in Denmark and Sweden, feeling the inflationary pressures but receiving very little of the benefits of the currency, are feeling frustrated by the euro and the negative economic consequences take precedence in their evaluations.
10 Note that Malta and Cyprus joined the eurozone in 2008, seven months after the data were collected.
11 Another strategy would be to use an instrumental variables approach. However, it is difficult to determine a priori which variables could serve as appropriate instruments to predict support for EU membership that would not be correlated with support for the euro.

REFERENCES

Anderson, C. and Reichert, M.S. (1995) 'Economic benefits and support for membership in the EU: a cross-national analysis', *Journal of Public Policy* 15(3): 231–49.
Angeloni, I., Aucremanne, L. and Ciccarelli, M. (2006) 'The euro and prices: did EMU affect price setting and inflation persistence?', *Economic Policy* 21(46): 353–87.
Banducci, S.A., Karp, J.A. and Loedel, P.H. (2003) 'The euro, economic interests, and multi-level governance: examining support for the common currency', *European Journal of Political Research* 42(5): 685–703.
Beck, N. and Katz, J.N. (1995) 'What to do (and not to do) with time series cross-section data', *American Political Science Review* 89: 634–47.

Dziuda, W. and Mastrobuoni, G. (2007) 'The euro changeover and its effects on price transparency and inflation'. Unpublished manuscript, Kellogg School of Management, Northwestern University.

Eichenberg, R.C. and Dalton, R.J. (1993) 'Europeans and the European Community: the dynamics of public support for European integration', *International Organization* 47: 507–34.

European Central Bank (2008) Statistical Data Warehouse, http://www.ecb.int/stats/prices/hicp/html

European Commission (2002) 'Qualitative study on EU citizens and the euro in the months following its introduction', Directorate General for Health and Consumer Protection.

Eurostat (2003) 'Euro-zone annual inflation down to 1.9%. Euro-indicators', Rapid STAT 69.

Evans, G. and Whitefield, S. (1995) 'The politics and economics of democratic commitment: support for democracy in transition societies', *British Journal of Political Science* 25(4): 485–514.

Gabel, M. (1998) *Interest and Integration: Market Liberalization, Public Opinion and European Union*, Ann Arbor, MI: University of Michigan Press.

Gabel, M. and Hix, S. (2005) 'Understanding public support for British membership of the single currency', *Political Studies* 53(1): 65–81.

Gabel, M. and Palmer, H.D. (1995) 'Understanding variation in public support for European integration', *European Journal of Political Research* 27(1): 3–19.

Gabel, M. and Whitten, G. (1997) 'Economic conditions, economic perceptions, and public support for European integration', *Political Behavior* 19(1): 81–96.

Gärtner, M. (1997) 'Who wants the euro – and why? Economic explanations of public attitudes towards a single European currency', *Public Choice* 93(3–4): 487–510.

Helleiner, E. (2003) *The Making of National Money: Territorial Currencies in Historical Perspective*, Ithaca, NY: Cornell University Press.

Hobolt, S.B. and Leblond, P. (2009) 'Is my crown better than your euro? Exchange rates and public opinion on the European single currency', *European Union Politics* 10(2): 209–32.

Howarth, D. and Loedel, P. (2005) *The New European Leviathan? The European Central Bank*, Basingstoke: Macmillan.

Jupille, J. and Leblang, D. (2007) 'Voting for change: calculation, community and euro referendums', *International Organization* 61(4): 763–82.

Kaltenthaler, K. and Anderson, C. (2001) 'Europeans and their money: explaining public support for the common currency', *European Journal of Political Research* 40(2): 139–70.

Karp, J.A. and Bowler, B. (2006) 'Broadening and deepening or broadening versus deepening: the question of enlargement and Europe's hesitant Europeans', *European Journal of Political Research* 45(3): 369–90.

Lewis-Beck, M.S. (1988) *Economics and Elections: The Major Western Democracies*, Ann Arbor, MI: University of Michigan Press.

Loedel, P. (1999) *Deutsche Mark Politics: Germany in the European and International Monetary System*, Boulder, CO: Lynne Rienner.

Meier, K. and Kirchler, E. (1998) 'Social representations of the euro in Austria', *Journal of Economic Psychology* 19(6): 755–74.

Mischler, W. and Rose, R. (2001) 'What are the origins of political trust? Testing institutional and cultural theories in post-communist societies', *Comparative Political Studies* 34(1): 30–62.

Risse, T. (2003) 'The euro between national and European identity', *Journal of European Public Policy* 10(4): 487–505.

Stimson, J.A. (1985) 'Regression in time and space: a statistical essay', *American Journal of Political Science* 29(4): 914–47.

Walstad, W.B. (1997) 'The effect of economic knowledge on public opinion on economic issues', *Research in Economic Education* 28(3): 195–205.

Wilson, S.E. and Butler, D.M. (2007) 'A lot more to do: the sensitivity of time-series cross-section analyses to simple alternative specifications', *Political Analysis* 15(2): 101–23.

EMU: the last stand for the policy convergence hypothesis?

David H. Bearce

To what extent can we observe economic policy convergence among the set of countries that gave up their national currencies for the euro in 1999?[1] Have these economic and monetary union (EMU) national economies converged on more similar economic growth, employment and inflation outcomes as a result of using a common currency and taking the same short-term interest rate from the European Central Bank (ECB)? How does the convergence experience within the euro area compare to that of Western European national economies remaining outside of the euro area?

These are important questions to answer because they have both policy and academic implications. In terms of public policy, these questions speak directly to the long-term viability of EMU. To the extent that macroeconomic policy convergence has occurred, it will become easier for the ECB to set a short-term interest rate that fits all participating national economies. However, if economic policy convergence has slowed or even reversed, then it will become increasingly difficult for the ECB to choose an appropriate regional monetary policy when there is variation in terms of economic growth, employment and inflation outcomes among participating national economies. Indeed, given sufficient macroeconomic policy divergence, there is no interest rate that the ECB could choose which would not create both winners and losers from among this set of national economies, thus heightening political divisions within EMU.

In terms of the academy, these questions bear on the validity and applicability of the so-called 'policy convergence hypothesis,' which was advanced in the international political economy (IPE) literature in the early 1990s, arguing that economic globalization forced the advanced industrial democracies to make more similar economic policy choices, leading to more similar macroeconomic policy outcomes. While this convergence hypothesis came under strong attack in the late 1990s, EMU represents the most favorable empirical domain to support the theoretical proposition of economic policy convergence.

At least among 'euro optimists,' it stands as a conventional wisdom that economic policy convergence has continued, even accelerated, among the EMU countries since the third stage was launched in 1999. Indeed, if some policy convergence was achieved during the second stage of EMU (1994–1998) when Western European governments retained their national currency unit and the potential for domestic monetary autonomy, then it seems reasonable to expect that policy convergence would become even more feasible in the third stage as EMU governments began operating with a common currency and under a regional monetary policy.

But it is also wise not to infer too much about Western European policy convergence after 2000 based simply on regional policy convergence during the late 1990s. Looking back, the late 1990s now appear as an unusual period when most of the advanced industrial democracies simultaneously experienced both high economic growth and low inflation.[2] If the 1970s can be identified as a period of 'stagflation' when governments were concomitantly plagued by slow growth and rising prices, the late 1990s might be conversely identified as an unusual period of 'non-inflationary growth.' With strong economic growth, tax revenues boomed, allowing Western European governments to reduce their budget deficits and retire public debt (Gobbin and Van Aarle 2001), often without substantial cuts in government spending. The lack of corresponding price pressures also meant that the Maastricht inflation target became relatively easy to achieve, permitting nominal interest rate convergence not only in Western Europe, but also in other regions of the Global North (Bearce 2007: 49–50). Indeed, many of the advanced industrial democracies outside of Western Europe would have effectively satisfied the Maastricht convergence criteria, although there was neither political pressure to do so nor any opportunity for these countries to enter into the euro area.

Given that we cannot confidently infer economic policy convergence during the third stage of EMU based simply on the Western European experience during the second stage, it becomes critically important to examine directly the extent of economic policy convergence in the region post-1999. Indeed, after ten years of experience with the common currency and regional monetary policy, there is now an historical opportunity to make such an examination.[3] In this regard, there is certainly no shortage of studies looking at the economic performance of certain countries in the euro area or at the economic performance of the euro area as a whole (e.g. Lane 2006; Wyplosz 2006). But there is much less research focusing directly on the *variation* in national economic performance within the euro zone, examining whether this variation is getting smaller or larger, and comparing it to the variation in a sample of national economies outside the euro zone.[4]

When looking at this variation, it is critically important to examine both economic outcomes and policy instruments because the two are theoretically related on a number of fronts. First, certain macroeconomic theories, including endogenous optimum currency area (OCA) theory, posit that using a common monetary policy instrument should promote convergence in terms of growth, employment and inflation outcomes, thus making it easier to set a regionally appropriate monetary policy. Second, political economy models commonly have governments using available economic instruments to hit their preferred policy targets. Thus, convergence (divergence) in the use of policy instruments should lead to convergence (divergence) in politically important macroeconomic outcomes, especially those related to growth, employment and inflation. Third, the IPE convergence literature explicitly connected policy instruments with macroeconomic outcomes, as will be discussed later.

This paper thus investigates euro zone convergence in terms of both economic policy outcomes and instruments. After describing a simple way to measure economic policy convergence among a set of countries, this paper will then present some new data on the extent of convergence within the euro area, comparing it to the extent of convergence among non-euro area countries in Western European. These data suggest that while there is evidence of euro area convergence in terms of long-term interest rates and the real exchange rate (which would be expected given the common currency and regional short-term interest rate), there is surprisingly little evidence of euro area policy convergence in terms of economic growth, employment, and inflation. Helping to explain the lack of economic convergence in terms of these primary policy outcomes, the data also show relatively little euro area convergence, even increased divergence, in terms of government spending, a primary fiscal policy instrument.

In short, a common regional monetary policy has not been sufficient to produce convergence in terms of the most politically important macroeconomic policy outcomes (e.g. growth, employment, and inflation) when there remains divergence among EMU member states in terms of their fiscal policies. Indeed, given the European Union's (EU's) inability to enforce the terms of its Stability and Growth Pact (SGP) and varying national preferences for fiscal policy expansion, economic policy divergence seems likely to persist, even expand as more (and less developed) national economies enter into the euro area.

The remainder of this paper is structured in three sections. The first lays out the policy convergence hypothesis from IPE. The second provides some evidence testing the convergence hypothesis as it applies to Western Europe beginning in 1999. With evidence of continued, even increased, EMU policy divergence, the third section of the paper discusses some policy implications associated with the lack of policy convergence within the euro area.

1. THE POLICY CONVERGENCE HYPOTHESIS

As mentioned in the introduction, the economic policy convergence hypothesis first entered into the IPE literature in the early 1990s (e.g. Scharpf 1991; Webb 1991; Garrett and Lange 1991; Goodman and Pauly 1993; Kurzer 1993; Notermans 1993; Andrews 1994; Moses 1994; Cerny 1995; Ohmae 1995). As it was originally advanced, convergence theory argued (in its simplest form) that competitive pressures from international trade and internationally mobile capital would constrain the economic policy options available to national governments. With increasing economic globalization, public sector actors would be forced to use their primary economic policy instruments (both fiscal and monetary) to achieve the economic policy outcomes favoured by internationally oriented private sector actors (namely, low inflation with exchange rate stability). Consequently, there would be much less space, if any, for left- and right-wing governments to pursue distinct macroeconomic strategies. As Garrett and Lange (1991: 543) nicely summarized on this point: 'in anything but the short run, the fiscal and monetary policies of governments of the left and right should converge.'

The original theoretical domain of the policy convergence hypothesis included at least the advanced industrial democracies. Perhaps policy convergence would not be expected to occur among developing countries with persistent trade barriers and capital account restrictions, but it was certainly expected among the developed national economies with integrated markets in terms of goods, services, capital and even labor. Especially with the achievement of a regional common market in 1992, most of the empirical analysis focused on countries in Western Europe and on economic institutions associated with the EU, namely the European monetary system (EMS) and the Maastricht convergence criteria.

Beginning in the mid-1990s, the policy convergence hypothesis came under attack from two different directions. The first line of attack came from scholars (e.g. Garrett 1995, 1998) who presented evidence consistent with the counter-proposition that economic globalization (namely, trade and capital mobility) actually led to greater fiscal policy *divergence* among the advanced industrial democracies. Other scholars (e.g. Iversen and Cusack 2000) disputed any direct connection between economic globalization and fiscal policy divergence, but they showed similar evidence of fiscal policy divergence (measured in terms of government consumption spending and transfer payments) among the advanced industrial democracies through at least the early 1990s. To complete the story of fiscal policy divergence, scholars like Basinger and Hallerberg (2004) provided evidence showing continued variation in tax rates across the advanced industrial democracies.

A second line of attack came from scholars who accepted the basic proposition of monetary policy convergence at least in Western Europe, but they disputed the underlying cause of this effect. While the original policy convergence hypothesis had identified international economic pressures as the proximate cause, McNamara (1998) instead argued that monetary policy convergence in Western Europe stemmed more from a new neoliberal policy consensus that had developed among national political elites after the failure of Keynesian policy in the 1970s. Also questioning extant explanations for monetary integration in Western Europe, Frieden (2002) argued that it was due to domestic lobbying pressure from private-sector actors, organized politically along economic sectors.

Put together, these counter-arguments to the original policy convergence hypothesis created an interesting tension in the IPE literature. On the one hand, most scholars seemed to accept the empirical evidence of fiscal policy *divergence* (although they continued to debate the causes of this phenomenon) while, on the other hand, they also accepted the theoretical proposition of monetary policy *convergence*, at least in Western Europe. As Mosley (2000: 739) wrote on this point: 'Studies of the advanced industrial democracies reveal a mixed pattern – sustained cross-national diversity in such areas as government consumption spending, government transfer payments ... but growing cross-national similarity in aggregate monetary' policy.

A number of scholars sought to address directly this potential contradiction (evidence of fiscal policy divergence coupled with theories of monetary policy convergence). Arguing that electoral factors would be sufficient to produce divergence in terms of both policy instruments and economic outcomes, Clark (2003) offered evidence consistent with both fiscal and monetary divergence among the advanced industrial democracies, including those in Western Europe, into the early 1990s. Arguing that partisan political considerations would also produce economic divergence at least in terms of policy instruments (although not necessarily in terms of economic outcomes like growth and inflation), Bearce (2007) also presented evidence showing fiscal, monetary and exchange rate divergence among the advanced industrial democracies through 1997.

With so much empirical evidence running contrary to the policy convergence hypothesis, one might simply argue that the proposition has been falsified. As Crystal (2004: 467) wrote on this subject: 'How many attacks on the conventional wisdom does it take before the wisdom is no longer conventional? The so-called globalization [convergence] hypothesis ... has undergone so much criticism in recent years that it is becoming difficult to find any adherents left in the scholarly literature.' Yet one could easily argue that the policy convergence hypothesis has not yet been completely falsified. First, recent arguments coming from the economics literature (e.g. Calvo and Reinhart 2002, Frankel *et al.* 2002) positing that national governments have been forced to surrender domestic monetary autonomy and adopt at least de facto fixed exchange rate regimes (the so-called 'fear of floating' hypothesis) have helped to revive the policy convergence hypothesis in the IPE community.

Second and more importantly for this paper, convergence theorists can still point to the third stage of EMU and argue that economic policy convergence is now finally taking place *at least among the countries participating in the euro area.* Endogenous OCA theory (Mundell 1961; McKinnon 1963) offers a theoretical basis for this argument. Even if Western Europe did not qualify as an OCA during the 1990s, it should have moved strongly in this direction beginning in 1999 when a large number of countries began to use a common currency and operate under a regional monetary policy based on the logic that monetary synchronicity would cause business cycle variables (e.g. growth, employment, and inflation) to converge, thus fulfilling a key OCA criterion. Consequently, even if policy convergence does not apply to all advanced industrial democracies and even if policy convergence did not describe the countries in Western Europe before 1999, convergence theory should still be applicable to the euro area national economies after 1999.

In this sense, EMU arguably represents the 'last stand' for the policy convergence hypothesis. If there is evidence of policy convergence among the EMU countries beginning in 1999, then a reduced and somewhat limited version of convergence theory could still be valid. But if there is no evidence in favor of policy convergence for this set of countries (euro zone national economies) in this temporal domain (post-1999), the convergence hypothesis might finally be falsified since this represents its most favorable empirical domain. In other words, if convergence theory is not valid among a most similar set of countries with developed economies and democratic polities operating with a common currency and regional monetary policy, it is hard to see how convergence theory could be valid in other regions of the globe and under other less favorable political-economy conditions.

2. EVIDENCE OF EMU CONVERGENCE/DIVERGENCE

Having laid out the policy convergence hypothesis and established EMU as its most critical case, this section of the paper will offer some new evidence on the extent of euro area policy convergence. The first task at hand is to establish how one might identify economic policy convergence. Simply defined, policy convergence implies that the units under study (in this case, Western European national economies) are becoming more similar both in terms of the use of their policy instruments (monetary and fiscal) and in terms of primary economic outcomes (growth, employment, and inflation). To see if this has indeed been the case, one can simply collect data on these different economic indicators for the set of euro area national economies at different points in time (in this case, on an annual basis). Then from these data, one can calculate the yearly variation within the sample using a simple statistical measure of variation such as the standard deviation.[5] One would also want to perform the same exercise for a sample of Western European countries retaining their national currency unit and potential domestic monetary autonomy for the purpose of a direct comparison to the euro area sample.

The policy convergence hypothesis makes two predictions with regards to these descriptive data, as illustrated in Figure 1. Plotting the annual variation over time, it first predicts that the sample of euro area countries should have

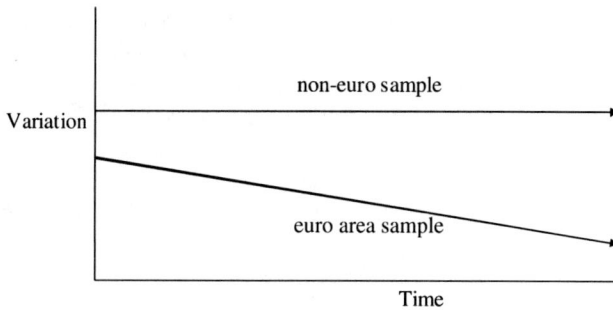

Figure 1 Variation expected by the policy convergence hypothesis

experienced reduced variation, indicating greater policy convergence after 1999, consistent with the use of a common currency and regional monetary policy. Such convergence would produce a negative slope for the euro line, although to the extent that EMU variation is already close to zero (indicating near complete policy convergence), this line may also be relatively flat. But in general, the euro line should *not* have a positive slope, which would indicate greater variation, or increased policy divergence.

Second, comparing the euro area sample to another sample of Western European countries outside of the euro zone, the policy convergence hypothesis also predicts that there should be greater variation in the non-euro sample since these countries do not share the same currency unit and retain the potential for national monetary policy autonomy. Thus as also shown in Figure 1, the line for the non-euro sample should lie above the line for the euro area sample. Furthermore, to the extent that policy convergence is an experience limited to those countries using the common regional currency, the non-euro line should *not* have a negative slope, thus indicating continued policy divergence outside of the euro zone.

Having mentioned the two samples that will be compared, it is now important to identify how the Western European countries are divided into these two samples. The euro area sample consists of the 11 countries that entered into the third stage of EMU on January 1, 1999: Austria, Belgium, Finland, France, Germany, Ireland, Italy, Luxembourg, the Netherlands, Portugal and Spain. The non-euro sample consists of the five Western European countries that continue to use their own national currency and retain at least the capacity for domestic monetary policy autonomy: Denmark, Norway, Sweden, Switzerland, and the United Kingdom.[6]

In the results reported below, I did not include Greece in either sample since it was a latecomer to the euro zone, joining in January 2001. However, if one were to assign Greece to either sample, then it more naturally belongs in the euro sample since it clearly prepared to use the common currency during the 1990s and has been within the euro zone for the most of EMU's third stage. This understanding has some important implications for the results that follow because Greece tends to be somewhat of an outlier among EU countries for many economic policy indicators. Thus, when I include Greece in the euro sample, its variation tends to increase for most economic indicators. Consequently, my exclusion of Greece tends to work *in favor* of the policy convergence hypothesis, and including Greece in the euro area sample only serves to produce even stronger evidence of EMU policy divergence.

Having described the basic research methodology, it is now important to demonstrate its validity. I do this by looking at two economic indicators where one would expect to see strong evidence in favor of euro area policy convergence. Given that they share the same regional currency and take the same short-term interest rate set by the ECB, we would expect to see relatively little variation in this sample of countries (when compared to the sample of Western European countries retaining their national currency unit) in terms of the long-term interest rate and the real exchange rate. Using data from the Organization for Economic Cooperation and Development's (OECD's) *Main Economic Indicators*, Figure 2 presents the annual standard deviation for the long-term interest rate,[7] and Figure 3 does the same for the change in the real exchange rate.[8]

In general, Figures 2 and 3 exhibit the general pattern expected by the policy convergence hypothesis, as illustrated earlier in Figure 1. Since the third stage of EMU was launched in 1999, euro area variation has been less than the variation within the sample of non-euro national economies in Western Europe for both the long-term interest rate and also for the change in the real exchange rate. In terms of the simple methodology used here, these results produce evidence consistent with monetary/exchange rate convergence within the euro area, as suggested by the policy convergence hypothesis. But most readers would probably identify these results as non-surprising, even trivial, since they represent the very first place that one would expect to see evidence in favor of EMU policy

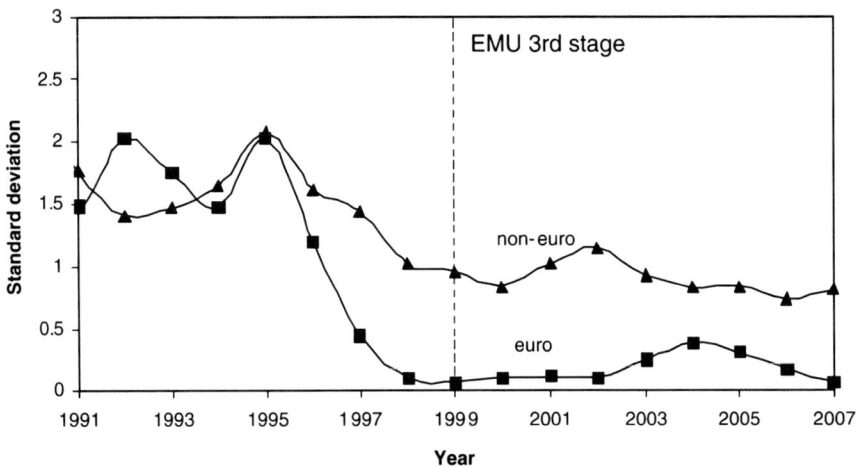

Figure 2 Variation in the long-term interest rate

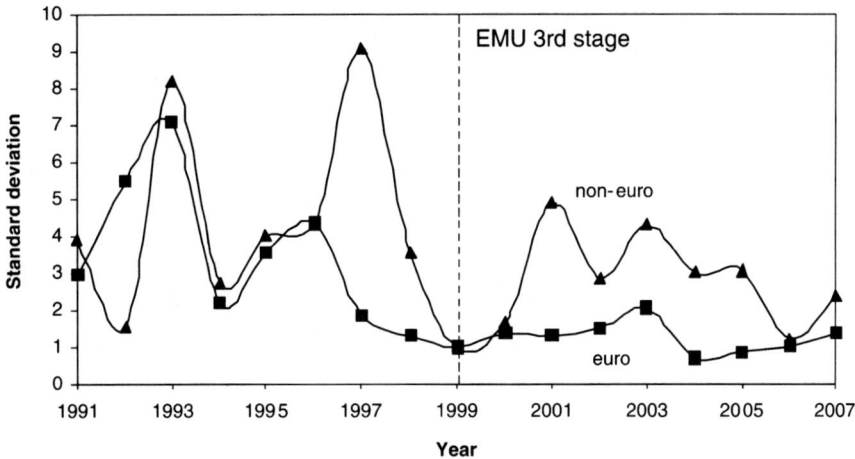

Figure 3 Variation in the real exchange rate

convergence given a common currency and regional monetary policy. Indeed, the real purpose of this exercise was simply to demonstrate that the methodology used here is not rigged against the policy convergence hypothesis and will yield evidence in favor of euro zone convergence, at least in terms of these monetary policy indicators.

Having established some methodological validity, we now need to ask the broader research question: has monetary convergence within the euro zone been accompanied by a pattern of policy convergence in terms of business cycle indicators like economic growth, employment, and inflation? This paper focuses on these three outcome variables because they constitute the basic indicators of a country's macroeconomic performance (Wyplosz 2006: 220). In this regard, it is useful to begin with economic growth because the 'growth rate of the economy is a central determinant of the likely long run success of the euro' since 'low growth, or very different rates of growth in differ-ent parts of the Euro area, would be likely to raise political questions and produce political tensions around the setting of the common or single monetary policy' (Bordo and James 2008: 19–20).

Figure 4 compares the variation between the euro and non-euro samples in terms of economic growth, measured in terms of the annual change in gross domestic product (GDP) (in constant terms) using data from the OECD's *Main Economic Indicators*. These results may surprise certain readers as they show more variation in every year after 1997 in the sample of euro countries than in the sample of non-euro countries. While one cannot read these results as an indication that a common monetary policy has produced growth divergence within the euro zone (more on this subject later), they can be read as evidence that monetary policy convergence has produced relatively little corresponding convergence in terms of economic growth.

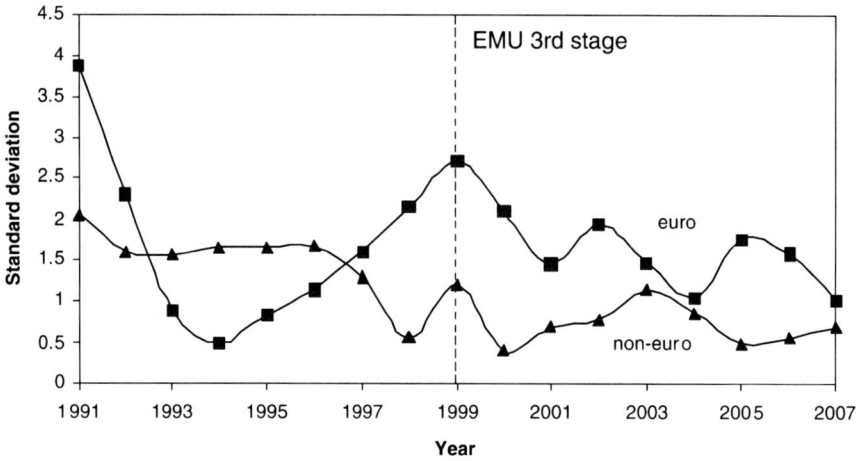

Figure 4 Variation in economic growth

But perhaps one would reach a different conclusion when looking at the annual variation in the unemployment rate, a policy indicator that is related to economic growth and also a politically important one for EMU member governments.[9] These results are presented in Figure 5. Indeed, if one looks only at the euro line, one may conclude that there is evidence of policy convergence as a result of using a common monetary policy since the euro line has a negative slope throughout the post-1999 period.

However, when one compares the euro line to the non-euro line, this conclusion seems somewhat premature. First, the non-euro sample shows less unemployment variation than the euro sample in *every* year post-1999.

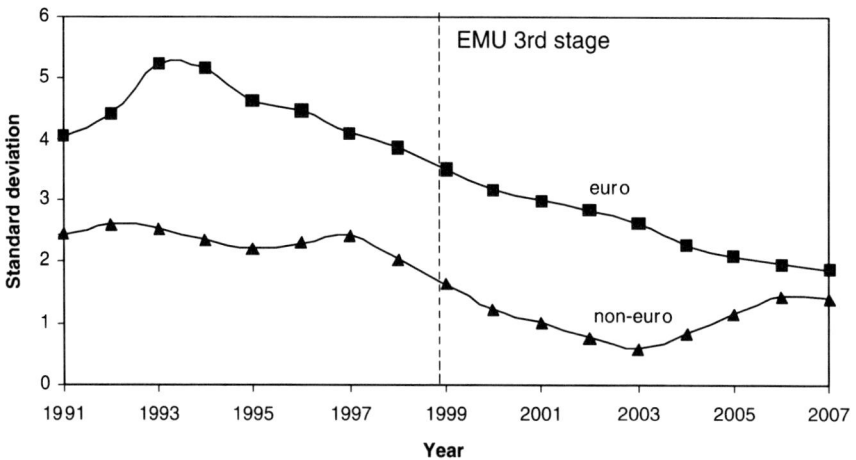

Figure 5 Variation in the unemployment rate

Second, there is also a negative slope to the non-euro line, which suggests that the observed pattern in terms of unemployment convergence is not unique to the countries using the common currency and regional monetary policy. Indeed, the negative slope for the euro line before these countries began using a common currency (i.e. the 1993–98 period) is also consistent with the conclusion that Western European convergence in terms of the unemployment rate cannot be easily explained by the use of a regional monetary policy instrument; it began before the third stage of EMU and has also been experienced by the European countries who retain domestic monetary autonomy.

If there is not much evidence of convergence in terms of economic growth and unemployment as a result of using a common currency and taking a regional monetary policy beginning in 1999, then perhaps there will be more evidence of convergence in terms of national inflation rates. Indeed, many convergence theorists (e.g. McNamara 1998) have identified domestic price stability as the primary goal underlying European monetary integration. So Figure 6 presents the data on variation in the inflation rate, measured in terms of the annual change in the consumer price index (CPI).[10]

While the euro area sample did show less variation than the non-euro sample from 1997 to 1999, consistent with the achievement of some (but certainly not complete) price convergence in the late 1990s to conform to the Maastricht convergence criteria, much of the inflation convergence that had been achieved in the late 1990s effectively evaporated by 2000. After this date, the variation among the euro area countries has been greater than that of the non-euro countries in every year except 2005 (when the standard deviation was effectively the same for both samples). This result is broadly consistent with Lane's (2006: 47) conclusion that '[t]here have been surprisingly persistent differences in national inflation rates within the euro area, such that the common monetary policy has not suited all member countries at all times.'[11]

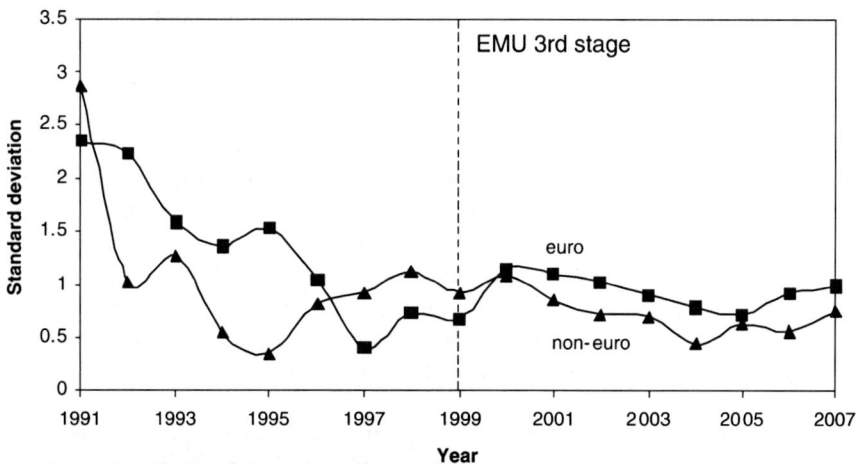

Figure 6 Variation in inflation

With evidence showing that there is as much, even more, post-1999 policy variation/divergence among the euro zone countries than among the non-euro countries in Western Europe in terms of basic macroeconomic indicators, a new research puzzle emerges: what explains the lack of EMU policy convergence in terms of growth, employment, and inflation? While it is beyond the scope of this paper to offer a comprehensive explanation for the lack of EMU policy convergence, one interesting possibility deserves to be briefly explored: fiscal policy divergence within the euro zone. As Bordo and James (2008: 19) wrote: 'The most obvious threat to the single currency is usually held to arise out of the imperfect control and coordination of national fiscal policies.' And as Dyson (2002) detailed, fiscal policy (unlike monetary policy) is still governed at the national level, making fiscal policy coordination difficult at the European level.

From the understanding that democratically accountable governments can be expected to use available policy instruments to hit nationally preferred economic targets, continued (even increased) divergence in the use of the fiscal policy instrument among EMU member governments may contribute to the lack of macroeconomic policy convergence. Stated somewhat differently, monetary convergence alone may not be enough to produce convergence in economic growth, employment and inflation given divergence in the governments' use of their fiscal policy instrument. In this sense, while monetary policy convergence may be a necessary condition for macroeconomic convergence, it is not a sufficient condition. Indeed, monetary policy convergence may even produce greater political pressure for fiscal policy divergence based on the logic that 'with a common monetary policy, national fiscal policies become the major tool by which governments can dampen fluctuations in output' (Lane 2006: 61).

To assess the extent of fiscal policy divergence within the euro area, this paper focuses on the annual variation in the change of government consumption expenditures, measured in constant prices using data from the OECD's *Main Economic Indicators*. This fiscal policy indicator is used, rather than the budget balance, because it more directly captures a policy instrument that governments can directly control. The budget balance is the difference between government expenditures and tax revenues, and while governments can choose their expenditure level, they do not directly choose their revenue level, which is a function of both the tax rate and the state of the national economy.[12] Furthermore, having just demonstrated euro area divergence in terms of economic growth, employment and inflation, all of which influence available tax revenues, budget balance divergence might stem as much from variation in these indicators as it does from variation in the fiscal policy instruments that governments can directly control, such as their level of consumption expenditures.

Figure 7 graphs the yearly standard deviation in the change of government consumption expenditures for the two samples, and the results show no evidence that can be read as consistent with fiscal policy convergence. Not only

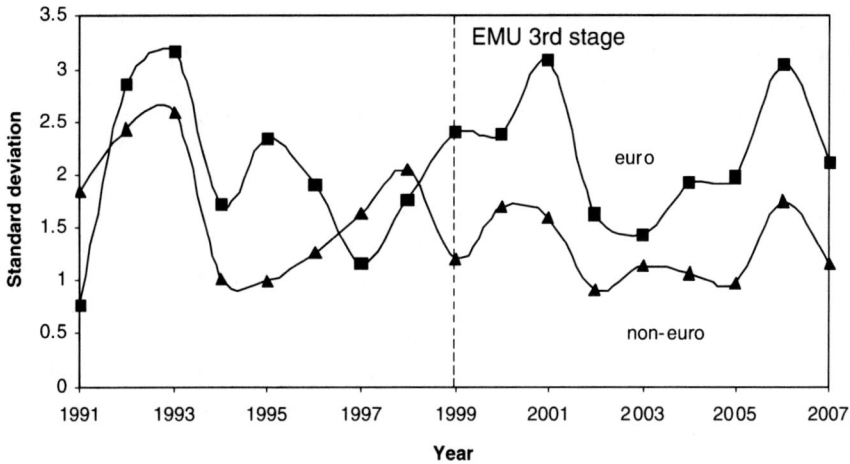

Figure 7 Variation in government consumption

is there more variation in the euro sample than in the non-euro sample for every year since the third stage of EMU began in 1999, there is not even a negative slope to euro line for most of the 1999–2007 period. This evidence accords with the inability of the EU to enforce the terms of its SGP. One would expect to see less fiscal variation had the SGP been successfully enforced. In fact, one would also expect to see less fiscal policy variation if all euro area governments were violating the terms of the agreement in a more or less similar fashion. But unfortunately for the policy convergence hypothesis, some EMU governments have constrained their spending to abide by the limits established under the SGP, but other governments have not, thus creating a situation of continued (even heightened) fiscal policy divergence within the euro area.[13]

3. DISCUSSION

Having shown that there is little evidence of macroeconomic convergence within the euro area and argued that the lack of such convergence may stem in part from continued fiscal policy divergence, one might offer three counter-arguments. First, one could respond that policy convergence must be understood as a long-term process, and that it remains too early to assess accurately the extent of EMU policy convergence. Second, it could also be argued that fiscal policy divergence is not a cause of macroeconomic divergence within the euro zone; instead it is the effect of participating governments using their fiscal policy instrument to achieve better (and presumably more similar) growth and inflation outcomes. In this sense, some fiscal policy divergence may be necessary to achieve greater macroeconomic convergence. Third, one might answer that while economic convergence remains incomplete, it will likely emerge with some EMU institutional reform, notably raising the ECB's inflation ceiling and/or allowing greater flexibility under the SGP.

In response to the first counter-argument that euro area policy convergence simply requires some additional baking time, it is important to point out that EMU policy convergence should only become even harder to achieve with the new EU member states (Lane 2006: 63). While Slovenia and Slovakia have been allowed to join the euro area (the former entered in 2007 with the latter entering in 2009), the ten other new EU member states (Bulgaria, Cyprus, the Czech Republic, Estonia, Hungary, Latvia, Lithuania, Malta, Poland, and Romania) remain outside the common currency arrangement. Furthermore, as described by Sadeh (2005), these countries all face significant adjustment costs in trying to qualify for the euro zone, a fact which presents the EU with a major political-economy dilemma.

On the one hand, these new EU member states could be held outside the monetary union until they achieve *complete* economic policy convergence, which will certainly take many years, even decades, to achieve. This decision would likely reinforce the notion that European integration has at least two speeds, perhaps setting an unfortunate precedent that could spill over into other EU projects and institutions. On the other hand, the new EU member states could be invited into the euro area as soon as it is politically possible to do so in order to avoid reinforcing the impression of a two-speed Europe. The latter seems to be the current strategy as Slovakia was invited to join the euro area despite concerns about its domestic price stability.

Indeed, these newer and less developed EU countries could also be invited into the euro area in an effort to achieve policy convergence in terms of yet another economic indicator: the level of economic development. However, achieving EU convergence in terms of economic development, or GDP per capita, would *necessarily* require different rates of economic growth or 'growth clubs.' More specifically, it would require the more developed countries to grow at slower rates and the less developed countries to grow at faster rates for an extended period of time. And different rates of national economic growth within the euro zone would likely engender even greater variation in national inflation rates, and additional variation in growth and inflation would only make it even harder for the ECB to choose an appropriate common monetary policy for all participating countries. Furthermore, convergence in terms of GDP per capita may also require even greater fiscal policy divergence with the less developed countries running a more expansionary fiscal policy to spur greater economic growth and the more developed countries running a more contractionary fiscal policy to restrain their growth. In short, if European convergence in terms of economic development is a major policy goal of the EMU project, then participating governments will need to accept even greater divergence in the years ahead, not only in terms of macroeconomic outcomes like growth and inflation, but also in terms of fiscal policy.

In response to the second counter-argument that fiscal policy divergence is a result, but not a cause, of EMU divergence in terms of economic growth, employment and inflation, one can simply point out that, even if this is true, it simply highlights the fact that there is incomplete policy convergence within the euro area and that member governments are struggling to cope with their divergent economic conditions. Indeed, having completely given away one of their two primary policy instruments (monetary) to the new regional central bank, euro zone governments can rely only on their fiscal policy instrument to adjust to asymmetric economic conditions and exogenous shocks.

Based on this understanding, violations of the SGP should not be at all surprising. Perhaps it was possible to sign the SGP in 1997 when economic conditions were relatively favorable throughout Western Europe (and elsewhere in the Global North) with EU governments reasoning that they did not need any policy instrument (either monetary or fiscal) to adjust their smoothly running national economies and that if any unfavorable economic shock did occur then a common monetary policy response would suffice. But this logic became unsustainable after 2000 when many (but not all) EMU national economies began to experience slower growth with the ECB dedicating the regional monetary policy to a price stability target with a 2 percent inflation ceiling. Under these less favorable and more variable economic conditions, democratically accountable governments needed at least one policy instrument to respond to rising societal demands for economic adjustment, and violating the SGP represented a less problematic political solution than exiting from the euro zone to regain national control of the monetary policy instrument.

But the euro's appreciation coupled with slow economic growth for some (but not all) EMU national economies has recently elevated discussion about the exit option. Public opinion polls conducted in euro area countries often report that a majority of citizens would prefer returning to their old national currency units. It is perhaps not surprising that societal opposition to the euro is strong in slower growth countries like Greece, Portugal, and Italy, but it is interesting to note that societal opposition is also high in Germany and the Netherlands where there are concerns that the ECB may not be able to hold the line on low inflation (Lane 2006: 64; Eichengreen 2007: 20, 46, 47).

Responding to the third counter-argument that euro area policy convergence will accelerate with some EMU institutional reform, it is important to consider that even if such reforms were politically feasible, many of the reform proposals are unlikely to speed up economic policy convergence and may even increase the extent of EMU policy divergence. One possible reform would be to raise the ECB's inflation ceiling above 2 percent. This would certainly allow for a more expansionary monetary policy, but if there remains significant economic policy divergence within the euro area, a more expansionary monetary policy would not change the fact that a common monetary policy creates a set of economic losers; instead it would just change the identity of those losers. With a more expansionary monetary policy and the potential for greater inflation, the euro zone losers would become the countries with strong national preferences for low inflation (Scheve 2004), namely Germany and the Netherlands. Furthermore, as Eichengreen (2007: 6) described, if a large country like Germany were to exit EMU, this would substantially reduce the benefits associated with using the euro for the remaining member countries, potentially leading to 'general disintegration.'

Another possible reform is even greater flexibility for the SGP, allowing for increased fiscal expansion on the part of EMU governments experiencing slower economic growth.[14] Further reforms in this direction might reduce the pressure currently being applied on the ECB for a looser monetary policy, but a less restrictive SGP only permits greater fiscal policy divergence within the euro area. And if fiscal policy divergence allows for greater variation in terms of national growth and inflation rates, as argued here, then further SGP flexibility would only reduce the odds of eventually achieving economic policy convergence in Western Europe.

To conclude, what have political scientists learned after ten years of experience with a common currency and monetary policy in Western Europe? Despite all the optimism associated with regional policy convergence during a period of favorable economic conditions in the late 1990s, we have learned that economic policy convergence among the euro area countries has not continued after 1999 and may have even reversed in certain dimensions. For policymakers, the lack of policy convergence means that European monetary union rests on a fragile foundation; indeed, this foundation will likely become even more problematic as the EU's new less developed national economies formally enter into the euro area. For IPE scholars, the lack of EMU policy convergence means that convergence theory has not demonstrated much validity even in its most favorable empirical domain. Although it may still be too early to declare it as dead, the convergence hypothesis appears to be on life support. Perhaps in another ten years, IPE scholars will have sufficient empirical evidence to make a final judgment as to its empirical validity.

ACKNOWLEDGEMENTS

My biggest thanks go to Mark Hallerberg who presented this paper on my behalf at the Hertie School of Governance conference in Berlin in April 2008 and also provided comments both before and after the presentation. I also thank two anonymous referees, Henrik Enderlein, Julia Gray, Amy Verdun, and the conference participants for their helpful comments, as well as Dan Tirone for his very capable research assistance on this project.

NOTES

1 From the outset, it is important to define the term 'economic policy convergence.' Convergence (divergence) implies that the variation within a sample of national economies is getting smaller (larger) over time in terms of various economic policy indicators. These indicators include both macroeconomic outcomes and specific policy instruments for reasons that will be discussed below.

2 Japan represents the obvious exception to this statement.

3 For the ten-year anniversary of EMU's third stage, the European Commission's Directorate-General for Economic and Financial Affairs commissioned a series of papers under a project titled email: EMU@10 Research. However, most of these papers do not deal directly with the topic of policy convergence; they are focused on other issues related to EMU. Of those that do focus on policy convergence, Bordo and James (2008) and Begg (2008) discuss the topic in the context of a broad synthetic overview, but present no new data on the subject. The Barrell *et al.* (2008) paper is more specifically focused on economic growth and employment, but it is also more a review of existing literature and does not present new quantitative analysis on the subject.

4 One important exception is Crowley and Mayes (2005).

5 The sample's standard deviation is calculated by squaring each observation's deviation from the sample mean. These squared deviations are then summed and divided by the sample size (minus one), yielding the standard deviation: $\sum (x - \bar{x})^2 / N - 1$. It is important to state that this statistic is not the only way to measure policy convergence/divergence, but it does have the advantage of being relatively straightforward in that it is easy to execute and the results are easy to understand and interpret. For an alternative strategy, see Crowley (2005); Crowley and Mayes (2005).

6 Since I focus here on the extent of policy convergence among the advanced industrial democracies in Western Europe, which is where the IPE convergence hypothesis predicted that economic policy convergence was the most likely to occur, my empirical analysis does not include the newly democratic and developing capitalist countries in Eastern Europe, although many of these countries did join the EU in 2004. I will, however, discuss in the next section of the paper what it likely means for EMU policy convergence when and if this set of less developed national economies enters into the euro area next to another set of more developed long-time EU member states.

7 The long-term interest rate is the yield on secondary markets of government bonds with residual maturities of ten years.

8 The real exchange rate takes account not only of the market exchange rate but also the variation in relative price levels.

9 These data also come from the OECD's *Main Economic Indicators*, which provides standardized unemployment rates, defined as the number of unemployed persons as a percentage of the civilian work force. Given that these are *standardized* unemployment rates, one has reason to believe that the sample variation does not represent differing national definitions of the unemployment rate, but does represent meaningful policy differences when using a common metric.

10 These data also come from the OECD's *Main Economic Indicators*. The CPI is an index of consumer prices for all items, food, energy, and an underlying or core inflation measure.

11 Indeed, Lane (2006: 49–50) goes further, arguing that the euro has even been a cause of macroeconomic policy divergence for at least two different reasons. First, lower interest rates within the euro zone led to a lending and housing boom in certain countries, but not others. Second, monetary union amplified the asymmetric impact of certain economic shocks due to differential trade and financial linkages with national economies outside of the euro zone.

12 As Wyplosz (2006: 237) similarly noted, '[s]ince the budget balance is endogen-
ously influenced by business cycles, it is beyond government control.'
13 It should be mentioned that there is evidence showing that euro area fiscal policies
have become more counter-cyclical (Wyplosz 2006), but this trend has not translated into anything that looks like fiscal policy convergence as shown here.
14 The 1997 SGP required countries to have less than -2 percent economic growth in
order to avoid the excessive deficit procedure. In 2005, this requirement was revised
to allow 0 percent growth, thus permitting somewhat greater fiscal policy flexibility.

REFERENCES

Andrews, D. (1994) 'Capital mobility and state autonomy: toward a structural theory of
international monetary relations', *International Studies Quarterly* 38: 193–218.
Barrell, R., Gottschalk, S., Holland, D., Khoman, E., Liadze, I. and Pomerantz, O. (2008)
'The Impact of EMU on Growth and Employment', European Economy Economic
Papers 318, European Commission, Economic and Financial Affairs Directorate-
General
Basinger, S. and Hallerberg, M. (2004) 'Remodeling the competition for capital: how
domestic politics erases the race to the bottom', *American Political Science Review* 98
(May): 261–76.
Bearce, D. (2007) *Monetary Divergence: Domestic Policy Autonomy in the Post-Bretton
Woods Era*, Ann Arbor, MI: University of Michigan Press.
Begg, I. (2008) 'Economic Governance in an Enlarged Euro Area', European Economy
Economic Papers 311, European Commission, Economic and Financial Affairs
Directorate-General.
Bordo, M. and James, H. (2008) 'A Long Term Perspective on the Euro', European
Economy Economic Papers 307, European Commission, Economic and Financial
Affairs Directorate-General.
Calvo, G. and Reinhart, C. (2002) 'Fear of floating', *Quarterly Journal of Economics*
CXVII (May): 379–408.
Cerny, P. (1995) 'Globalization and the changing logic of collective action', *Inter-
national Organization* 49 (Autumn): 595–625.
Clark, W. (2003) *Capitalism, Not Globalism: Capital Mobility, Central Bank Indepen-
dence, and the Political Control of the Economy*, Ann Arbor, MI: University of
Michigan Press.
Crowley, P. (2005) 'An intuitive guide to wavelets for economists', Bank of Finland
Discussion Paper 1/2005.
Crowley, P. and Mayes, D. (2005) 'Differences in the euro area: a wavelet approach',
Bank of Finland Bulletin 4: 21–35.
Crystal, J. (2004) 'Globalization and economic policy: what has changed?,' *International
Studies Review* 6 (September): 467–9.
Dyson, K. (2002) 'Conclusions: European states and euro economic governance', in
K. Dyson (ed.), *European States and the Euro: Europeanization, Variation, and
Convergence*, Oxford: Oxford University Press, pp. 335–66.
Eichengreen, B. (2007) 'The breakup of the euro area', NBER Working Paper No.
13393, Cambridge, MA: National Bureau of Economic Research.
Frankel, J., Schmukler, S. and Serven, L. (2002) 'Global transmission of interest rates:
monetary independence and currency regime', NBER Working Paper No. 8828,
Cambridge, MA: National Bureau of Economic Research.
Frieden, J. (2002) 'Real sources of European currency policy: sectoral interests and
European monetary integration', *International Organization* 56 (Autumn): 831–60.
Garrett, G. (1995) 'Capital mobility, trade, and the domestic politics of economic
policy', *International Organization* 49 (Autumn): 657–87.

Garrett, G. (1998) *Partisan Politics in the Global Economy*, Cambridge: Cambridge University Press.

Garrett, G. and Lange, P. (1991) 'Political responses to interdependence: what's "left" for the Left?' *International Organization* 45 (Autumn): 539–64.

Gobbin, N. and Van Aarle, B. (2001) 'Fiscal adjustments and their effects during the transition to the EMU', *Public Choice* 109: 269–99.

Goodman, J. and Pauly, L. (1993) 'The obsolescence of capital controls? Economic management in an age of global markets', *World Politics* 46 (October): 50–82.

Iversen, T. and Cusack, T. (2000) 'The causes of welfare state expansion: deindustrialization or globalization?', *World Politics* 52 (April): 313–49.

Kurzer, P. (1993) *Business and Banking: Political Change and Economic Integration in Western Europe*, Ithaca, NY: Cornell University Press.

Lane, P. (2006) 'The real effects of European monetary union', *Journal of Economic Perspectives* 20(4): 47–66.

McKinnon, R. (1963) 'Optimum currency areas', *American Economic Review* 53 (September): 717–24.

McNamara, K. (1998) *The Currency of Ideas: Monetary Politics in the European Union*, Ithaca, NY: Cornell University Press.

Moses, J. (1994) 'Abdication from national policy autonomy: what's left to leave?', *Politics and Society* 22 (June): 125–48.

Mosley, L. (2000) 'Room to move: international financial markets and national welfare states', *International Organization* 54 (Autumn): 737–73.

Mundell, R. (1961) 'A theory of optimum currency areas', *American Economic Review* 51(September): 657–65.

Notermans, T. (1993) 'The abdication from national policy autonomy: why the macroeconomic policy regime has become so unfavorable to labor', *Politics and Society* 21 (June): 133–67.

Ohmae, K. (1995) *The End of the Nation State: The Rise of Regional Economies*, New York: Free Press.

Sadeh, T. (2005) 'Who can adjust to the euro?', *World Economy* 28 (November): 1651–78.

Scharpf, F. (1991) *Crisis and Choice in European Social Democracy*, Ithaca, NY: Cornell University Press.

Scheve, K. (2004) 'Public inflation aversion and the political economy of macroeconomic policymaking', *International Organization* 58 (Winter): 1–34.

Webb, M. (1991) 'International economic structures, government interests, and international coordination of macroeconomic adjustment policies', *International Organization* 45 (Summer): 309–42.

Wyplosz, C. (2006) 'European monetary union: the dark sides of a major success', *Economic Policy* 21: 207–61.

Wage inflation and labour unions in EMU

Alison Johnston and Bob Hancké

In this article we examine the evolution of wages and of wage-setting systems before and after the introduction of the euro in 1999. We concentrate on wage restraint – the change in nominal wage growth minus the change in labour productivity growth (a negative outcome indicates wage *restraint* as opposed to wage *excess*, see note 1 for further details). During the Maastricht period, aggregate nominal wage restraint cycles of some European monetary union (EMU) candidate countries and Germany, as well as wage restraint cycles of the exposed and sheltered sectors, were highly synchronized. After the introduction of the euro, nominal wage growth remained low compared to the Maastricht period – but after 1999 different trajectories emerged between EMU member states, including those that previously belonged to the highly disciplined Deutschmark bloc, and between wage-setting in the exposed and sheltered sectors within countries.

The evolution of wage restraint in EMU raises questions about most arguments on the political economy of wage-setting in EMU. Three possible scenarios have dominated that debate: one predicts *across-the-board wage increases* because the central bank can no longer effectively punish wage excess; the second predicts *increased wage flexibility* and wage moderation as a result of further integration of the European economy; and the third possibility is of pan-European *wage co-ordination* as a result of labour unions reorganizing to match the structure of the centralized monetary authority. Yet in most countries national-level wage co-ordination has persisted (and therefore neither international co-ordination nor wage flexibility prevailed) and in many of them wage restraint remained stable or increased in comparison to the 1990s – in Austria, Belgium, Finland, France and Germany – while in Ireland, Italy, the Netherlands, Portugal and Spain, wages grew faster than labour productivity.[1]

What has led to these divergent outcomes (a) between the countries which previously were members of the core Deutschmark bloc (Austria, the Benelux countries, France and Germany) with highly synchronized wage restraint cycles, and (b) within countries between the exposed and the public sectors? And what are the wider implications for wage-setting in EMU? These are the questions that this article addresses. We approach these problems by analysing the different constraints that unions in the exposed and the sheltered sectors face, and which, we think, have resurfaced since the introduction of the euro. Before EMU, when currencies were pegged to the Deutschmark and member states committed to the Maastricht inflation criteria, wage increases in the sheltered and exposed sectors were constrained because inflationary increases in either of the sectors would be punished by the national central bank. After 1999, national central banks disappeared in that capacity and were replaced by the European Central Bank (ECB). The effect of a world in which central banks no longer disciplined wage-setters was, in the Hall and Franzese (1998) and Iversen and Soskice (1998) analyses, a significant increase in nominal wage pressures across all sectors and countries. These analyses correctly identified the changing institutional context as the driving force; however, they ignored the incentives for wage restraint that both labour unions and employers in the exposed sector continued to face. For unions in the exposed sector, competitiveness matters; they are therefore unable to claim excessive wage increases without facing employment losses. Unions in the sheltered sector, in contrast, were subject to softer constraints which excluded competitiveness. Without the central bank's threat, they are, in principle, free to claim excessive wages. But why, then, the different patterns of linkages between the exposed and the sheltered sectors across EMU?

The argument that we develop here is that EMU member states with collective bargaining institutions that constrain wage-setters in the sheltered sector, either by tying their wage increases to developments in the exposed sector, by imposing a hard ceiling on wage increases, or through both mechanisms, have been more effective at maintaining wage restraint than countries where such institutional constraints were absent. We develop two additional substantive points to support this argument. The first is that asymmetries are built into EMU's design (cf. also Verdun 1996). Germany was at the core of the exchange rate mechanism (ERM) of the European monetary system and, despite the formal symmetric structure of EMU, remains so since directly or indirectly it is the largest trading partner of most other EMU member states (Andrews 2001). The second is that the incentives for the sheltered sector to align moderate wage increases with the exposed sector have weakened significantly with the introduction of the euro (and, in fact, as a result of the institutional design of EMU itself). With the appearance of the ECB, the domestic monetary constraint that targets national wage-setters has disappeared, and wages in the exposed and sheltered sectors diverge where additional incentives and constraints for the sheltered sector are missing.

This article is organized as follows: after a short review of the main positions in the debate on wage-setting in EMU, we discuss our methodology for examining the impact of EMU on wage-setting. We then move on to analyse the difference between the Maastricht period and EMU with special attention to the changes in the role of Germany in both institutional arrangements, discuss the different incentives for exposed and sheltered sectors in this new regime, and conclude the analysis by linking these outcomes to the different political-institutional frameworks on wage-setting in different countries.

1. UNDERSTANDING WAGE-SETTING IN EMU

Wage-setting behaviour in EMU has received much attention, both before the introduction of the euro in 1999 and after. Political economists argued that in EMU, with its specific asymmetric structure which consisted of a centralized monetary policy and separate wage-bargaining systems, national wage-setters are no longer constrained by their central bank and would therefore pursue high wage increases when monetary policy authority was transferred to the ECB (Hall 1994; Hall and Franzese 1998; Iversen and Soskice 1998; Soskice and Iversen 2000; Cukierman and Lippi 2001). The creation of the ECB, thus the argument goes, significantly reduces the size of individual wage-setters with respect to the monetary authorities, and thus effectively moved the wage-setting structure towards a situation in which national labour unions might be strong enough to extract high wage increases yet would be small enough not to bear the full cost of inflation (Calmfors and Driffill 1988).

Whilst this approach helps us to understand very well what happened before 1999, when countries such as Italy, generally seen as having a very low capacity for wage moderation, brought wage inflation under control, it gives us less analytical leverage over what happened afterwards: annual outliers in the Maastricht period aside, wage moderation remained, as Figure 1 shows, strong in some countries but not in others. A parallel group of arguments (Calmfors 2001; Sibert and Sutherland 2000) went further by predicting that inflation-averse policy-makers who were presented with a high-wage inflation situation would opt for nominal wage flexibility in the absence of monetary policy, and therefore introduce labour market reforms which would lead to overall wage moderation. Neither of these scenarios ensued: wage explosions did not take place, and while labour market reforms have been introduced in most EMU member states, wage-setting has, on the whole, not been decentralized.

Where the political economy literature predicted a lapse in wage restraint, economic theory suggested the opposite effect: market forces would continue

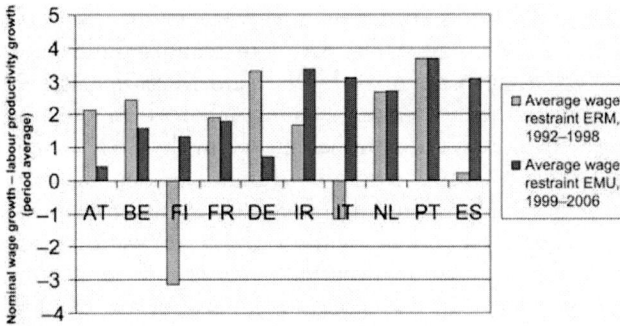

Figure 1 Wage restraint under ERM and EMU
Note: Nominal wage growth data from AMECO and labour productivity growth data from OECD.

to constrain unions and impose wage moderation. Against the background of the single European market, transparent pricing in a single currency area further underlined the need for competitiveness in the EMU member states. Without the nominal exchange rate as an adjustment mechanism, the only policy instrument left to enhance national competitiveness, which operates via the real exchange rate (the ratio between the price of a good expressed in domestic currency and in foreign currency), was wage restraint. Competitiveness constraints would therefore restrain the ability of wage-setters to demand higher wages, in the context of a highly integrated product market which EMU was intended to reinforce (Danthine and Hunt 1994; Calmfors *et al.* 2001). Beside the basic observation that this did not happen everywhere, perhaps the most puzzling finding against this argument is that the country within EMU where wage moderation was highest – Germany – has only the seventh largest export share, while two countries with among the highest export shares in EMU – the Netherlands and Ireland – also have among the highest average levels of wage excess after 1999.

The stylized facts on wage-setting in EMU thus leave us with a puzzle. Wage restraint has neither increased nor decreased across the board for all EMU member states since 1999: in some countries wage restraint continued, while in others (Ireland, the Netherlands, Portugal, Italy and Spain) it fell quite dramatically. Moreover, wage performance in EMU does not seem to be explained through standard explanations such as small versus large economies, high versus low export shares, or high versus low growth. How, then, do we account for these differences in wage performance?

In order to make sense of these differences in wage restraint since 1999, we start by thinking of wage-setting in EMU as a series of nested interactions across international and domestic levels. EMU produced a profound shift in the institutional regime that governs wage bargaining, with consequences at the international (European Union (EU)) level and in the domestic political economies. This has led to a wage-setting regime in EMU in which wage-setters are considerably less constrained than they were in the 1990s. This point is based on three related insights. The first is that under the fixed exchange rate regime of the ERM, and supported by the hard Maastricht criteria, Germany *de facto* imposed its macro-economic policy choices on the rest of Europe: since the Bundesbank was the nominal anchor in the ERM, other prospective EMU members were forced to import Bundesbank policy or face currency speculations or devaluations. In addition, the combination of the Maastricht inflation and exchange rate criteria reinforced this imposition of German monetary policy on the other national central banks, and these, in turn, imposed it upon 'their' wage-setters. In EMU, Germany has not lost this leadership role, but this time it is forced to adjust to what others do instead of impose its policies. The second insight is that under EMU, individual trade unions in the member states no longer face the hard monetary constraint imposed by their national central bank. However, inflationary wage explosions did not occur because competitiveness concerns (over the real exchange rate or RER henceforth) kept wage developments in the exposed (tradable goods and services) sector under control. The third insight is based on the dual-sector framework that we introduce: whereas wage pressures from unions in the exposed sector are limited through competitiveness concerns, unions in the sheltered (non-tradable goods and services) sector of the economy do not face such constraints. The struggles over wage-bargaining agendas that are emerging within some EMU member states between labour unions in export sectors and in sheltered private and public services are thus the logical outcomes of the different constraints that these sectors face. Countries where the constraint imposed by a strong, independent central bank is not replaced by hard incentives and constraints that link wage-setting in the sheltered and exposed sectors thus face significant divergence between wages in the two sectors and possibly higher wage inflation rates as a result.

The balance of this article develops these points. After discussing our methodology, we start with a comparison of the Maastricht and EMU periods (1992–1998 and 1999–present) to highlight the institutional shift that has taken place and analyse Germany's new position in EMU. We then examine the different incentives for exposed and sheltered sectors, and finish with a return to the role that domestic wage-setting institutions play in this process.

2. MEASURING WAGE RESTRAINT ACROSS COUNTRIES AND SECTORS

When examining the impact of EMU on wage-setting, standard regression analysis is very difficult because of the very small number of observations (eight years of data for ten countries, i.e. the original EMU minus Luxembourg and Greece). Whilst panel data analysis is, in principle, possible, this method has several problems. The most important problem is that different trajectories of wage moderation, with about half the countries setting moderate wages and the other half at excessive levels, make it unlikely that the regression coefficients will show a significant common trend for the ten countries under analysis. In a pooled data set, positive correlations between an EMU time dummy variable and wage restraint performance will again yield insignificant beta coefficients for similar reasons. Several preliminary panel regression analyses that we conducted indeed yielded mostly insignificant results. The only independent variables which did have significant coefficients were the changes in inflation and labour productivity.[2]

We therefore deployed an alternative method: a pair-wise cross-correlation analysis of seven to eight years of data for each (pre- and post-EMU) period. Cross-correlation analysis has been used in business cycle analysis (see Artis and Zhang 1997 among others) to determine whether national European business cycles are becoming more or less synchronous with increased trade integration. Using a cross-correlation analysis for examining wage growth and wage restraint cycles has several advantages. One advantage is that since it is a measurement of synchronicity between two functions, and not of causation, it does not require control checks, which would have to be severely limited in any case owing to degrees of freedom problems. In addition, cross-correlation analysis can be conducted on time series with as few as seven observations and since our two periods (1991–1998 and 1999–2005/6) do not contain more than one business cycle, the data for this method do not need to be de-trended.[3] Finally, cross-correlation analysis enables us to examine patterns within individual EMU member states before and after 1999, something regressions would not allow.

We performed two correlation analyses on the aggregate and sectoral wage restraint and wage growth cycle data. The first one consisted of a comparison of pair-wise correlation coefficients on annual nominal wage restraint between the different EMU countries for the 1991–1998 (Table 1) and 1999–2006 (Table 2) periods. Because of the *de facto* central role of the Bundesbank and the German inflation rate for the Maastricht criteria, we focused on correlations between Germany and other prospective member states, expecting pair-wise correlation coefficients to be higher in the 1990s and lower in the 1999–2006 period.

We then examined correlations for three-year moving averages in wage restraint between the exposed and sheltered sectors within each one of the countries for the same periods.[4] One pair-wise correlation coefficient is between wage restraint cycles for a country's total manufacturing sector (International Standard of Industrial Classification (ISIC) tabulation category D) and a country's personal services sector (community social and personal services, ISIC tabulation category O). These are reported in the middle columns of Tables 3 and 4. We use these as proxies for a given country's (relatively highly unionized) exposed and (relatively lowly unionized) sheltered sectors. The second pair-wise correlation coefficient is between wage restraint cycles for a country's total manufacturing sector and a country's non-market services sector (a composite of public administration and defence, education, and health and social work – ISIC tabulation categories L, M, and N respectively); we use the latter as a proxy for a given country's (relatively

Table 1 Correlations between national nominal wage restraint: 1991–1998

Country	Austria	Belgium	Finland	France	Germany	Ireland	Italy	Netherlands	Portugal	Spain
Austria	1									
Belgium	0.97***	1								
	(0.000)									
Finland	−0.45	−0.40	1							
	(0.259)	(0.329)								
France	0.81**	0.75**	−0.63*	1						
	(0.016)	(0.033)	(0.094)							
Germany	0.96***	0.93***	−0.54	0.83**	1					
	(0.001)	(0.003)	(0.210)	(0.022)						
Ireland	−0.33	−0.29	−0.34	−0.33	−0.25	1				
	(0.419)	(0.480)	(0.416)	(0.430)	(0.595)					
Italy	−0.59	−0.48	0.13	−0.37	−0.64	0.56	1			
	(0.123)	(0.231)	(0.756)	(0.361)	(0.118)	(0.149)				
Netherlands	0.97***	0.94***	−0.50	0.79**	0.98***	−0.31	−0.58	1		
	(0.000)	(0.000)	(0.210)	(0.021)	(0.000)	(0.461)	(0.134)			
Portugal	0.18	0.27	0.03	−0.03	0.30	0.40	0.48	0.25	1	
	(0.674)	(0.516)	(0.944)	(0.935)	(0.520)	(0.332)	(0.232)	(0.551)		
Spain	−0.09	−0.00	0.11	−0.12	−0.04	0.33	0.69*	0.01	0.91***	1
	(0.825)	(0.997)	(0.804)	(0.779)	(0.936)	(0.430)	(0.061)	(0.978)	(0.002)	

Notes: Nominal wage growth data from AMECO (2007) and labour productivity growth data from OECD. The table presents pair-wise correlation coefficients of annual nominal wage restraint between the prospective EMU countries from 1991 to 1998. P-values in parenthesis. *, **, and *** indicate significance on a 90 per cent, 95 per cent and 99 per cent confidence interval.

Table 2 National nominal wage restraint correlations: 1999–2006

Country	Austria	Belgium	Finland	France	Germany	Ireland	Italy	Netherlands	Portugal	Spain
Austria	1									
Belgium	0.79** (0.019)	1								
Finland	0.56 (0.147)	0.71** (0.048)	1							
France	0.71** (0.047)	0.51 (0.194)	0.32 (0.446)	1						
Germany	0.41 (0.317)	0.22 (0.606)	0.42 (0.300)	-0.08 (0.856)	1					
Ireland	-0.82** (0.014)	-0.49 (0.216)	-0.08 (0.854)	-0.73** (0.039)	-0.33 (0.418)	1				
Italy	0.40 (0.323)	0.09 (0.828)	0.44 (0.275)	0.52 (0.183)	0.07 (0.871)	-0.15 (0.728)	1			
Netherlands	0.56 (0.147)	0.57 (0.141)	0.55 (0.156)	0.47 (0.239)	0.66* (0.074)	-0.55 (0.162)	0.17 (0.685)	1		
Portugal	0.45 (0.366)	0.57 (0.240)	0.36 (0.479)	0.49 (0.325)	0.58 (0.231)	-0.55 (0.262)	-0.33 (0.517)	0.74* (0.090)	1	
Spain	-0.12 (0.772)	-0.27 (0.515)	0.41 (0.311)	-0.12 (0.777)	0.37 (0.364)	0.35 (0.397)	0.66* (0.075)	0.17 (0.696)	-0.59 (0.216)	1

Notes: Nominal wage growth data from AMECO and labour productivity growth data from OECD. The table presents pair-wise correlation coefficients of annual nominal wage restraint between the EMU member-states from 1999 to 2006. P-values in parenthesis. *, **, and *** indicate significance on a 90 per cent, 95 per cent and 99 per cent confidence interval.

Table 3 Sectoral nominal wage restraint correlations, 1991–1998

	Manufacturing and personal services[†]	Manufacturing and non-market services[°]
Austria	0.18	0.91***
	(0.664)	(0.002)
Belgium	0.73**	0.85***
	(0.041)	(0.008)
Finland	0.78**	0.91***
	(0.022)	(0.002)
France	0.20	0.53
	(0.642)	(0.172)
Germany	0.54	0.95***
	(0.166)	(0.000)
Ireland	0.44	0.15
	(0.280)	(0.720)
Italy	0.65*	0.93***
	(0.080)	(0.001)
Netherlands	0.42	0.86***
	(0.305)	(0.006)
Portugal	0.98***	0.99***
	(0.000)	(0.000)
Spain	0.81**	0.97***
	(0.014)	(0.000)
EMU average	0.57	0.81
Denmark	0.55	0.90***
	(0.158)	(0.002)
Sweden	0.92***	0.92***
	(0.001)	(0.001)
NON-emu average	0.74	0.91

Source: Data from EU KLEMS Database.

Notes: The table presents pair-wise correlation coefficients of annual nominal wage restraint for three-year moving averages in wage restraint between the manufacturing and personal/non-market services sectors. P-values in parenthesis. *, **, and *** indicate significance on a 90 per cent, 95 per cent and 99 per cent confidence interval.

[†]Personal services include relatively low skilled services.

[°]Non-market services include public sector services such as health, education, and administration.

highly unionized) public sector. These are reported in the right-hand columns of Tables 3 and 4. We expect pair-wise coefficients between both the public and private sheltered sectors and the exposed sector to be higher in the 1991–1998 period than in the EMU period because of the similar hard monetary constraint imposed by the Maastricht criteria and national central banks on all three sectors in the economy.

Table 4 Sectoral nominal wage restraint correlations: 1999–2005

	Manufacturing and personal services	Manufacturing and non-market services
Austria	−0.51	−0.84**
	(0.242)	(0.017)
Belgium	0.45	0.06
	(0.311)	(0.904)
Finland	−0.88***	−0.42
	(0.010)	(0.352)
France	0.84**	0.49
	(0.017)	(0.263)
Germany	0.56	0.15
	(0.193)	(0.750)
Ireland	0.73*	−0.03
	(0.063)	(0.952)
Italy	0.80**	0.88***
	(0.030)	(0.009)
Netherlands	0.35	0.40
	(0.440)	(0.375)
Portugal	0.32	0.90***
	(0.480)	(0.006)
Spain	−0.67*	0.63
	(0.100)	(0.126)
EMU average	0.20	0.22
Denmark	0.25	0.70*
	(0.788)	(0.081)
Sweden	0.72	0.79**
	(0.691)	(0.034)
NON-emu average	0.50	0.74

Source: Data from EU KLEMS Database.

Notes: The table presents pair-wise correlation coefficients of annual nominal wage restraint between the manufacturing and personal/public services sectors. P-values in parenthesis. *, **, and *** indicate significance on a 90 per cent, 95 per cent and 99 per cent confidence interval.

In addition to this analysis of wage moderation, we also conducted a similar pair-wise correlation analysis of *wage growth* cycles between the manufacturing and the non-market services sectors for the EMU ten countries (Table 5) to determine whether co-ordination in wage *growth* between these relatively unionized sectors changed significantly under EMU. Since wage co-ordination usually transpires through wage increases and not through wage restraint, a significant divergence between wage growth cycles across these sectors would imply that the divergence in wage moderation would be due to a collapse of inter-sectoral wage co-ordination rather than the central bank and competitiveness-centred mechanisms.

Table 5 Nominal wage growth correlations for the manufacturing and public services sectors: ERM and EMU

	ERM period	EMU period
Austria	0.82**	0.86**
	(0.013)	(0.013)
Belgium	0.47	0.73*
	(0.242)	(0.061)
Finland	0.88***	0.08
	(0.004)	(0.863)
France	0.42	0.85**
	(0.299)	(0.016)
Germany	0.98***	0.80**
	(0.000)	(0.030)
Ireland	0.80**	−0.88***
	(0.017)	(0.010)
Italy	0.84***	0.85**
	(0.010)	(0.016)
Netherlands	0.95***	0.31
	(0.000)	(0.502)
Portugal	0.98***	0.95***
	(0.000)	(0.001)
Spain	0.93***	0.62
	(0.001)	(0.135)
EMU average	0.81	0.52
Denmark	0.70*	−0.66
	(0.052)	(0.104)
Sweden	0.92***	0.94***
	(0.001)	(0.002)
NON-emu average	0.81	0.21

Source: Data from EU KLEMS Database.
Notes: The table presents pair-wise correlation coefficients of annual nominal wage restraint between the manufacturing and public services sectors. P-values in parenthesis. *, **, and *** indicate significance on a 90 per cent, 95 per cent and 99 per cent confidence interval.

3. GERMANY BEFORE AND AFTER EMU

The unique institutional design of the Maastricht period implied that Germany dominated the regime, while the Maastricht criteria *de facto* imposed Germany's inflation rate as the target on the rest of the ERM countries. Germany's central role resulted from the position of the Bundesbank, which had, after the emergence of the Deutschmark (DM) bloc in the 1980s, become the *de facto* monetary authority for the entire European economy. Within the fixed exchange rate regime of the ERM, other central banks were forced to follow the Bundesbank's interest rate policy in order to avoid their currencies sliding against the DM, as a result of their inflation rates rising above the German rate. As the high cross-correlations in Table 1 demonstrate, wage restraint was highly synchronized between several EMU candidate countries and Germany (note the core DM bloc countries, with correlation coefficients above 0.8 and 0.9, in particular). Since central banks constrained *all* domestic wage-setters, both exposed and sheltered, the latter were forced to moderate wage increases and pursue wage restraint. The cross-correlation coefficients in Tables 3 and 5 suggest a high degree of wage restraint and wage growth synchronicity between the exposed sector and the sheltered sectors.

The robust pan-European disinflationary system that existed during the Maastricht period changed dramatically under EMU. In a single currency area, without a single target inflation rate for every individual member state and without a non-accommodating national central bank to enforce this target, the discipline imposed by such an asymmetric multiple-player system disappeared. The divergence in the RER as a result is a normal response by markets to the political fixing of the nominal exchange rates in 1998 at the levels at which countries joined the euro: it is, in this perspective, nothing more than a key mechanism of inter-country adjustment (Allsopp and Artis 2003). However, even though EMU removed one half of the unique institutional design of the Maastricht period – the national central banks and the shadowing mechanism of German monetary policy – the other half, which consists of wage-setting institutions and collective bargaining frameworks, remained in place. Given this shift in the links between central banks and wage-setters, it is hardly surprising that under EMU we see both a dramatic drop in the links between wage restraint cycles both within countries (only two of the ten countries we survey have wage restraint correlation coefficients between the exposed and the sheltered sector above 0.8 under EMU, compared to eight out of ten under ERM – see Table 4) and across. In the absence of a German anchor to shadow, and lacking an agent such as a national central bank to enforce wage restraint, pair-wise cross-correlations between EMU candidate countries and Germany, presented in Table 2, have decreased significantly, with coefficients between the core DM bloc countries and Germany halving or more than halving their value for the ERM period.

One important continuity between the pre- and post-EMU periods, however, is the position of Germany at the centre of EMU – but this time as a *regime-taker* instead of a regime-setter. The size of its economy, as well as the volume at which other EMU member states trade with Germany, make it the natural target for any RER adjustment strategy of other countries. A RER depreciation through disinflation against Germany will have proportionately larger positive demand effects for a smaller economy with a high export share than it would have for a large economy against a smaller trading partner. In addition, the system now produces one particularly perverse effect when inflation rates outside Germany rise. Since the ECB's EMU-wide 2 per cent inflation target is the composite weighted inflation rate across the Euro-zone, a rise of inflation in some member states above this target implies that some member states have to disinflate to the parallel (weighted) extent to bring the aggregate inflation rate down to the target 2 per cent. In principle, nothing precludes any country or even a group of small countries from playing this anchor role and disinflating when others inflate, but collective action problems both invite free-riding on the German position and make co-ordination difficult for a larger group of other countries. One could imagine that in one-shot games, Germany would play this stabilizing role once and then abandon it, leaving the others to sort out their high inflation rates. But this argument ignores the role of the ECB as last-mover, which is very likely to adopt a restrictive policy at the sign of inflationary pressures (a scenario which is certain to ensue when Germany inflates or even refuses to disinflate alongside others). Against the background of the hard ECB constraint imposed by the 2 per cent inflation target, Germany is therefore structurally forced to maintain low inflation when others inflate (Hancké and Soskice 2003). With the monetary constraint on domestic inflation lifted, and given the inter-country adjustment pressures, national inflation rates were bound to diverge, if not for all of EMU, then at least between the core DM bloc countries. In an ideal 'symmetric' world, all countries would share this disinflationary burden by rotating the cost of adjustment. In EMU, however, the largest economy, which also happened to be the stabilizing anchor in the ERM regime, bears the burden more or less alone.[4]

This structural regime argument steps perhaps somewhat lightly over the many additional reasons that Germany may have had to disinflate, such as the need to regain competitiveness after the revaluations of the early 1990s following German monetary unification and the realignment during the ERM crisis, or compensation for the overvalued entry of Germany into EMU. However, heavy German wage restraint started too late (in 1996, i.e. four to five years after the 1991–92 appreciations) for the former argument to be persuasive, and too early to compensate for the high DM–euro exchange rate.

4. CONSTRAINTS ON THE EXPOSED AND THE SHELTERED SECTOR

This shift in the international political economy of EMU has important consequences for domestic wage-setters in the member states. Expanding the Calmfors–Driffill (1988) model slightly to include central banks, in which intermediate wage-bargaining co-ordination leads to high inflation – exactly the situation in EMU today with multiple wage-bargaining regimes coexisting within one monetary union – leads us to expect a significant fall in wage restraint across the board for all countries. Contrary to that intuition, however, wages remained moderate in many EMU member states, and when high inflation occurred, it was by no means excessive compared to the pre-1992 period. The main reason is that for wage bargainers in the exposed sector, a hard constraint on excessive wage inflation continues to exist under EMU via the RER. If domestic prices rise too much as a result of wage excess, firms in the export sector lose competitiveness, demand for their goods falls, which prompts employers to cut employment. By maintaining wage restraint, unions in export sectors thus avoid a fall in competitiveness and a parallel drop in employment. In almost all the countries we examine, except Italy and Portugal, wage restraint in the manufacturing sector is considerably higher than in the unionized and non-unionized sheltered sectors in the economy.[5]

Unions in the sheltered sector, however, do not face such a hard RER constraint. Since the introduction of the euro implied that the domestic monetary constraint on high wage settlements was lifted as well, they are in principle free to pursue inflationary wage settlements, which would translate into a sharp divergence between wage rates in the exposed and sheltered sectors. The data in Table 4 confirm this: the correlation coefficients between wage restraint in the export (manufacturing) and sheltered (public services and personal services) sectors fell sharply after 1999. Out of the ten pair-wise correlations between wage restraint in the manufacturing and non-market services sectors, there are only two cases (Italy and Portugal) where the correlation remained stable, and in both of these cases, the stability in the correlation coefficient can be attributed to the fact that wage-setters in both sectors pursued excessive wage increases after 1999. In all the other instances, correlation coefficients have fallen – quite dramatically in some instances.

The pair-wise coefficients for Sweden and Denmark, two countries where the national central bank still has the power to punish excessive wage settlements, provide an interesting comparison. Even though they decrease for the EMU period, their values remain much higher than those of most EMU countries (see Table 4), suggesting that in those countries wage restraint remains co-ordinated in the shadow of the central bank.

The fall in synchronized wage moderation throughout EMU is not due to a collapse in wage co-ordination after 1999, however. In practice, centralized and patterned bargaining wage agreements co-ordinate wage-setters around wage growth rates, *not* wage restraint. Table 5 presents pair-wise cross-correlations of wage *growth* cycles between sectors and demonstrates that these remained stable or even increased for six of the countries we examine: Austria, Belgium, Germany, France, Italy and Portugal.[6] Combined, the data in Tables 4 and 5 suggest that the relevant shift therefore lies in the extent to which the exposed sector still internalizes the inflationary effects of wage-setting whilst the sheltered sector no longer does so.

Inflationary wage settlements in the sheltered sector often translate relatively quickly into an unsustainable wage/price level because these sectors cover the largest part of the active population. High domestic inflation will have negative effects on the RER and thus lower international competitiveness, a situation which is likely to produce tensions between wage-setters in the exposed and sheltered sectors, particularly in small open economies where the domestic inflation rate is the main determinant of the RER. The next section explores the variation due to the different institutional, political and legal constraints that wage-setters in the sheltered sector face.

5. THE ROLE OF WAGE-BARGAINING INSTITUTIONS IN WAGE RESTRAINT

The stylized picture that we have developed so far is that since the introduction of the euro, one group of countries – Austria, Belgium, Finland, France and Germany – have managed to maintain wage restraint (below the EU average), whereas Italy, Spain, the Netherlands, Ireland and Portugal have not. Whilst low (or even lack of) wage moderation in countries such as Ireland and Spain could be explained by their high gross domestic product (GDP) growth over this period, GDP growth does not explain the entire picture. High growth countries such as Finland did not display more wage excess than EMU countries with lower growth, while Italy and Portugal, two countries with low growth over this period, have adopted more expansive wage settlements than most other EMU member states. Our argument is that the institutions that govern wage bargaining explain the capacity of domestic wage-setters to keep wage moderation intact.

Unlike wage restraint in the manufacturing sector, which has either continued or increased under EMU (except in Italy and Portugal), wage restraint in the sheltered sectors (both in non-market and personal services) has followed very different paths in the EMU member states. In some countries (Austria, Germany and France), wage growth in the non-market and personal services sectors has been contained by productivity increases, while in other countries (Portugal, Ireland, Italy and the Netherlands), wage excess became a persistent problem under EMU. We hypothesize that the nature of the wage-bargaining frameworks which keep sheltered unions in check is the key explanation for this divergence in sheltered sector wage restraint. We identify three different scenarios.

In the first, the sheltered sectors continue as they did in the ERM period, and comply with wage restraint, for while the monetary constraint may have disappeared, national legal and institutional constraints have not. Institutions that govern wage-setting matter a great deal in this respect. In Belgium, for example, the 1996 law on wage competitiveness establishes a hard wage target that all sectors have to adopt, and the synchronization of wage growth between the sheltered and exposed sectors (predictably) increases substantially after 1999. A similar evolution might also exist in countries where inter-industry co-ordination of wage bargaining remains strong. Austria and Germany might be cases of the latter: both have pattern bargaining systems where wage-setters in all sectors (usually) shadow the metalworking sector. In these countries, the pair-wise cross-correlation coefficients between wage growth cycles remain high between the manufacturing and non-market services sectors under EMU.

The second scenario which could arise is that the sheltered sector pushes for excessive wage increases (above labour productivity), but does not receive them. This is likely to lead to wage militancy and possibly protracted social conflicts in the public sector, and would be particularly relevant to unions in countries where governments have imposed hard fiscal constraints through domestic rules or have them imposed through compliance with the Stability and Growth Pact. The dynamics in France since the late 1990s seem to capture this case: secure jobs in the public sector and a high unionization rate have pushed civil servants in France to claim wage increases which go against the disinflationary wage settlements in the private sector.

In the third scenario the sheltered sector could push for excessive wage increases and receive them, as happened in Ireland and the Netherlands after 2000. However, these countries also demonstrate the importance of wage-setting institutions. Both Ireland and the Netherlands introduced emergency social pacts in 2003 that curbed wage growth in the face of inflationary pressures, bringing the sheltered sector back in line with wage restraint in other sectors.

Divergence in nominal wage restraint performance across EMU thus consists of two components: competitiveness-driven restraint in the exposed sector, and wage increases beyond productivity in the sheltered sector. Low levels of wage inflation in the sheltered sector can be relatively easily compensated by productivity gains in the exposed sector, thus re-balancing the aggregate level of wage restraint between these two sectors in an economy. Higher levels, however, are more problematic as they impose disinflation or a less competitive RER on the exposed sector. The exact mix between the two sectoral inflation rates is determined by the relative power of wage-setters in the exposed and sheltered sectors and especially by the extent to which the leadership role of the exposed sector is institutionalized in wage bargaining systems.

Table 6 presents the high and low wage restraint countries identified in Figure 1, and relates them to wage-bargaining systems (that typology is taken from Traxler *et al.* 2001). The high wage moderation countries share one

Table 6 Wage moderation under different wage-bargaining regimes

High wage moderation *Difference in nominal wage growth and* *labour productivity growth is less than* *EMU average – 2 per cent*	*Low wage moderation* *Difference in nominal wage growth and* *labour productivity growth is greater than* *EMU average – 2 per cent*
Austria (pattern bargaining – exposed sector leads)	Ireland (state-sponsored co-ordination with time-irregular social pacts)
Belgium (state-imposed wage law)	Italy (inter-associational bargaining)
Finland (time-regular incomes policies)	Netherlands (state-sponsored co-ordination with time-irregular social pacts)
France (state-co-ordinated – exposed sector leads)	Portugal (intra-associational bargaining)
Germany (pattern bargaining – exposed sector leads)	Spain (intra-associational bargaining)

Source: Traxler *et al.* 2001.

characteristic of wage co-ordination: they all have strong frameworks that can contain sheltered sector wage growth. In Austria and Germany, the metalworking sector (IG Metall in Germany and GMT in Austria) leads negotiations, setting wage increases equal to the increase in the national aggregate labour productivity rate. All other sectoral unions then shadow these increases in a pattern bargaining model. Unsurprisingly, as we already indicated in Table 5, wage growth correlations between exposed and sheltered sectors have remained high and relatively stable for both countries for the ERM and EMU periods.

Belgium's restraints lie in its wage law on competitiveness, introduced in 1996 on the failure to arrive at voluntary wage moderation via the previous (softer) law on competitiveness in 1989 and the failed social pact of the early 1990s (Pochet 2004). This law implemented a ceiling on all wage developments within the country, mandating that annual increases should not exceed the average wage increases of Belgium's largest trading partners – France, Germany and the Netherlands (Pochet 2004) – and has remained so under EMU. Since 1996, wage moderation performance in Belgium has increased considerably, and correlations in wage growth between the exposed and the sheltered sectors doubled under EMU.

Finland's use of centralized incomes policies has provided the important institutional component which has enabled the country to realize a stable course of wage moderation between 1999 and 2006. Finland has experienced much greater wage moderation during times when central agreements were reached and implemented (see Johansson 2006), and since 1998, social partners have agreed upon four two-year incomes policies, which cover approximately 90 per cent of the workforce. Because these policies set pay increases for the economy as a whole, any excess in wage inflation in the sheltered sector, due to its lower productivity, will be regained by wage restraint incurred in the export sector, due to its higher productivity. Since 1999, this disinflationary component has become quite apparent in sectoral wage restraint. Differences in nominal wage restraint between the manufacturing and the public services sectors have increased by 71 per cent under EMU, compared to the ERM period. Nevertheless, if one averages the levels of wage restraint in manufacturing and the public and personal services sectors, the average level of wage moderation is relatively equal to the labour cost increases agreed to in the national biannual policies.

France, finally, offers yet a different form of inter-sectoral wage co-ordination, which relies on the large multinational firms and the state. One of the paradoxes to be explained in this case is that unions are too weak to count for much in collective bargaining, but that the bargaining coverage rate (the proportion of eligible workers covered by collective bargaining) is one of the highest in the Organization for Economic Co-operation and Development (OECD) countries. The answer to this paradox is that the wage-bargaining system is largely organized around the needs of the large firms in France, which set wages for their workers as a function of relative unit labour costs. These wages are then proposed to the unions in branch-level bargaining rounds, and extended by the Ministry of Labour to cover the sector as a whole. In a second round, the government uses these wage rates as targets for public sector bargaining, thus completing coverage.

In contrast to the group of countries which adopted high wage moderation policies, those countries which experienced lower nominal wage restraint do not possess institutional frameworks that consistently bind wage-setters in the sheltered sector. One country, the Netherlands, can *temporarily* bind the sheltered sector from making inflationary wage settlements by establishing national wage freezes in social pacts. In 1999, differentials in wage restraint between the manufacturing and the public services sectors doubled from 1998, and then doubled again in 2000, almost breaching 5 per cent in 2001. This inflationary wage growth ultimately resulted in two social pacts, in 2003 and 2004, which imposed a wage ceiling in 2003 and wage freezes for 2004 and 2005. Though these social pacts were effective at reining in wages in the Netherlands after 2003, their temporary and reactive nature has failed to place a strong enough constraint on wage-setters in the sheltered sector to contain wage excess for the entirety of the EMU period.

Contrary to the Netherlands, Italy had neither a permanent nor a temporary constraint on wage-setters in the sheltered sector. The competitiveness constraint on wages for exposed sector unions was also not particularly effective, as wage excess increased quite substantially, sometimes even exceeding wage excess in public services. The government establishes, in the Document for Economic and Financial Planning, an annual inflation target, which is intended to act as a target for wage increases. Yet exposed and sheltered sector unions have consistently overshot these targets. The lack of constraints on wage-setters in the sheltered sector and the ineffectiveness of the competitiveness constraint on wage-setters in the exposed sector have contributed to Italy's poor wage restraint performance.

6. CONCLUSION

This article explored two crucial shifts in wage-setting and wage inflation since the introduction of the euro: the different evolution of wage restraint across different EMU member states after 1999 for countries with previously highly synchronous wage restraint cycles in the ERM/Maastricht period (the core DM bloc), and the increasing divergence between wage-setting in the exposed and sheltered sectors. Our argument has been that the shift from ERM to EMU lifted the robust monetary constraint on wage-setters, with different effects on wages in the exposed and the sheltered sectors. For unions in the tradable sector, not all that much appears to have changed, as competitiveness constraints (expressed in the RER) replaced the previous monetary constraint. This constraint, however, does not apply to the sheltered sector. Inflationary pressures seem to be mounting significantly for some countries, and the resulting divergence contributed to a growing cleavage between wage-setters in these two sectors. These tacit conflicts played out differently in different settings: in some countries institutional and legal arrangements still imposed low inflation on the sheltered sector, while they did not in others.

The implications of this analysis, both for research and policy, may be important. What it suggests, first of all, along the lines of Verdun's (1996) work, is that standard frameworks for political-economic and especially macro-economic analysis, which treat developments in countries (still) as more or less symmetric – where, in the limiting case, Luxembourg is analysed alongside Germany as an equally relevant observation – are problematic. If EMU is, despite the formal symmetry in its design, an asymmetric system in which developments in Germany have a proportionate impact on the rest of EMU, these standard approaches are likely to miss an important structural dimension.

The second contribution opens an older debate on the way wage-setting institutions and practices operate. The idea of different sectors in a national economy responding differently to similar shocks is not new (see Rogowski 1989; Franzese 2001). But we suggest that these cleavages between sectors in an economy are highly contingent upon the nature of the international regime itself, and the national institutions within it: lifting the monetary constraint has produced very different sets of incentives for exposed and sheltered sector unions in EMU, with the exposed sectors on the whole continuing to pursue low-inflation strategies in order to safeguard competitiveness, while the sheltered sectors are now able, to some extent, to free-ride on the capacity of the exposed sectors to produce low inflation. The comparison with the ERM/Maastricht period in the 1990s is instructive: the monetary constraint operated in such a way that wage inflation in the exposed and sheltered sectors converged, while under EMU, sheltered sectors are, other things being equal, no longer forced to play that game. New expressions of old cleavages thus emerged, and the politics underlying these are worth exploring in their own right.

Finally, the article raises some questions about the institutional design of EMU. EMU is regarded as a symmetric arrangement, but actually operates in an asymmetric way. The ECB is constitutionally bound to target Euro-zone inflation rates. Given that the ECB has established a strict 2 per cent target, if two large economies – Germany and France – have a very low inflation rate (of around 1 per cent), the ECB is unable to loosen monetary policy to reward them if aggregate inflation is moving above 2 per cent. This would be relatively unproblematic if those countries could rely on fiscal policy to boost their economies (while relying on wage-setting to keep inflation under control), but the Stability and Growth Pact, even though it might seem like a paper tiger to many, in effect precludes that. While problems of fiscal governance in EMU are beyond the scope of this article, the constraints that EMU places on fiscal policy as a demand management tool mean that the ECB's strict monetary target will be even more problematic for wage-setters in large countries which have adopted a wage moderation strategy. For smaller countries that have substantial export shares, wage restraint could be beneficial since it raises aggregate demand. However, as we are beginning to learn from Germany, there may be only so much a large economy can do with competitive exports to stimulate aggregate demand. For the time being, the centralized authority of the ECB seems able to hold on to this status quo – but recent disgruntled noises amongst German (and French) public sector unions suggest that some larger member states are questioning the legitimacy of using wage restraint as an adjustment policy.

Looking at EMU loosely as a series of nested games, in which incentive structures shift as a result of the institutional design itself, thus offers a useful way of making sense of this new political-economic framework. It allows us to explore new cleavages, and differential effects depending on the structural position of an economy. However, it is more than a mere academic exercise: trying to understand EMU with these lenses also alerts us to new conflicts that might be emerging and which produce effects that question both the institutional design underpinning the euro and the organization of wage-setting systems in some individual EMU member states. Further research on the spill-over effects of wage restraint policies in large and small countries could be insightful here: ten years on, we see that small countries have been able to retain most of their wage-bargaining institutional structure intact, while for larger countries (Germany specifically), the preservation of these institutions is increasingly being called into question.

ACKNOWLEDGMENTS

The authors wish to thank the Anglo-German Foundation and the Hans-Böckler Foundation (Project 2000-203-1) for financial support, and Michael Artis, Dorothee Bohle, Richard Bronk, Anil Duman, Bela Greskovits, Anke Hassel, Costanza Rodriguez- d'Acri, Waltraud Schelkle, David Soskice, three anonymous reviewers, and participants in the PERG seminar at the CEU and a conference at the Hertie School of Governance for helpful discussions. The usual exculpations apply.

NOTES

1 Our calculation of wage restraint differs from Oliver Blanchard's (2006) efficiency wage measurement, only in terms of the nominal weight: Blanchard uses real wage

growth minus labour productivity growth while we use nominal wage growth minus labour productivity growth. We use nominal wages rather than real wages to differentiate between productivity-driven and inflation-driven wage restraint. Also, since ours is an actor-centred approach, nominal wage growth is a more optimal dependent variable as, unlike real wage growth, actors have greater influence over it.

Aggregate calculations are computed using nominal compensation data from the AMECO database and labour productivity data from the OECD. Sectoral calculations are computed using data from the EU KLEMS database. We divided total compensation by number of hours worked to obtain the nominal wage per hour, and sectoral gross value added was used for labour productivity.

2 We used the Phillips curve as our baseline model for preliminary regression analyses. Time series data spanned from 1991 to 2006 for national level analysis and 1991 to 2005 for sector level analysis.

3 We thank Michael Artis for this point.

4 Since our approach requires us to compare countries with some degree of co-ordinated labour markets, we do not include the UK, the only EU15 country whose labour market lacks any wage co-ordination. We have included Sweden and Denmark, but were unable to include Norway or Switzerland as non-EMU control cases owing to the absence of data in the EU KLEMS database for these countries.

5 This continuing central role of Germany in EMU has primarily historical reasons. Since the country was the anchor of the ERM until EMU with one of the lowest inflation rates, it remained in that position after the introduction of the euro. It would not have mattered who the actual anchor was at the time (although the large trade volumes with Germany would make it more of an anchor than others); however, once EMU came into existence, the country in the anchor position remained there as a result of the institutional design.

6 Data on wage restraint by sector for the EMU10 (Luxembourg and Greece excluded) are available upon request.

REFERENCES

Allsopp, C. and Artis, M.J. (2003) 'The assessment: EMU, four years on', *Oxford Review of Economic Policy* 19(1): 1–29.

AMECO (2007) (European Commission's Directorate General for Economic and Financial Affairs. Annual Macro-Economic Database, last update: 9 November 2007). http://ec.europa.eu/economy_finance/indicators/annual_macro_economic_database/ameco_en.htm. Accessed January–February 2008.

Andrews, D. (2001) 'Currency coalitions and the monetary balance of power', Working Paper, European Centre of California.

Artis, M.J. and Zhang, W. (1997) 'International business cycles and the ERM: is there a European business cycle?', *International Journal of Finance and Economics* 2: 1–16.

Blanchard, O. (2006) 'European unemployment: the evolution of facts and ideas', *Economic Policy* 21(45): 5–59.

Calmfors, L. (2001) 'Wages and wage bargaining institutions in the EMU – a survey of the issues', *Empirica* 28: 325–51.

Calmfors, L and Driffill, J. (1988) 'Bargaining structure, corporatism and macroeconomic performance', *Economic Policy* 6: 12–61.

Calmfors, L., Booth, A. and Burda, M. (2001) 'The future of collective bargaining in Europe', in T. Boeri (ed.), *The Role of Unions in the Twenty-First Century: A Report for the Fondazione Rodolfo Debenedetti*, Oxford: Oxford University Press, pp. 1–134.

Cukierman, A. and Lippi, F. (2001) 'Labour markets and monetary union: a strategic analysis', *The Economic Journal* 111: 541–65.

Danthine, J.-P. and Hunt, J. (1994) 'Wage bargaining structure, employment and economic integration', *Economic Journal* 104: 528–41.

EU KLEMS Database. Last update: November 2007. http://www.euklems.net/index.html. Accessed January–February 2007.

Franzese, R.J. (2001) 'Institutional and sectoral interactions in monetary policy and wage/price-bargaining', in P.A. Hall and D. Soskice (eds), *Varieties of Capitalism: The Institutional Foundations of Competitiveness*, Oxford: Oxford University Press, pp. 104–44.

Hall, P.A. (1994) 'Central Bank independence and coordinated wage bargaining: the interaction in Germany and Europe', *German Politics and Society* 31(Spring): 1–23.

Hall, P.A. and Franzese, Jr. R.J. (1998) 'Mixed signals: central bank independence, coordinated wage bargaining, and European monetary union', *International Oraganization* 52(3): 505–35.

Hancké, B. and Soskice, D. (2003) 'Wage-setting and inflation targets in EMU', *Oxford Review of Economic Policy* 19(1): 149–60.

Iversen, T. and Soskice, D. (1998) 'Multiple wage bargaining systems in the single European currency area', *Oxford Review of Economic Policy* 14(3): 110–24.

Johansson, Å. (2006) 'Wage setting in Finland: increasing flexibility in centralized wage agreements', OECD Economics Department Working Paper No. 503, July.

OECD Statistics Portal Frequently Requested Statistics. http://www.oecd.org/document/15/0,3343,en_2649_201185_1873295_1_1_1_1,00.html. Accessed January–February 2008.

Pochet, P. (2004) 'Belgium: monetary integration and precarious federalism', in A. Martin and G. Ross (eds), *Euros and Europeans: Monetary Integration and the European Model of Society*, Cambridge: Cambridge University Press, pp. 201–25.

Rogowski, R. (1989) *Commerce and Coalitions: How Trade Affects Domestic Political Alignments*, Princeton: Princeton University Press.

Sibert, A. and Sutherland, A. (2000) 'Monetary union and labour market reform', *Journal of International Economics* 51(2): 421–35.

Soskice, D. and Iversen, T. (2000) 'The non-neutrality of monetary policy with large price or wage setters', *Quarterly Journal of Economics* 115(1): 265–84.

Traxler, F., Blaschke, S. and Kittel, B. (2001) *National Labour Relations in Internationalized Markets: A Comparative Study of Institutions, Change, and Performance*, Oxford: Oxford University Press.

Verdun, A. (1996) 'An asymmetrical economic and monetary union in the EU: perceptions of monetary authorities and social partners', *Journal of European Integration* 20(1): 59–81.

Political science and the 'Cinderellas' of economic and monetary union: payment services and clearing and settlement

Lucia Quaglia

In the run-up to and early years of economic and monetary union (EMU) the literature in political science focused on the making of EMU, especially the negotiations on the Treaty on European Union (TEU), the institutional set-up of EMU and the European Central Bank (ECB), member states' adaptation to EMU, and so on. So far, very limited attention has been devoted by political scientists to the less 'fashionable' parts of EMU: first and foremost, the 'plumbing' of the single currency, that is the payment services and the clearing and settlement of securities. These policy areas are usually regarded as the 'Cinderellas' of EMU because they are perceived as less important in terms of their overall contribution to the functioning of the single currency and as less politically salient, owing to their largely technical content.

This perception is incorrect and ten years after the establishment of EMU it is time for political scientists to focus their research on these activities for two main reasons. Empirically, payment services and the clearing and settlement of securities have become some of the most active areas of European Union (EU) policy-making after 1999. They are crucial for the functioning of the Eurozone and there is a considerable degree of politics involved, as evidenced in this analysis. Since they are very technical policy areas, the representatives of the finance ministries and the finance ministers themselves have limited interest and subject-specific knowledge to participate in the policy process, unlike, for example, in other EMU-related policies, such as fiscal policy and structural reforms. By contrast, the Commission and the ECB, and specific parts of the financial industry, identified below, tend to be more heavily involved.

Moreover, in the field of monetary policy there is an established body of literature on central bank independence and credibility that considers central banks as social-welfare maximizers serving the public interest (for a review, see Cukierman 1992; de Haan *et al.* 2005), whereas there is not such an assumption in the policy areas examined in this paper. This entails the possibility of the ECB acting as a 'traditional' bureaucracy, according to the public choice approach. For both of these reasons, political science, particularly bureaucratic politics approaches, contributes to a better understanding of what has been happening in these under-studied policy areas.

Theoretically, whereas theories of European integration, such as liberal inter-governmentalism and neofunctionalism, have been used to explain the establishment of EMU (for a review, see Verdun 2002), other theoretical approaches used in political science have often been overlooked in the study of EMU and the EU more generally. As this paper demonstrates, payment services and the clearing and settlement of securities provide useful testing grounds for bureaucratic politics approaches applied to the European Commission and the ECB. The latter plays an important role in these activities, and has sought to expand its competence over time, as explained in this paper.

By testing the analytical leverage of theories that have previously rarely been used by political scientists to explain the existence and the functioning of EMU, this paper tackles the first question informing the special issue, namely, what contributions can the discipline of political science make to the understanding of EMU? The answer to this question also identifies a gap (or blind spot) in the literature, which has not focused to date on some complementary (but very important) parts of EMU. Examining a variety of case studies in both policy areas is instrumental in gaining a better understanding of the explanatory power of bureaucratic politics approaches. This, in turn, helps to address the question of what political science can learn from EMU, specifically in the case of the 'Cinderellas' of EMU. Finally, this research contributes to bodies of scholarly works on the interaction between EU institutions and the institutional set-up and behaviour of the ECB.

Empirically, as far as payment services are concerned, this paper will look at the Single Euro Payments Area (SEPA), an industry-led initiative strongly backed by the European Commission and the ECB, and the Payment Services Directive (PSD). The Trans-European Automated Real-time Gross Settlement Express Transfer system (TARGET) 2, the payment system set up by the ECB, building on TARGET 1, which was established when the final stage of EMU began, is not examined because the project was not controversial, unlike TARGET 2 Securities. The policy-making process of TARGET 2 was internal to the ECB and the Eurosystem and no other EU body or national governments were involved in the discussion. As far as the clearing and settlement of securities are concerned, this paper will look at the short-lived proposal for an EU directive, subsequently set aside by the Commission, which preferred a voluntary code of conduct adopted by industry, and the controversial ECB project TARGET 2 Securities (also known as T2S), which is a platform for the settlement of securities attached to TARGET 2. It is argued that an adapted version of the theory of bureaucracy sheds new light on the policy process and the bureaucracies involved in it, namely the Commission and the ECB.

THE ANALYTICAL FRAMEWORK

A vast array of theoretical tools has been applied to the study of EMU (for an overview, see Verdun 2002). Two of the most well-known approaches, which have also traditionally been used to explain the process of European integration, are supranational governance (Sandholtz and Stone Sweet 1998) and liberal intergovernmentalism (Moravcsik 1993, 1998). According to the supranational governance approach, which to a large extent subsumed the neofunctionalist theory (cf. Haas 1968), the 'push factors' in the process of integration are transnational exchange stimulated by industry, legal provisions framing integration and the entrepreneurship of well-resourced supranational institutions (Sandholtz and Stone Sweet 1998). By contrast, liberal intergovernmentalism portrays the process of European integration as the result of a series of rational choices made by powerful national governments pursuing the interests of prevailing domestic groups and negotiating in intergovernamental arenas (Moravcsik 1993, 1998).

   These integration theories aim to explain why and how integration occurs, and tend to focus on 'history-making events' and broad stages of integration (Peterson 1995). However, they are less useful in explaining the day-to-day policy evolution. By contrast, other theoretical approaches developed in political science, such as bureaucratic politics, seem to be well suited to shedding some light on ordinary policy-making processes in the EU, especially those in which technical supranational bureaucracies are heavily involved. Yet, this approach has hardly ever been used in the study of EMU and has been substantially overlooked in the study of the EU more generally (for some exceptions, see Peters 1992, 1997; Radaelli 1999; Christiansen 1997).

   There are several theoretical approaches to bureaucratic politics (for a review, see Peters 2002), all of which are informed by the assumption that bureaucracies tend to engage in self-interested activities for a variety of reasons, such as to increase their power *vis-à-vis* other institutions, to maximize their budget, to expand their tasks, and to maximize their status and the quality of their work. This produces two main interrelated phenomena, which also correspond to the main streams of research on bureaucratic politics. The first phenomenon is *bureaucratic competition* for power in order to increase the influence of various bodies on policy-making processes and outcomes (cf. Allison 1971). The second phenomenon is *bureaucratic expansion*, that is, attempts by bureaucracies to expand their structure, organization, tasks and budget – this is captured by the so-called 'budget maximization' model (cf. Niskanen 1971; Tullock 1976, 1967). An adapted version of the 'bureau shaping' model can be seen as a variant of bureaucratic expansion, as it exposes one main tenet: bureaucracies try to expand their tasks, provided this is in line with an ideal configuration conferring high status and agreeable work tasks (Dunleavy 1991: 209).

Similarly, in the EU, bureaucratic politics can take two main forms. First, there is 'bureaucratic competition' between and within institutions in the EU policy process (Radaelli 1999). This aspect of bureaucratic competition involves not only the two main EU bureaucracies, the Commission and the ECB, but can be extended to examine the behaviour of all the main EU institutions involved in the EU policy process (the European Parliament (EP) and the Council of Ministers), whenever they compete to defend their institutional prerogatives, or to exert power in the policy process. Second, 'bureaucratic expansion' consists of attempts by the main EU bureaucracies, namely the Commission and the ECB, to expand their policy competence and tasks, as predicted by the 'budget maximization' approach. An adapted version of the 'bureau shaping' approach predicts that EU bureaucracies will try to expand their competence and tasks only if this increases their status and is in line with their remit.

It should be noted that there are some similarities between neofunctionalism, supranational governance and bureaucratic politics, which are complementary, rather than mutually exclusive, explanations. They both postulate an active role of EU supranational bureaucracies in EU policy-making, hence leading to similar observable implications. The main difference is that whereas the first approach assumes that the actions of supranational bureaucracies are 'in the interest of Europe', and have the main objective of promoting European integration, the second approach assumes that these bureaucracies are also aware of, and try to promote, their own self-interest. If the second explanation is correct, there should be some evidence of self-interested behaviour in the empirical record, with the caveat that such evidence is unlikely to be clearcut.

PAYMENT SERVICES IN THE EU

Payments services fall into two main categories: wholesale, which are large-value payments made by major financial players, such as banks and other large financial companies; and retail, used by consumers and business for the payment of goods and services. Payment services can be provided by banks and non-bank payment institutions, which are the parts of the financial industry most affected by the regulation of payment services. In EMU, wholesale payments are dealt with by TARGET 2. By contrast, before the twenty-first century, the markets for retail payments in the EU varied considerably owing to different technical standards, national legislation and domestic customers' preferences for different payment instruments. In the first decade of the twenty-first century, there were two parallel initiatives under way in the EU in order to promote an internal market for retail payments: the SEPA and the PSD.

The SEPA

The background to the SEPA programme and the creation of the European Payments Council (EPC) was the adoption by the Commission of the 'Regulation on cross-border payments in euro' issued in 2001, shortly before the physical introduction of the single currency. The regulation brought the cost of cross-border card transactions, electronic cash withdrawals and bank transfers in euro into line with the cost of national transactions. This provided an incentive for the modernization of the payment industry, streamlining cross-border payment infrastructures. The objective of the SEPA was to remove the barriers to the movement of funds across borders and reduce the cost of euro payments to the level of domestic transfers through the delivery of common standards and services for euro payments by 2010. The project involved all the countries in the Eurozone, both for domestic payments as well as those made across borders to other SEPA countries.

The creation of the SEPA was promoted by the European Commission and the ECB working with the Eurosystem – they were agenda-setters and remained important players throughout the process of setting it up. As evidenced by their public statements, both the Commission and the ECB promoted the project as a way to increase economic efficiency, thus completing the single market, and demonstrating some concrete benefits from EMU. These two supranational bureaucracies were at the centre of EMU: first and foremost the ECB and second the Commission, which had also been a vocal advocate of both projects. Arguably, they both had a bureaucratic self-interest in the successful outcome of these projects, as well as a concern for the way in which they were perceived by the public.

The Commission did not specify how the SEPA was to be achieved technically because it preferred to leave it to the market. As far as the ECB was concerned, it held the opinion that TARGET, a large-scale payment system run by the ECB, was a pan-European system of wholesale payments that was unsuitable for retail payments. Both the ECB and the European Commission were reluctant to build a separate retail system, which could be seen as a non-'agreeable task', according to the bureau shaping theory, and they were eager to persuade the banks to do it themselves, as evidenced, for example, by the joint statement of the Commission and the ECB 'SEPA' in May 2006 (Commission and ECB 2006).

As far as industry was concerned, the SEPA project was led by the EPC, established in 2002 with the purpose of promoting the creation of the SEPA through industry self-regulation. The EPC brought together the main EU banking associations from the 27 member states. However, it had problems in reaching an internal consensus. On the one hand, pressure for change came from large companies. On the other hand, smaller companies were concerned about the cost and the disruption that change could bring (*The Economist*, 21 May 2005). One reason for the banks' inertia and that of most of their customers (except for the biggest companies) was that, by and large, national payment systems worked well. Moreover, payment systems were costly to build and small cross-border payments accounted for only a small percentage of the overall volume in 2004. Some bankers thought that 'building a single pan-European system makes about as much sense as buying a Rolls-Royce for monthly visits to the hairdresser' (*The Economist*, 21 May 2005).

The financial industry's reluctance, which emerged in particular in 2004, was overcome by the strong insistence, if not outright pressure, exerted by the ECB and the Commission, which mentioned the possibility of undertaking legislative action or other forms of public intervention if the industry failed to achieve the SEPA.[1] The EP and the member states gathered in the Council were not involved in the policy making process of this initiative.

The PSD

The PSD, also known as 'New Legal Framework for Payments in the Internal Market', harmonized the legal basis to be applied to all types of payment service providers throughout the EU. It was intended to facilitate the achievement of the SEPA, provide the legislative framework to license payment service providers, and pave the way for the introduction of European-wide payment services for credit transfers and direct debits. The directive applied to all member states and EU currencies.

After the creation of EMU, although the Eurozone member states had a single currency (the euro), there was no common legal framework for non-cash payments in the EU. Consequently, service providers were effectively blocked from competing and offering their services throughout the EU. In December 2003, the Commission issued a Communication on a New Legal Framework for Payments in the Internal Market, inviting responses on the proposed content for the new directive. In light of the comments received by industry and national authorities, the Commission set the agenda and adopted a formal proposal for a directive on a New Legal Framework for payments in December 2005.

In March 2007, the text was examined in a trialogue with representatives of the EP, the Commission and the Council represented by the Presidency, with an attempt to reach an agreement in the first reading. In the same month, in the Economic and Financial Affairs (ECOFIN) Council the finance ministers unanimously adopted a general approach on a compromise text for the PSD. In April 2007, the Members of the European Parliament (MEPs) in plenary session approved the compromised text without further changes.

Some of the most controversial issues during the negotiations were the appropriate prudential framework for payment institutions, the activities that payment institutions could undertake, and the possibility to waive the application of parts of the directive either for certain small institutions and natural persons,[2] or for certain instruments used primarily for payments of small amounts. Another issue was whether the directive should apply only to payments in the EU and in euros. Finally, there was the issue of consumer protection, which cut across some of the specific points mentioned above.

Let us examine in more detail the preferences of the main players as this is important in order to explain how they behaved in the policy process and influenced the outcome. The Commission drafted the directive after public consultation; however, many observers noticed that the proposal, as originally drafted, did not sufficiently take into account the policy preferences expressed by banks and member states with a 'traditionalist' approach to financial services, such as France, Italy, Spain, and also Germany, as elaborated below. This explains why painstaking negotiation took place in the Council and the related provisions had to be changed before eventually being approved by the Council and the EP. Reportedly, the Commission was more sympathetic to the 'liberal' camp, represented by the UK and the Nordic countries, until it realized that there was a blocking minority in the Council and a compromise between the two coalitions was needed.

In its official opinion on the proposed PSD, the ECB (2006) suggested introducing some capital requirements for payment institutions, to prevent them from carrying out credit functions, and to limit the ancillary services they could offer. This position was close to the preferences expressed by banks and 'traditionalist' member states (first and foremost, Germany, France and Italy), as elucidated below.

The EP, especially the Committee on Economic and Monetary Affairs, reflected the views of industry (especially the banks) as well as consumers in its report on the draft directive. It favoured a higher level of regulation than initially proposed by the Commission, with a view to improved consumer protection, but it also embraced some issues that were important to industry, such as limiting the scope of the directive (EP 2004; see also EP 2006).

The member states were also divided into two main camps. The countries with a 'traditionalist' outlook on financial activities, such as France, Italy and Spain, insisted that non-bank payment companies should have strict capital requirements to put them on a level playing-field with banks. The 'liberal' countries, such as the UK, Sweden and the Netherlands, wanted to widen the innovative use of payment cards and credit, and were more relaxed about the rules to be imposed on non-bank payment institutions (*Financial Times*, 26 March 2007). Some new member states, especially Poland and the Czech Republic, sided with the 'liberal' camp because they already had non-bank payment institutions operating domestically. By contrast, the German government was especially concerned about the competitiveness of the public banks, which constitute approximately half of the banking system in Germany (*Financial Times*, 28 February 2007). Germany's role was pivotal because the country had the presidency in the first semester of 2007, when the directive was eventually agreed upon.

THE CLEARING AND SETTLEMENT OF SECURITIES IN THE EU

Clearing and settlement of securities are so-called post-trading activities that take place after securities have been traded and are necessary in order for the transaction to be completed. International Central Securities Depositories (ICSD) are central securities depositories that clear and settle international securities or cross-border transactions in domestic securities. In Europe, there are two main ICSD: Clearstream and Euroclear. The Central Securities Depositaries (CSDs) are entities for holding securities, which enable securities transactions to be processed by book entry. In addition to safekeeping, a central securities depository may incorporate clearing and settlement functions. The 'intermediaries' are usually 'custodian banks', that is, banks that hold securities on behalf of institutional investors. Stock exchanges are also involved because some conduct both trading and post-trading activities – the so-called 'vertical model', explained below.

After the establishment of EMU, cross-border arrangements for the clearing and settlement system of securities in the EU remained complex and fragmented. As a result, the costs of cross-border clearing and settlement in Europe were much higher than in the United States (London Economics Report 2005). At the same time, the two ICSDs operating in Europe had expanded their market power and operated as a sort of private monopoly in the settlement of securities. They had also been criticized for their opacity. As in the case of the payment services, the view of the ECB and the Commission was that this limited efficiency prevented the reaping of all the benefits ensuing from EMU, and therefore a solution needed to be found.

The code of conduct

In the policy-making process concerning clearing and settlement, the Commission was assisted by a group of experts chaired by the economist Alberto Giovannini (the Giovannini Group on Cross-Border Clearing and Settlement Arrangements), which produced two reports on this topic in 2002 and 2003 respectively. In response to the second Giovannini report, and after public consultation which revealed that there was a large majority in favour of a high-level, Lamfalussy-type directive, subject to a cost-benefit analysis,[3] the Commission issued a communication in April 2004. The communication outlined the actions that it intended to undertake in order to improve clearing and settlement arrangements, proposing the preparation of a framework directive. The directive would introduce rights of access for clearing and settlement providers to all EU markets and would ensure choice for investment firms, banks, central securities depositaries and markets. It would set up a common regulatory framework concerning clearing and settlement, allowing the mutual recognition of clearing and settlement systems across the EU. The directive would also contain rules – disclosure requirements, accounting separation and unbundling of specific services – for bodies that play a determining role in the clearing and settlement process.

In June 2005, the EP adopted a Report on Clearing and Settlement in the European Union to respond to the second Commission communication. The report was rather lukewarm towards the prospect of legislating on clearing and settlement, and urged an impact assessment by the Commission before proposing legislation, as the EP was concerned about potentially over-burdensome legislation (EP 2005a; see also EP 2005b).

In March 2006, the Competition and Internal Market Commissioners issued a joint statement, pointing out that they would act unless there was further action from the industry before the summer. In July 2006, Commissioner McCreevy made it clear that he favoured an industry-led approach, as opposed to proposing a directive. Following this, the three main industry associations – the Federation of European Securities Exchanges, the European Association of Central Counterparty Clearing Houses and the European Central Securities Depositories Association (ECSDA) – prepared a code of conduct that was signed by all their members in November 2006. The measures detailed in the code addressed three main issues: (i) the transparency of prices and services; (ii) access and interoperability; and (iii) the unbundling of services and accounting separation.

Let us look in more detail at the preferences of the main policy actors in order to gauge their influence on the outcome. The Commission was somewhat internally divided on the directive: some favoured legislation, others did not. It should be noted that the change in the College of Commissioners, and especially the Internal Market Commissioner, made a difference; the Barroso Commission was in favour of 'better regulation', meaning less regulation and self-regulation, whereas Commissioner Charles McCreevy seemed to be closer to an Anglo-Saxon approach. It was not a coincidence that the draft directive initiated by the previous commissioner was eventually set aside by the new commissioner. Moreover, it was clear that there was not a critical mass of member states in favour of a directive (interview, Brussels, 13 June 2007). On the one hand, the agenda-setting power of the Commission was limited by the member states. On the other hand, the Commission itself had changed its preferences with the change of its most senior officials. The episode also underscored the Commission's power to keep items off the legislative agenda.

In its response to consultation, the ECB, which supported the main goals of the directive, was keen to point out that, given the fact that there was no corresponding Level 2 committee that could draft the Level 2 implementing measures of the directive, this task should be assigned to the European System of Central Banks (ESCB) and the Committee of European Securities Regulators (CESR), which were already working together on this issue. This could be seen as an attempt to expand the prerogatives of the ECB and the national central banks.

Some member states and policy stakeholders were against a directive, preferring to rely on market forces. This is generally the approach preferred by the British authorities, and this was clear in the joint response to consultation issued by the British Treasury, the Financial Services Authority and the Bank of England. The German government opposed an EU directive on this issue, preferring a code of conduct, because a directive would challenge the 'vertically integrated model' of stock exchange (also referred to as the 'silos model') used by the German bourse (which is the largest vertical silo in Europe) and the Spanish and Italian bourses (*Financial Times*, 11 July 2006). In a vertically integrated model, the stock exchange incorporates trading and post-trading services of clearing and settlement. The new member states and the Nordic member states tended to be closer to the British position (interviews, Brussels, June 2007). French policy-makers were the main advocates of a directive on clearing and settlement. French banks were also in favour of this, although they were concerned about the length of the negotiations and what would be the final outcome (interview, Paris, July 2007).

TARGET 2 Securities

The last important development in the field of clearing and settlement of securities was the ECB's decision in 2007 to set up its own platform for the settlement of securities – T2S – which would be attached to the TARGET 2 platform, discussed above. The objective of T2S was to provide efficient settlement services for securities transactions in central bank money, leading to the processing of both securities and cash settlements on a single platform through common procedures. The ECB made it clear that T2S would be a 'settlement platform', not a CSD, hence it would not be dealing with activities such as dividend payments, redemptions, etc.; it would not open securities accounts for the users (i.e. the banks), an activity that would remain with the CSDs, and joining it would be voluntary.

In July 2006, the Governing Council of the ECB decided to consult market participants concerning the setting up of a new service for securities settlement in the euro area. Several meetings took place between the ECB/Eurosystem, market participants and market infrastructures in December 2006 and January 2007, when the ECB requested that market participants comment on a document entitled 'Governance of Target 2 Securities: A possibility'. In February 2007, the ECSDA wrote to the ECB asking for a delay in the project and calling for the ECB to engage in more market consultation (ECSDA 2007; *Financial Times*, 17 April 2007).

According to the ECB, the rationale for the setting up of T2S was to improve the efficiency of the system for clearing and settlement (Godeffroy 2006). The argument used by the ECB was that it had an interest in the proper functioning of securities clearing and settlement systems because any major malfunction could endanger the implementation of monetary policy, the functioning of payment systems, and the overall stability of the financial system in the euro area. Moreover, custodian banks were increasingly involved in operating securities settlement systems and some central securities depositories had bank status, hence co-operation with prudential supervisors was also important (ECB 2007).

Critics argued that this was an attempt by the ECB to expand its competence; it could potentially be detrimental to the primary task of the ECB, namely conducting monetary policy with a view to maintaining price stability. Additionally, it would lead to the creation of a public monopoly in this field. As the economist Willem Buiter argued (*Financial Times*, 19 January 2007), whereas the strong degree of independence of the ECB could find some justification in the realm of monetary policy, this was not acceptable in performing the tasks envisaged as part of T2S, which should be subject to public scrutiny. Initially, the consultation process of the ECB was criticized for being limited and not fully transparent (*Financial Times*, 17 April 2007; ECSDA 2007), although these criticisms receded as the project progressed. Moreover, in line with a 'budget-maximizing' (to be precise, a 'budget-protecting') bureaucratic explanation, several individuals interviewed for this research pointed to the need for national central banks to undertake new tasks and redeploy their personnel, once the conduct of monetary policy was transferred at the Eurozone level.

The T2S project was also a way of ending the internal rift within the ECB/Eurosystem (Norman 2007). Companies providing settlement services use central bank money to reduce the risk involved. Whereas some central banks, such as the Banque de France, allowed the operation of such accounts by the private sector, others, such as the Bundesbank, did not (*Financial Times*, 17 April 2007). Market operators wanted some harmonization, so as to create a level playing-field in the euro area. Consequently, the ECB/Eurosystem faced two choices: either out-source the use of central bank money, or in-source the settlement of securities, with T2S (Norman 2007). This was not a minor technical choice. On the contrary, it stirred a robust debate between national central banks in the Eurosystem and within the ECB Governing Council for over a year, without reaching a compromise solution until the T2S project was proposed.

Allegedly, T2S was relatively controversial both within the Governing Council of the ECB and in the ECOFIN Council where it was also discussed. Within the ECB, the members of the Executive Board tended to be in favour of T2S. However, some national central bank governors sitting on the Governing Council, for example, the central bank of Finland, were not supportive of the project, which was seen as being beyond the remit of the ECB/Eurosystem (interview, Brussels, 13 June 2007). Although they did not declare this officially, the Belgian authorities were not particularly supportive of the project either, owing to the importance of Euroclear's activities in Belgium (interview, Brussels, March 2007).

By contrast, the national central banks of the three (subsequently four) large countries in charge of setting up TARGET 2 backed the T2S project. National central banks have significant exposure and resources deployed in payment systems and, in contrast to monetary policy, the division of labour between the national central banks and the ECB is not so clearcut. It is thus not a complete surprise that TARGET 2 and T2S are to be provided by the three or four large national central banks; these central banks have accepted centralization in exchange for playing a dominant role in building and running the centralised systems.[4] This is an instance of 'in-house' bureaucratic politics in the Eurosystem.

This positioning in favour or against T2S was more or less reflected in the ECOFIN Council, with the difference that in these fora there was also the UK, which was lukewarm at best towards T2S, even though it was clear that the UK could not prevent the project from moving ahead. In February 2007, the finance ministers requested a more elaborate business plan, with clear information on how T2S would comply with EU competition policy and the intended governance structure from the ECB (*Financial Times*, 8 March 2007). The Heads of State and Government endorsed the project in May 2008, and in July 2008 the Governing Council of the ECB decided to launch T2S.

The Commission, for whom making the clearing and settlement of securities more efficient was a priority, supported the setting up of T2S. Reportedly, there were good and constructive relations between ECB officials and Commission officials in Directorate-General (DG) Internal Market dealing with the project (interviews, Brussels, March 2007; Frankfurt, September 2007). The main concern was whether the creation of what would be a public monopoly would infringe upon EU competition rules and DG Competition pledged to look into the matter.

The EP, traditionally wary of increasing the ECB's tasks, given its high degree of institutional independence, did not substantially oppose the project. Reportedly, this was because MEPs were concerned that the large US clearing and settlement groups could take over this function in the EU, which is also why some of the MEPs (especially from the socialist group) were keen on a directive on clearing and settlement (interview, London, 2 July 2007).

Industry was divided on the project. In the euro area, the banking sector reacted positively, although it should be said that the European Banking Federation, for example, questioned the need for ECB intervention and was internally divided on the issue of T2S. This is because, even if in principle banks would gain from T2S, in some countries they had spent considerable funding to adapt to the existing system and it would be costly to change. Euroclear, the ICSD that already provided similar services, objected to the ECB's plans, warning that it would fragment the industry by splitting securities settlement from other services and settlements in different currencies (*Financial Times*, 29 September 2006). The CSDs had mixed feelings, especially those likely to lose part of their business.

AN OVERALL ASSESSMENT

The empirical record suggests that a variety of actors were involved in the policy-making process concerning payment services and the clearing and settlement of securities. As elaborated below, specific parts of the financial industry proved to be influential lobbies in line with a supranational governance and, more generally, a pluralist account of policy-making. Member states' preferences were played out, at times forcefully, in the Council of Ministers, as predicted by liberal intergovernmentalism, and the EP was involved through co-decision. However, the Commission and the ECB were the key actors: they acted as agenda-setters, in line with a supranational governance approach but also a bureaucratic politics one.

The reminder of this section teases out the main findings in a systematic way, discussing to what extent they fit with intergovernmentalist, supranationalist and bureaucratic politics approaches. It is concluded that traditional integration theories do not provide a satisfactory explanation, and bureaucratic politics should be brought in for a thorough account. This paper does not claim that bureaucratic politics was the only driver of the 'Cinderellas' of EMU. It argues instead that such an approach sheds new light on the policy process, and is instrumental in order to conceptualize the role of the main policy-makers and their influence on the outcome.

The Commission was particularly influential at the agenda-setting stage concerning the 'plumbing' of the single currency by proposing legislation or threatening to do so in order to spur the market to act. Arguably, as explained before, this was 'in the interest of Europe', but it was also in the bureaucratic interest of the Commission. The Commission consulted with industry and national authorities on whether or not to undertake legislative action in addition to action on the specific content of directives. Obviously, the Commission needed a critical mass of member states and policy stakeholders supporting its proposals, as the case of the non-proposed directive on the clearing and settlement of securities made clear.

However, the case of the non-proposed directive on clearing and settlement also highlighted the importance of the preferences at the top level of the Commission in charting its course of action – the top echelons of DG Internal Market did not want a directive. It also highlighted a particular aspect of agenda-setting: the power of keeping certain items off the agenda. The Commission's preference for market-led action through the SEPA and the code of conduct does not contradict a bureaucratic politics explanation because the Commission's power in the making of these 'soft law' measures tends to be enhanced as compared to traditional legislation, which involves co-decison between the Council and the EP. By contrast, the EP and the Council were not formally involved in the introduction of the SEPA and the code of conduct, hence they were kept 'out of the game'.

The ECB is not a traditional regulatory body: it is, first, a central bank overseeing the functioning of the payments system. It has minimal prudential supervisory functions, and some regulatory powers in its areas of activity. In certain areas, such as the SEPA, the ECB, like the Commission, was keen for certain market-led activities to take place with the back-up of public authorities, which had agenda-setting power. On one occasion, involving T2S, the ECB's view was that direct public intervention was necessary. The benign view was that the ECB genuinely aimed at correcting market failures by intervening in the market, even if this resulted in a de facto public monopoly, which was nevertheless preferable to de facto private monopolies. The less benign view is that the ECB behaved as a traditional bureaucracy, trying to expand its competence while keeping in line with its remit and objectives, as predicted by the bureau shaping theory, rather than acting in the public interest (a benevolent welfare maximizer), as generally assumed by mainstream theories of monetary policies and central bank independence. Moreover, the ECB was also internally affected by bureaucratic politics, as it was divided on the choice of outsourcing (or not) central bank money – and the T2S project provided a solution to the impasse in the Eurosystem.

The EP was not formally involved in several of the policy initiatives considered in this paper (the SEPA, TARGET 2, T2S, the code of conduct), some of which are soft law. It was, however, a powerful player at the decision-making stage in the making of the PSD, which was substantially redrafted to incorporate the amendments put forward by the EP and also supported by some member states negotiating in the Council. Overall, the EP was sympathetic to the view of industry and acted as a channel through which the latter could articulate its policy preferences in the policy-making process, aside from lobbying the Commission and the national authorities who negotiated in the Council. In a few cases, the policy preferences of different parts of industry, played out in the EP, causing heated internal debates.

In the Council, the member states generally tried to push through or promote the preferences of national industry or companies based on their territory. Preferences in the Council are the most difficult to examine because this is an opaque body. However, unlike in other policy areas related to EMU (e.g. fiscal policy, structural reform, etc.), the involvement of finance ministry officials and finance ministers was relatively limited, partly because of the technical nature of the issues involved and partly because the policy measures were not adopted through co-decision.

Like the EP, the Council was not formally involved in the SEPA, TARGET 2, T2S or the code of conduct. Inherently, these measures tend to give more power to the EU bureaucracies (the Commission and the ECB) underpinning them, which contributes to explaining why the Commission was eager to make use of soft law and the ECB decided to undertake T2S. In a way, the limited involvement of the member states (intergovernmental politics) and the EP (supranational politics) was compensated by the heavy involvement of European bureaucracies (bureaucratic politics). Specific parts of the financial industry were also involved (interest group politics). However, in all the initiatives examined, it was the Commission and the ECB, not the private sector, which drove the projects forward, trying to reconcile the (at times competing) interests of industry.

One could argue that the SEPA and T2S were spillovers from monetary union and the single market project, as predicted by neofunctionalist theory:

lobbyists and bureaucrats pushed for integration in fields adjacent to already integrated policy fields. This would also feed into a pluralist (industry-led) view of the policy process. However, as the empirical account shows, the main impulse for these initiatives did not come from industry, which, most of the time, was divided on this issue. These policy measures were primarily driven by the Commission and the ECB, often according to their own preferences.

Although the empirical evidence is not clearcut because the data presented could be interpreted in different ways and certain sources of information are not available to the public, it is possible to suggest that the two supranational bureaucracies, the ECB and the Commission, sought to expand their functions and policy tasks concerning payments services and clearing and settlement. This enhanced their status, was in line with their overall remits, and was instrumental in pursuing specific objectives, namely demonstrating the benefits ensuing from the single currency and safeguarding financial stability. These activities also contributed to furthering European integration; however, the way in which this objective was pursued was in line with the specific preferences of the two bureaucracies primarily involved in the process. This last point flags up the fact that it is sometimes difficult to separate neatly bureaucratic politics explanations from a supranational governance approach. Since the latter has been in favour in the study of the EU, revisiting some supranational governance explanations by adopting a bureaucratic politics perspective allow us to cover some blind spots.

CONCLUSIONS

Bureaucratic politics theories have a good explanatory mileage in accounting for the 'plumbing' of EMU, even though they have not been used to explain the introduction of the single currency. Perhaps this is not surprising, given the fact that the main 'traditional' theories of European integration are better suited to explaining the high politics of EMU, i.e. the history-making events that led to the creation of the single currency, whereas the low politics of EMU can be better accounted for by traditional theories of policy-making (Peterson 1995). That said, there are relatively few works that apply bureaucratic politics approaches to the study of the EU; this work argues that there might be significant added value in doing so.

The main theoretical insight that can be gained for the discipline of political science from the study of the 'Cinderellas' of EMU is the usefulness of considering theories of bureaucracies with reference to the Commission and the ECB, as these approaches can be useful in shedding novel light on the behaviour of these supranational institutions. The analytical leverage of bureaucratic politics tends to be greater when the degree of intergovernmental politics involved in the EU processes under scrutiny is low. The main empirical insight that can be gained for political science from the 'Cinderellas' of EMU is the importance of analysing the politics involved in these seemingly 'technical' activities. Payment services and clearing and settlement of securities are often regarded as among the most 'technical' areas of EMU. Yet, the analysis conducted in this paper suggests that politics matter a great deal in the governance of these financial activities.

ACKNOWLEDGEMENTS

Financial support from the British Academy (Grant SG 45759) is gratefully acknowledged. I wish to thank the 15 practitioners who made themselves available for interview. I am also grateful to the anonymous referees, the editors and the participants at the conference in Berlin for their perceptive comments on an early draft of this paper. All errors and omissions are mine.

NOTES

1 http://www.ecb.int/pub/pdf/other/singleeuropaymentsarea200412en.pdf
2 The term 'natural person' is used to distinguish an actual human being from a 'legal' or 'juridical' person, an organization or corporation which may, in certain circumstances, be given rights of a person under the law.
3 http://ec.europa.eu/internal_market/financial-markets/docs/clearing/2004-consulta tion/reponses_en.pdf
4 I wish to thank one referee for pointing this out to me.

REFERENCES

Allison, G.A. (1971) *The Essence of Decision: Explaining the Cuban Missile Crisis*, Boston: Little, Brown.
Christiansen, T. (1997) 'Tensions of European governance: politicized bureaucracy and multiple accountability in the European Commission', *Journal of European Public Policy* 4(1): 73–90.
Commission of the European Communities (CEC) and the European Central Bank (ECB) (2006) *Single Euro Payments Area*, joint statement, 4 May 2006.
Cukierman, A. (1992) *Central Bank Strategy, Credibility, and Independence: Theory and Evidence*, Cambridge, MA: MIT Press.
De Haan, S., Eijffinger, S. and Waller, S. (2005) *The European Central Bank: Credibility, Transparency, and Centralization*, Cambridge, MA: MIT Press.
Dunleavy, P. (1991) *Democracy, Bureaucracy and Public Choice*, Hemel Hempstead: Harvester Wheatsheaf.

The Economist, several issues.

European Central Bank (ECB) (2006) *Opinion of the European Central Bank (ECB) of 26 April 2006 on a Proposal for a Directive on Payments Services in the Internal Market*, OJEC C109/10.

European Central Bank (ECB) (2007) *Reply to the Letter from ECSDA to ECB on Target 2 Securities*, http://www.ecb.int/paym/market/secmar/integr/pdf/ECB-012.pdf

European Central Securities Depositories Association (ECSDA) (2007) *Letter From ECSDA to ECB on Target 2 Securities*, http://www.ecb.int/paym/market/secmar/integr/pdf/T2SECSDAletter.pdf

European Parliament (EP) (2005a) *Report on Clearing and Settlement in the European Union*, Committee on Economic and Monetary Affairs, 6 June 2005.

European Parliament (EP) (2005b) *Resolution on Clearing and Settlement in the European Union*, 2004/2185INI, P6 TA(2005)0301.

European Parliament (EP) (2006) *Report on the Proposal for a Directive on Payment Services in the Internal Market*, Committee on Economic and Monetary Affairs, 20 September 2006.

The Financial Times, several issues.

Godeffroy, J. (2006) Speech by Jean-Michel Godeffroy to the British Bankers Association, London, 20 September 2006

Haas, E. (1968) *The Uniting of Europe: Political Social and Economic Forces 1950–57*, Stanford, CA: Stanford University Press.

London Economics (2005) *Securities Trading, Clearing, Central Counterparties and Settlement in EU 25 – An Overview of Current Arrangements: Report*, 30 May 2005, London.

Moravcsik, A. (1993) 'Preferences and power in the European Community: a liberal intergovernmental approach', *Journal of Common Market Studies* 31(4): 473–524.

Moravcsik, A. (1998) *The Choice For Europe*, London: UCL Press.

Niskanen, W. A. (1971) *Bureaucracy and Representative Government*, New York: Aldine-Atherton.

Norman, P. (2007) *Plumbers and Visionaries*, Chichester: John Wiley & Sons.

Peters, G.B. (1992) 'Bureaucratic politics and the institutions of the European Community', in A. Sbragia (ed.), *Europolitics. Institutions and Policy-making in the 'New' European Community*, Washington, DC: Brookings Institution, pp. 75–122.

Peters, G.B. (1997) 'Escaping the joint-decision trap: repetition and sectoral politics in the European Union', *West European Politics* 20(2): 22–36.

Peters, G.B. (2002) *The Politics of Bureaucracy*, London: Routledge.

Peterson, J. (1995) 'Decision-making in the European Union: towards a framework for analysis', *Journal of European Public Policy* 2(1): 69–93.

Radaelli, C.M. (1999) 'The public policy of the European Union: whither politics of expertise?', *Journal of European Public Policy* 6(5): 757–74.

Sandholtz, W. and Stone-Sweet, A. (1998) *European Integration and Supranational Governance*, Oxford: Oxford University Press.

Tullock, G. (1967) *The Politics Of Bureaucracy*, New York: Public Affairs Press.

Tullock, G. (1976) *The Vote Motive*, London: Institute of Economic Affairs.

Verdun, A. (ed.) (2002) *The Euro: European Integration Theory and Economic and Monetary Union*, Lanham, MD: Rowman & Littlefield.

Index

Page numbers in *Italics* represent tables.
Page numbers in **Bold** represent figures.